Secularism, Religion and
Multicultural Citizenship

The Islamist attacks of 9/11, the Danish cartoon affair and rioting by Muslim youths in France are just some of the events that have caused the 'Muslim question' to become a key issue of public debate in many western democracies. *Secularism, Religion and Multicultural Citizenship* argues that the Muslim case raises important questions about how we understand western secularism and respond to new religious claims in multicultural democracies. The contributors challenge prevailing assumptions about the history and practice of western secularism and recover the pragmatism behind liberal principles in negotiating new conditions. By situating the Muslim experience in relation to western secularism and liberal democratic practice, and through examining a variety of national contexts (including Britain, Germany, France, the United States, Australia and India), this book extends thinking about our contemporary condition and considers the broader significance for multicultural liberal democracies.

GEOFFREY BRAHM LEVEY teaches political theory and was founding Director of the Program in Jewish Studies, at the University of New South Wales, Sydney.

TARIQ MODOOD is Professor of Sociology, Politics and Public Policy, and founding Director of the Centre for the Study of Ethnicity and Citizenship at the University of Bristol.

Secularism, Religion and Multicultural Citizenship

GEOFFREY BRAHM LEVEY AND
TARIQ MODOOD
FOREWORD BY CHARLES TAYLOR

CAMBRIDGE UNIVERSITY PRESS
Cambridge, New York, Melbourne, Madrid, Cape Town, Singapore, São Paulo,
Delhi, Dubai, Tokyo

Cambridge University Press
The Edinburgh Building, Cambridge CB2 8RU, UK

Published in the United States of America by Cambridge University Press, New York

www.cambridge.org
Information on this title: www.cambridge.org/9780521695411

First published 2009
Reprinted 2010

Printed in the United Kingdom at the University Press, Cambridge

A catalogue record for this publication is available from the British Library

Library of Congress Cataloguing in Publication data
Secularism, religion, and multicultural citizenship / [edited by] Geoffrey Brahm Levey,
Tariq Modood.
  p. cm.
Includes bibliographical references and index.
ISBN 978-0-521-87360-4 (hardback) – ISBN 978-0-521-69541-1 (pbk.)
1. Secularism. 2. Multiculturalism. 3. Religious pluralism. 4. Islam–Relations.
I. Levey, Geoffrey Brahm. II. Modood, Tariq. III. Title.
BL2747.8.S345 2008
322′.1–dc22
2008031152

ISBN 978-0-521-87360-4 hardback
ISBN 978-0-521-69541-1 paperback

Contents

Tables

Contributors

VEIT BADER is Professor of Sociology and of Social and Political Philosophy at the University of Amsterdam, and a member of the Institute for Migration and Ethnic Studies. He is the author of numerous articles on religious diversity, cultural identity and associative democracy, and of *Secularism or Democracy? Associational Governance of Religious Diversity* (2007); editor of *Religious Pluralism, Politics, and the State* – a special volume of *Ethical Theory and Moral Practice* (2003) – and *Citizenship and Exclusion* (1997), and coeditor of *Associative Democracy: The Real Third Way?* – a special volume of *Critical Review of International Social and Political Philosophy* (2001).

RAJEEV BHARGAVA is Professor and Director of the Centre for the Study of Developing Societies, Delhi. His main fields include political theory, the history of political thought and the philosophy of social science. He is editor of *Secularism and Its Critics* (1998); coeditor of *Multiculturalism, Liberalism and Democracy* (1999) and of *Civil Society, Public Sphere and Citizenship: Dialogues and Perceptions* (2005); and author of *Individualism in Social Science* (1992).

JOSÉ CASANOVA is Professor of Sociology and Senior Fellow in the Berkeley Center for Religion, Peace, and World Affairs at Georgetown University, Washington DC. He was previously Professor of Sociology at the New School for Social Research, New York, from 1987 to 2007. His research focuses on religion, democratisation and social change in Latin America, Southern Europe and Eastern Europe. His publications include *The Opus Dei and the Modernization of Spain* (Cambridge, forthcoming), and *Public Religions in the Modern World* (1994).

IAN HUNTER is an Australian Professorial Fellow at the University of Queensland, Brisbane. He works on early modern political, philosophical and religious thought. His most recent monograph is

Rival Enlightenments: Civil and Metaphysical Philosophy in Early Modern Germany (Cambridge, 2001). With David Saunders, he has edited *Natural Law and Civil Sovereignty: Moral Right and State Authority in Early Modern Political Thought* (2002). He and David Saunders have also completed a new edition of Andrew Tooke's first English translation of Samuel Pufendorf's *De officio hominis et civis: The Whole Duty of Man* (2003).

GEOFFREY BRAHM LEVEY teaches political theory and was founding Director of the Program in Jewish Studies at the University of New South Wales, Sydney. He writes on issues in contemporary political theory, the philosophy of social science, and Jewish political thought and behaviour. He is editor of *Political Theory and Australian Multiculturalism* (2008), and coeditor of *Jews and Australian Politics* (2004).

TARIQ MODOOD is Professor of Sociology, Politics and Public Policy, and the founding Director of the Centre for the Study of Ethnicity and Citizenship at the University of Bristol. He is coeditor of the journal *Ethnicities*. His many publications include, as author, *Multicultural Politics: Racism, Ethnicity, and Muslims in Britain* (2005) and *Multiculturalism: A Civic Idea* (2007); and as coeditor, *The Politics of Multiculturalism in the New Europe* (1997), *Ethnicity, Nationalism and Minority Rights* (Cambridge, 2004), *Ethnicity, Social Mobility, and Public Policy: Comparing the USA and UK* (Cambridge, 2005) and *Multiculturalism, Muslims, and Citizenship: A European Approach* (2005).

ABDULLAH SAEED is Professor and Head of Arabic and Islamic Studies at the University of Melbourne. His publications cover Islamic finance, Muslim communities in Australia, Islamic law and freedom of religion, Christian–Muslim relations, Islamic thought in Indonesia, Qur'anic hermeneutics, Islam and human rights, and Islamic law reform. He is author of *Islamic Banking and Interest* (1996, 1999), *Islam in Australia* (2002), *Approaches to the Qur'an in Contemporary Indonesia* (2005) and *Interpreting the Qur'an: Towards a Contemporary Approach* (2006); coauthor of *Freedom of Religion, Apostasy and Islam* (2004); and coeditor of *Islam and Political Legitimacy* (2003) and *Muslim Communities in Australia* (2001).

DAVID SAUNDERS is Professor Emeritus in the Faculty of Arts at Griffith University, Brisbane, and currently lives in Paris. His research concerns the historical relations of law, politics and religion. He is author of *Anti-Lawyers: Religion and the Critics of Law and State* (1997) and, with Ian Hunter, has published a re-edition of Andrew Tooke's 1691 *The Whole Duty of Man*, the first English translation of Samuel Pufendorf's *De officio hominis et civis* of 1673 (2003). Also with Ian Hunter, he has edited *Natural Law and Civil Sovereignty: Moral Right and State Authority in Early Modern Political Thought* (2002).

S. SAYYID is a Research Fellow in the School of Sociology and Social Policy, and Director of the Centre of Ethnicity and Racism Studies at the University of Leeds. His research area covers issues of Islamic identity and Islamophobia. He is the author of *A Fundamental Fear: Eurocentrism and the Emergence of Islamism* (1997, 2nd edn 2003), and coeditor of *A Postcolonial People: South Asians in Britain* (2006).

CHARLES TAYLOR is Board of Trustees Professor of Law and Philosophy at Northwestern University, Chicago. Winner of the 2007 Templeton Prize, he is a former Chicele Professor of Moral Philosophy at Oxford and Professor Emeritus of Political Science and Philosophy at McGill University. Among his publications are *Hegel* (Cambridge, 1975), *Philosophical Papers* (2 vols., Cambridge, 1985), *Sources of the Self* (1989) and *A Secular Age* (2007).

Foreword
What is secularism?

CHARLES TAYLOR

It is generally agreed that modern democracies have to be 'secular'. There is perhaps a problem, a certain ethnocentricity, involved in this term, but I'll leave this aside for the moment, and take it up in the next section. Even so, the term is not limpid. What in fact does it mean? A great deal of discussion seems to assume that we're all quite clear about this, and the only possible discussion concerns whether we're for or against.

That is why this collection is so timely. The essays in this book probe the multiple meanings of the term, and moreover show how these are embedded in different historical and political contexts.[1] The reader may not be clearer after she finishes this book, but at least she'll have begun to recognise her confusions. This is a Socratic mode of wisdom that we all stand in need of in this domain.

If I can parade my own confusions in the next few pages, I think that there are at least two rather different models of what constitutes a secular regime that are going the rounds today.

Both involve some kind of separation of church and state. The state can't be officially linked to some religious confession, except in a vestigial and largely symbolic sense, as in England or Scandinavia. But secularism requires more than this. The pluralism of society requires that there be some kind of neutrality, or 'principled distance', to use Rajeev Bhargava's term.[2]

Secularism involves, in fact, a complex requirement. There is more than one good sought here. We can single out three, which we can class

---

[1] The essays in Part I (Chapters 2 to 5) of this volume explore some of the great range of historical contexts in which something like a secular regime has been sought. The chapters by Hunter and Saunders have the great advantage of making us take a certain distance from our usual exclusive focus on contemporary societies.

[2] See his contribution to this volume (Chapter 4, pp. 103–106), but also Bhargava (1998c: esp. 493–4, 520) for 'principled distance', and Bhargava (2007: esp. 39–41).

in the three categories of the French Revolutionary trinity: liberty, equality, fraternity. First, no one must be forced in the domain of religion, or basic belief. This is what often defined a religious liberty including, of course, the freedom not to believe. This is what is also described as the 'free exercise' of religion, in the terms of the US First Amendment. Second, there must be equality between people of different faiths or basic belief; no religious outlook or (religious or areligious) *Weltanschauung* can enjoy a privileged status, let alone be adopted as the official view of the state. Then, thirdly, all spiritual families must be heard, included in the ongoing process of determining what the society is about (its political identity), and how it is going to realise these goals (the exact regime of rights and privileges). This (stretching the point a little) is what corresponds to 'fraternity'.

These goals can, of course, conflict; sometimes we have to balance the goods involved here. Moreover, I believe that we might add a fourth goal: that we try as much as possible to maintain relations of harmony and comity between the supporters of different religions and *Weltanschaungen* (maybe this is what really deserves to be called 'fraternity', but I am still attached to the neatness of the above schema, with only the three traditional goods).

One kind of secularism claims to have resolved the question of how to realise these goals. It is claimed that one can determine the proper method in the realm of timeless principle, and that no further input, or negotiation, is required to define them for our society now. The basis for these principles can be found in reason alone, or in some outlook that is itself free from religion, purely *laïque*. Jacobins are on this wavelength, as was the first Rawls.

The problem with this is that (a) there is no such set of timeless principles that can be determined, at least in the detail they must be for a given political system, by pure reason alone; and (b) situations differ very much, and require different kinds of concrete realisation of agreed general principles; so that some degree of working out is necessary in each situation. It follows that (c) dictating the principles from some supposedly higher authority above the fray violates the third category of secularism, listed above. It deprives certain spiritual families of a voice in this working out.

We have a good illustration of (b) in the way that the issues concerning secularism have evolved in different western societies in recent decades, because the faiths represented in those societies have changed. We need to alter the way in which we proceed when the range of religions or basic philosophies expands: for example, contemporary Europe or America with their Muslims.

In relation to (c), we have the recent legislation in France against wearing the *hijab* in schools. Normally, this kind of thing needs to be negotiated. The host country is often forced to send a double message: (i) you can't do that here (kill Salman Rushdie, practice female genital mutilation), and (ii) we invite you to be part of our consensus-building process. These tend to run against each other; (i) hinders (ii) and renders it less plausible. All the more reason to go as easy as possible on (i). Religious groups must be seen as much as interlocutors and as little as menace as is possible.

These groups also evolve if they're in a process of redefinition of this kind in a democratic, liberal context. José Casanova in this volume and elsewhere points out how American Catholicism was originally targeted in the nineteenth century as inassimilable to democratic mores, in ways very analogous to the suspicions that nag people over Islam today. The subsequent history has shown how American Catholicism evolved, and in the process changed world Catholicism in significant ways. There is no reason written into the essence of things why a similar evolution cannot take place in Muslim communities. If this doesn't happen, it will in all likelihood be because of prejudice and bad management.

Let's pause and look at how this could happen (perhaps is happening). There is substantial suspicion of Islamic immigrants in many European countries today, and of Islam in general in the western media and public.

'Multiculturalism' has become a suspect term in much of Europe today. People say things like: 'I used to be for openness and toleration of difference, but now I see where it's leading.' Where is it leading? This is all about Islam. Rather simple requests, like that of schoolgirls to wear a headscarf, are suddenly freighted with immense significance.

In part, this is because of a rather simple and unreal understanding of multiculturalism that was abroad earlier. It meant on this view limitless acceptance of different forms of life, which could allow at the limit the evolution of a society with self-contained ghettos. This was absurd on two levels: first, in its original notion (for instance, in the Canadian case) multiculturalism was seen as a procedure for integration: precisely the idea that the norms and accommodations to which we would all come to adhere were to be negotiated between new and old citizens, and not simply taken over without change from the past.

But second, this whole idea was absurd in another way. The tremendous assimilative force of the way of life in advanced liberal, consumer-capitalist society is so great that there is no question of communities integrally retaining their whole original life-form, unless they go to great lengths to isolate themselves from the mainstream – as, for instance, the Amish have done, and also certain communities of Orthodox Jews. The danger of a society of ghettos is a totally unreal one. The real menace is that of failed integration, where young people, who have lost much of their original language and culture, nevertheless cannot make a go of their lives in our societies, because they lack the skills and training (including crucially the linguistic skills), or because they suffer discrimination. This is the situation we see in some *banlieues* of Paris, and in certain parts of German cities. This is a really tragic plight. It is the worse in that it breeds a sense of alienation and resentment, which can then emerge in violent action, and even in resistance to further efforts to bring about integration.

In other words the real danger is not that immigrants retain their original identities unchanged, but that they develop alienated counter-identities, which are very much in the society they have joined (e.g., they speak some version of French, or German; they aspire to a job, prosperity), but not of it (they feel themselves outsiders, and want to strike back.) We have here a phenomenon that is familiar from other societies, like the United States and Canada – only there it is to be found not so much among immigrants, as among African Americans (for the USA), and some communities of First Nations (in the Canadian case).

Add of course, in the Muslim case, that the building of a counter-identity is further encouraged by the global backlash that we now see in many Muslim countries, and which focuses in general on the West as an enemy. It is tempting for disoriented young people, frustrated in their ambitions for themselves, to draw on, sometimes partly and provisionally, sometimes with deadly intent, these 'Islamic' counter-identities, which grab so much attention and headlines everywhere.

To the extent that this happens, it must not be seen simply as a reflection of 'Islam', but also and especially as a phenomenon generated by the failed relationship of frustrated integration.

But unfortunately, it is all too often seen in the first light. This brings us back to the phobia about Islam in the West. Why do demands by schoolgirls to wear headscarves provoke such a disproportionate reaction?

The feeling often is: this simple-seeming proposal is really part of a package. The package is 'Islam', and it includes such terrible things as we can read of in the press daily, happening in Nigeria, or Saudi Arabia. If you reply that the girls in question aren't living in Nigeria or Saudi Arabia, and almost certainly don't share, say, extreme Wahabi views, people in Europe today may look at you with that kind of almost indulgent pity reserved for the terminally naive; or they will tell you stories about how imams are twisting the girls' arms, making them into unwilling stalking-horses for 'Islam'.

You can't just talk about headscarves as an issue on its own, and all the sociological evidence about the (in fact very varied) motives of the girls themselves is swept aside as irrelevant.

Here is a classic example of block thinking, which seems to have made huge strides in Europe in recent years. John Bowen's book, *Why the French Don't Like Headscarves* (2006) documents this shift for the French case.

Block thinking fuses a very varied reality into one indissoluble unity, and this on two dimensions: first, the different manifestations of Islamic piety or culture are seen as alternative ways of expressing the same core meanings; and second, all the members of this religion/culture are seen as endorsing these core meanings. That actually a girl's wearing the headscarf might express a rebellion against her parents, and their kind of Islam, that others might be deeply pious while being utterly revolted by gender discrimination or violence – all this is lost from view.

Block thinking is an age-old phenomenon, and we all do it to some degree. In another age, we might be indulgent, but today it has explosive potential. People who think like this are prime recruits for Huntington's theory of the 'clash of civilisations'. What's worse, the way they then act tends to edge us closer to this nightmare scenario, because by treating all the varied segments of Islam as though they belonged to one threat, they make it harder for Muslims to stand out and criticise their own block thinkers, who are busy fighting their own gigantic, unified enemy. 'Christians and Jews', says Osama bin Laden – that takes in quite a lot of people. Block thinkers on each side give aid and comfort to block thinkers on the other, and with each exchange they edge us closer to an abyss. We're still very far from the edge, but still, the sooner we stop this madness, the better.

How to stop this dialectic? Well, it works in part because the critics of block thought on each side are unknown to the others. How many times does the European critic meet this kind of response: 'But where are the Muslims who are criticising extremist Islam?' Of course, you patiently explain that you're not likely to meet them in the drawing rooms of Paris journalists or the French political class. But this will never have the impact of a real connection to the multi-faceted discourse of the other side. Developing this type of discourse is an urgent necessity in the West today. Contributions like those of Tariq Modood and Abdullah Saeed to this volume (Chapters 7 and 9) are urgently needed to impart further depth and realism to the often frighteningly unidimensional western debate on Islam.

But to return to the main line of my argument above, we have to turn to the other basic model of secularism. This means not one based on an antecedently available set of principles, but one that builds an overlapping consensus, of the kind that Rawls was tending towards, without perhaps fully reaching it. Here there is no canonical justification; the principles are agreed, the basis on which we coexist, but each spiritual family justifies them in their own way. Why respect human life? Because of the nature of humans as rational, because humans are in the image of God, or whatever.

The actual principles are what we can come to agree on, as something we can all justify from our own point of view. This means that in any concrete situation, we cannot know beforehand (before negotiating) what they are. This would be scandalous if we were using the overlapping consensus as a *criterion* of right principles; then the principles I accept would be hostage to some illiberal gang that I have to include in the negotiation. No, each of us must determine from their point of view what is right. But what will be established as the ruling regime must be negotiated. Democracy doesn't permit of anything else.

This allows us to respect our third goal, really to give the different spiritual families a voice in the determination of the rules by which they will live.

In the discussion of secular regimes above, which appeal to timeless principles, I invoked the extreme variety of situations in which we must try to realise these principles, in which we have to work out what they mean. But this variety includes societies outside the West. Is there a problem involved in even speaking of 'secularism' here, in view of the fact that the key term 'secular' is one that belongs to the historical language of Latin Christendom?

We live in a world in which ideas, institutions, art styles, and formulae for production and living circulate among societies and civilisations that are very different in their historical roots and traditional forms. Parliamentary democracy spread outward from England, among other countries, to India. And the practice of non-violent civil disobedience spread from its origins in Gandhi's practice to many other places, including to Martin Luther King's civil rights movements, to Manila in 1983 and the Velvet Revolution in 1989, and eventually to the Orange Revolution of our time.

But these ideas and forms don't just change place as solid blocks; they are also modified, reinterpreted, given a new spin and meaning in each transfer. This can lead to tremendous confusion when we try to follow these shifts and understand them. One possible course of confusion comes from taking the word too seriously: the name may be the same, but the reality will often be different.

This is evident in the world 'secular'. We tend to think of 'secularisation' as a process that can occur anywhere (and for some people, is occurring everywhere). And we think of secularist regimes as options for any country, whether they are adopted or not. And certainly, these *words* crop up everywhere. But do they really mean the same thing? Are there not, rather, subtle differences, which can bedevil cross-cultural discussions of these matters?

I think there are, and that they do make problems for our understanding. Either we stumble through cross-purposes; or else, a rather minimal awareness of the differences can lead us to draw far-reaching conclusions that are very wrong: as when people argue that since the 'secular' is an old category of Christian culture, and since Islam doesn't seem to have a corresponding category, including such notions as distinction of church and state, *therefore* Islamic societies cannot adopt secular regimes. Obviously, they will not be just like those in Christendom, but maybe the idea here can travel in a more inventive and imaginative way.

Let's look at some of the features of the 'secular' as a category developed within Latin Christendom. First, it was one term of a dyad. The secular had to do with the 'century' – that is, with profane time – and contrasted with what related to the eternal, or higher time.

Certain times, places, persons, institutions, actions were seen as closely related to the sacred or higher time, and others as 'out there' in profane time. That's why the same distinction could often be made by use of the dyad 'spiritual–temporal' (e.g. the state as the 'temporal arm'). Ordinary parish priests are 'secular' priests, because they operate out there in the 'century', as opposed to within monastic institutions under rules (the 'regular' priests).

So there was an obvious meaning for 'secularisation', which goes pretty far back – to the aftermath of the Reformation. When certain functions, properties, institutions were transferred out of church control to that of laymen, this was 'secularisation'.

These moves were originally made within a system in which the dyad held; things were moved from one niche to another within a standing system of niches. This feature, where it still holds, can make secularisation a relatively undramatic affair, a rearrangement of the furniture in a civilisation whose basic features remain unchanged.

But from the seventeenth century on, a new possibility arose. A new conception of social life came gradually to be defined, in which the 'secular' was all there was. Since 'secular' originally applied to a kind of time – profane or ordinary time, seen in relation to higher times – what was necessary was to come to understand profane time as all there is: to deny any relation to higher time. The word could go on being used, but the meaning was profoundly changed, because what it contrasted with was quite altered. The contrast was not another time-dimension, in which 'spiritual' institutions found their niche; rather the secular was in the new sense defined over and against claims on resources or allegiance made in the name of something transcendent to this world and its interests. Needless to say, those who imagined a 'secular' world in this sense saw these claims as ultimately unfounded, and only to be tolerated to the extent that they didn't challenge the interests of worldly power and well-being.

Because many people went on believing in the transcendent, it could even be necessary that churches continue to have their place. They could in their own way be essential to the well-functioning of society. But this good function was to be understood in terms of 'this-worldly' goals and values (peace, prosperity, growth, flourishing etc.).

Obviously, this way of putting things depends on a clear distinction being made between 'this world', or the immanent, and the transcendent. This very clear-cut distinction is itself a product of the development of Latin Christendom, and has become part of our way of seeing things in the West. We tend to apply it universally, even though nothing this hard and fast exists in any other human culture in history. What does seem, indeed, to exist universally is some distinction between higher beings, or spirits, or realms, and the everyday world we see immediately around us. But these are not usually sorted out into two distinct realms, where the lower one can be taken as a system understandable purely in its own terms. Rather, the levels usually inter-penetrate, so that the lower can't be understood without the higher. To take an example from the realm of philosophy, for Plato, the existence and development of the things around us can only be understood in terms of the corresponding Ideas, and these exist in a realm outside time. The clear separation of an immanent from a transcendent order is one of the inventions (for better or worse) of Latin Christendom.

The new understanding of the secular I have just been describing builds on this clear separation. It affirms, in effect, that the 'lower', immanent or secular order is all there is; that the higher, or transcendent is a human invention. Obviously, the prior invention of the clear-cut distinction between the levels prepared the ground for this 'declaration of independence' of the immanent.

The first unambiguous assertion of this self-sufficiency of the secular came with the radical phases of the French Revolution, although there were ambiguous regimes in the century that preceded it, like the attempts of 'Enlightened' rulers such as Frederick the Great and Joseph II to 'rationalise' religious institutions, in effect treating the church as a department of the state.

This polemic assertion of the secular returns in the Third Republic, whose *laïcité* is founded on these ideas of self-sufficiency and the exclusion of religion. Marcel Gauchet shows how Renouvier laid the grounds for the outlook of the Third Republic radicals in their battle against the church. The state has to be *moral et enseignant*. It has *charge d'âmes aussi bien que toute Eglise ou communauté, mais à titre plus universel*. Morality is the key criterion. In order not to be under the church, the state must have *une morale indépendante de toute religion*, and enjoy a *suprématie morale* in relation to all religions. The basis of this morality is liberty. In order to hold its own before religion the morality underlying the state has to be based on more than just utility or feeling; it needs a real *théologie rationnelle*, like that of Kant (Gauchet 1998: 47–50).

Needless to say, this spirit goes marching on in contemporary France, as one can see in the discussion about banning the Muslim headscarf. The insistence is still that the public spaces in which citizens meet must be purified of any religious reference.

And so the history of this term 'secular' in the West is complex and ambiguous. It starts off as a term in a dyad, which distinguishes two dimensions of existence, identifying them by the kind of time that is essential to each. But then building on the clear immanent–transcendent distinction, it mutates into a term in another dyad, where 'secular' refers to what pertains to a self-sufficient immanent sphere, and its contrast term (often identified as 'religious') relates to the transcendent realm. This can then undergo a second mutation, via a denial of this transcendent level, into a dyad in which one term refers to the real (the secular), and the other to what is merely invented (the religious); or where 'secular' refers to the institutions we really require to live in 'this world', and 'religious' or 'ecclesial' to optional extras that often disturb the course of this-worldly life.

Through this double mutation, the dyad itself has thus profoundly changed; in the first case, both sides are real and indispensable dimensions of life and society. After the mutation, secular and religious are opposed as true–false, or necessary–superfluous.

Then this term, with all its baggage of ambiguity, and its depth assumptions of a clear immanent–transcendent distinction, begins to travel. No wonder it causes immense confusion. Westerners are themselves frequently confused about their own history. Notwithstanding this, a common outlook embraces the true–false view, but sees the earlier two-dimensions conception as having created the necessary historical preconditions for its arising. One way of stating this is to understand western secularism as the separation of religion and state, the excision of religion into a 'private' zone where it can't interfere with the common life. Then the earlier western distinction between church and state, which eventually led to a separation of church and state, is seen as the run-up to the finally satisfactory solution, where religion is finally hived off.

But these stages are not clearly distinguished. Thus American secularists often confuse totally separation of church and state from that of religion and state. Rawls at one point wanted to ban all reference to the grounds of people's 'comprehensive views' (these included religious views) from public discourse.

And this leads to disastrously ethnocentric judgements. If the canonical background for a satisfactory secularist regime is the three-stage history: distinction church–state, then separation church–state, then sidelining of religion from state and public life; then obviously Islamic societies can never make it.

Or again, one often hears the judgement that Chinese imperial society was already 'secular', totally ignoring the tremendous role played by the immanent–transcendent split in the western concept, a split that had no analogue in traditional China. Ashis Nandy (2002), in discussing the problems that arise out of the uses of the term 'secular', shows up the confusions that are often involved in analogous statements about the Indian case, e.g., that the Emperor Asoka was 'secular', or that the Mughal Emperor Akbar established a 'secular' form of rule.

But this kind of statement can also reflect a certain wisdom. In fact, Nandy distinguishes two quite different notions that consciously or unconsciously inform the Indian discussion. There is the 'scientific-rational' sense of the term, in which secularism is closely identified with modernity, and a variety of 'accommodative' meanings, which are rooted in indigenous traditions. The first attempts to free public life from religion; the second seek rather to open space 'for a continuous dialogue among religious traditions and between the religious and the secular' (Nandy 2002: Chapter 3, esp. 68–9 and 80).

The invocation of Akbar's rule as 'secular' can then be a way of redefining the term, rather in the sense of my attempt earlier; that is, one defines secularity as an attempt to find fair and harmonious modes of coexistence among religious communities, and leaves the connotations of the word 'secular' as these have evolved through western history quietly to the side. This takes account of the fact that formulae for living together have evolved in many different religious traditions, and are not the monopoly of those whose outlook has been formed by the modern, western dyad, in which the secular lays claims to exclusive reality (Nandy 2002: 85).[3]

What to do? It's too late to ban the word 'secular'; too many controversies have already been started in these terms. But 'secularism', as an essential feature of religiously diverse societies, aiming to secure

---

[3] Amartya Sen (2005) also makes use of a similar point about Akbar's rule to establish the roots of modes of secularism in Indian history.

freedom of both belief and unbelief as well as equality between citizens, is much too important a matter to be left to 'secularists', by which I mean those who are deeply into the true–false dyad arising out of the history of Latin Christendom. (I apologise to Clémenceau for parodying his famous dictum on war.)

We need to take a deep breath, and start again, at another point. And that is why, taking a leaf from the book of Rajeev Bhargava (1998a) thinking about the Indian context, I proposed above that we start by articulating afresh the basic goals we seek in secularist regimes. As a starting point, we might take my trilogy of 'liberty, equality, fraternity'. People can relate to those coming out of very different religious traditions. And they can devise ways of securing them that make sense in very different religious environments. Let us tune out the mantras chanted in certain western societies with self-endowed vocations to universal validity, like 'separation of church and state' or *laïcité*, and look at our real situations in the light of the indispensable values of democratic society.

Acknowledgements

This book is the outcome of an international symposium on *Religion and Multicultural Citizenship* held at the University of New South Wales in Sydney on 11–13 July 2005 – as it happened, days after the bombings on London transport. We first began discussing such a collaborative venture in 2000, when the subject of Muslim integration into western societies was little discussed. That, of course, is no longer the case. With the Islamist attacks of September 2001 and subsequently, public controversies over such issues as Muslim clothing, gender relations and free speech, and rioting by Muslim youth in Paris and elsewhere, the 'Muslim question' is now widely canvassed. The symposium sought to examine the Muslim case from a broader perspective than is usual: namely, the relation between religion and politics as governed by the original religious settlements in western states. Our belief was and is that the Muslim case has a significance that extends beyond Muslims and their integration: that it, in fact, raises fundamental questions about our assumed liberal-democratic principles and practices in multicultural societies. We hope the book contributes to this enlarged thinking about our contemporary condition.

The symposium was jointly organised by the editors and Ien Ang, Director of the Centre for Cultural Research at the University of Western Sydney. We especially wish to thank Ien for her extensive and gracious input into the planning and staging of the symposium. Thanks are due also to the University of Western Sydney's David Burchell for his contribution. We are indebted to the three institutions that sponsored the symposium: the University of New South Wales Faculty of Arts and Social Sciences (under its 'Large Conference Grant' programme), the Centre for Cultural Research at the University of Western Sydney, and the Centre for the Study of Ethnicity and Citizenship at the University of Bristol through the generosity of the Lord Ashdown Charitable Trust.

We are grateful to all those who participated in the symposium. The intellectual exchange was enhanced by papers from Danielle Celermajer, Marion Maddox and Samina Yasmeen, and by several people who served as discussants: David Burchell, Moira Gatens, Shakira Hussein, Clive Kessler, Jeffrey Minson and Helen Pringle. Our joint essay on the Danish cartoon affair was written after the symposium; we thank our commissioning editor John Haslam for suggesting it. Versions of this essay were presented to the Social and Political Theory seminar at the Australian National University (2006), the School of Social Sciences and International Studies seminar at the University of New South Wales (2007), and the Ethnicity and Democratic Governance conference on *Immigration, Minorities and Multiculturalism in Democracies* in Montreal (2007). We are grateful to the audience members on those occasions for their comments.

The chapters in this book have been peer-reviewed, and though they cannot be named, we wish to acknowledge the anonymous reviewers for their critical input. It is an honour to be able to thank Charles Taylor for his generous Foreword to the book. Finally, we owe a special thanks to John Haslam for his support of the project.

An earlier version of Chapter 4 appeared as 'Political secularism', in *A Handbook of Political Theory*, ed. J. Dryzek, B. Honnig and A. Philips (Oxford University Press, 2006), pp. 636–55, and is modified here by permission of Oxford University Press.

Chapter 6 originally appeared as 'Immigration and the new religious pluralism: a European Union/United States Comparison', in *Democracy and the New Religious Pluralism*, ed. T. Banchoff (New York: Oxford University Press, 2007), pp. 59–83, and is reprinted here by permission of Oxford University Press, Inc.

1 | Secularism and religion in a multicultural age

GEOFFREY BRAHM LEVEY

What should be the relation between religion and the state in liberal democracies today? The original liberal settlements of this question, forged against the background of protracted sectarian conflict in early modern Europe, devised a pragmatic solution of separation between the two domains. This move – generally subsumed under the rubric of secularism or a secular state – arguably has been a stunning achievement for the past few centuries. But liberal societies today are under serious strain and facing new challenges brought on by radically transformed conditions. Suddenly, questions are now being posed that previously were considered settled.[1]

Until recently, the prevailing view was that religiosity in western democracies would attenuate with each generation, reflecting the march of secularisation and the forces of modern consumer societies. This attenuation, it was believed, would parallel the expected eclipse of ethnic identities more generally. Such expectations have been roundly shaken. When Nathan Glazer and Daniel Patrick Moynihan (1963: 290) famously concluded – after surveying the scene in New York City in the early 1960s – that '[t]he point about the melting pot is that it did not happen', the signs were there for religious identity as well. By the 1980s, evangelical groups and the 'Moral Majority' had become significant players in American politics. It has taken another two decades, however, for the global resilience and significance of religious identity to be fully recognised. 'The belief that outbreaks of politicized religion are temporary detours on the road to secularization was plausible in 1976, 1986, or even 1996', observe Timothy Shah and Monica Toft (2006: 43). 'Today, the argument is untenable.' Even as traditional, institutional forms of religiosity, such as church

---

[1] I thank Tariq Modood for his comments and an anonymous reader for his/her questions in relation to earlier versions of this chapter.

attendance, were dissipating across continental Europe, Britain and its offshoots such as Canada and Australia, new forms of religious expression and the intensification of religious sentiment were being observed. As Ronald Inglehart and Pippa Norris report, 'the world as a whole now has more people with traditional religious views than ever before – and they constitute a growing proportion of the world's population' (quoted in Shah and Toft 2006: 40).

Western democracies today are being challenged by religion along three intersecting 'fault-lines'. The first is the background context of all discussion of religion in the modern West – the aforementioned traditional liberal quest to separate religion and politics for the sake of peace and the mutual protection of both. While there is, of course, wide variation among liberal democracies in the way that it is institutionalised and practised, church–state separation remains a defining feature of all liberal societies. Part of the dispute at this level is the time-honoured one of sorting out the appropriate demarcation of the private and public domains as new cases present themselves. But the arguments also run much deeper as to how the separation between the two domains should be understood.

The second fault-line is much more recent. It emerges with the rise of identity politics in the United States and beyond in the 1960s, and the advent of multiculturalism as state policy in places such as Canada and Australia in the 1970s. On this newer, 'multicultural' model, the emphasis has been on publicly supporting, accommodating and even celebrating ethnic diversity. Again, there is wide variation among liberal democracies in this respect. Not all democracies have experimented with official policies of multiculturalism. Some, like the United States, allow for cultural diversity in a more decentralised, piecemeal fashion through different jurisdictions of public law and policy. Others, such as France, have generally discouraged the expression and accommodation of minority cultural differences. Nevertheless, it is fair to say that all liberal democracies have felt the tension between the old liberal 'separationist' model devised for religion and the increasing demands for cultural recognition and accommodation in the name of multiculturalism. A central question, here, has been whether multiculturalism violates or better realises fundamental liberal-democratic values like equality, autonomy and toleration.

The third fault-line has opened up more recently again. It is a product of significant Muslim immigration to the West – especially

Europe – and of the nature of Islam as a 'public religion'.[2] Cases such as Salman Rushdie's *Satanic Verses* in Britain, the slaying of Dutch filmmaker Theo Van Gogh, the Danish cartoons of Muhammad, and the wearing of headscarves at state schools in France, have left many people in these countries asking whether Muslims can be successfully integrated into their societies. These impressions have, of course, only been compounded by the actions of militant Islamists around the world. In Europe, but also in Canada and the antipodes, the view is increasingly put that the Muslim presence challenges the liberal secular state *and* condemns the liberal multicultural state. On this account, the 'Muslim question' requires an ever more resolute insistence on 'core' liberal values and the established liberal settlements governing religion and politics, while multiculturalism is blamed for encouraging cultural relativism and social segregation, and for sowing confusion about the appropriate boundaries of the tolerable.

These three intersecting 'fault-lines' – religion–politics, religion–multiculturalism, and Islam–Muslims/multiculturalism – raise a number of pressing questions. How should liberal democracies respond to their growing Muslim communities? What is the appropriate liberal response to a girl wearing a headscarf to a French school, or to an Islamic organisation's request for public funding in the UK, or to a request that images of the Prophet Muhammad not be published in newspapers? Should these cases be seen as instances of 'multiculturalism' and 'diversity', which contemporary liberalism should defend and celebrate? Or are they rather examples of a dangerously theocratic impulse, which threatens the social peace and the liberal separation of religion and the state? Should places like France, Germany and the UK adjust their legal codes in order to accommodate a religious tradition that was not a party to the original peace compacts, and that may not accept some of the limiting terms of modern liberalism?

---

[2] Substantial Muslim populations have lived in the Balkans and Eastern Europe for centuries, a fact underscored by the long Ottoman rule in those regions. There also has been a Muslim presence in western Europe for centuries. For example, the first sizeable group of Muslims arrived in Britain from India in the eighteenth century (Foreign and Commonwealth Office 2006: 4). However, the large Muslim populations in western Europe today are chiefly a product of post-World War II immigration (Fetzer and Soper 2005: 2). For figures on the Muslim communities in Europe and the United States, see the chapters by Casanova (Chapter 6) and Saeed (Chapter 9) in this volume.

This book tackles these and related questions. The first part of the book seeks to clarify the history, terms and limits of western secularism. The second part explores the Muslim experience in relation to western secularism today and the ramifications of this relationship for both. For the remainder of this chapter, I want to connect the historical picture of western secularism to contemporary developments by suggesting where problems lie and where, perhaps, they do not. I shall proceed by pursuing three further questions. Is religious identity different from other forms of cultural identity? Does the Islamic experience differ significantly from that of other religions in the West? And have the original liberal settlements regarding religion outlived their usefulness in light of contemporary developments?

Is religious identity different?

Secularism denotes the idea that the state or political authority should not be in the business of imposing or advancing or privileging any particular religion or religious belief or religion in general.[3] The initial aim was to create a space in which different faith communities might coexist amicably. This elementary idea of state neutrality has been variously practised or advanced on the basis of prudence, toleration, indifference and respect for persons. Whatever the underlying principle or posture, there are at least two senses in which religious identity must be credited as being different or special in the context of any liberal society.

One is that religion is integral to the history of liberalism. It was out of the bloody religious wars and persecutions of the sixteenth and early seventeenth centuries that liberal ideas and institutions evolved. While some have traced the idea of religious toleration back to medieval political thinkers (e.g. Nederman and Laursen 1996; Laursen and Nederman 1998), the prevailing view continues to link it to the changing attitudes to heresy and heretics – chiefly, the acceptance of

---

[3] A distinction is sometimes drawn between secular, secularism and secularisation, where 'secular' refers to a delimitation or principled exclusion of religion, 'secularism' to an ideological opposition to religion, and 'secularisation' to the waning of religious belief and observance among a group or in society. In this book, we do not attach such a narrow or negative meaning to 'secularism', but rather employ the term to denote the various understandings of what the secular state was, is and should be.

religious coexistence over persecution – that took hold in the wake of the religious conflicts and Protestant Reformation in the sixteenth century (Zagorin 2003). The attempt to avoid religious conflict was one of the main motivations behind the idea of separating a 'public' sphere of activity appropriate for political concern and intervention from a 'private' sphere where the state ought not to concern itself. Moreover, as Jonathan Israel (2006: 65) notes, early Enlightenment thinkers (1650–1740s) drew on and reinterpreted scripture to fashion their arguments for toleration, since religion was then all-dominant and its vocabulary was the only language everyone understood. This formative relationship has bestowed on religion a special significance and sensitivity in liberal thought and in the affairs of liberal societies, and likely always will.

It is, however, a later historical development that has increasingly distinguished religion from other forms of cultural identity in liberal societies. The rise of the nation-state from the late eighteenth century witnessed the conjuncture of political authority and the consolidation of particular language and cultural identities (Taylor 1997). The religion model and the nation-state model thus have different logics and press in opposite directions: whereas secularism aims to preclude government from discriminating on the basis of a particular religion, the nation-state aims to produce and reproduce a particular language and culture. To be sure, both models witness many variations. Some liberal democracies continue to have state or established churches, though protecting the religious freedom of other faith communities (e.g. England, Greece and Denmark); some have official ties to a particular faith, such as the Catholic concordat in Spain, Portugal and Italy; while others honour religious neutrality by supporting or accommodating many religions (e.g. Germany, Sweden and India) or by privatising all religion (France, the United States). At the same time, liberal nation-states are limited in how far they can impose a particular national identity courtesy of their commitment to individual and democratic rights, although, here again, there is considerable variation among actual cases. The point nevertheless remains: the nation-state model aligns the state with a particular cultural identity in a way that the religion model generally seeks to preclude regarding religious identity.

So religion is uniquely situated in relation to the liberal state. At the same time, religious identity is also *akin* to other cultural identities in many respects. For one thing, many ostensible religious practices and traditions are observed by members of faith communities for broadly cultural or even social rather than religious reasons. For example, many Christians who baptise their children, many Jews who attend synagogue on the High Holidays and many Muslims who have their infant sons circumcised do these things – and sometimes little else – in order to 'identify' with their group rather than out of religious belief or observance. Second, some putatively 'religious' groups embrace other dimensions of membership, such as ethno-national criteria in the case of the Jews, and political communal criteria in the case of Muslims, as S. Sayyid notes in Chapter 8. Third, religion and ethnicity or national background also often overlap and mutually shape each other in particular communities: for example Turkish Muslims in Germany, North African Muslims in France, Pakistani Muslims in Britain, and German and Scandinavian Lutherans and Irish and Italian Catholics in the United States. Finally, religious groups, like other cultural groups, wish to observe and reproduce their traditions.

In many ways, the debate surrounding religion in democracies turns on the implications of this tension in religion being both different from and similar to other forms of identity. Most contemporary liberals readily grant the special *historical* relationship between religion and liberalism. However, the question of whether or in what sense religious identity should be treated differently has proven more contentious and, indeed, vexatious. This is true even – or perhaps especially – with liberals who are sympathetic to the claims of culture.

Consider, for example, the approach of Will Kymlicka, the influential philosopher of multiculturalism. Kymlicka accepts that the 'religion model is altogether misleading as an account of the relationship between the liberal-democratic state and ethnocultural groups' (Kymlicka 2002: 345). However, he understands the religion model to involve a very strict and complete separation between church and state. As he puts it, liberal neutrality actually allows the state to promote a particular religion on the same terms that it does a particular language – namely, as long as it is done for some 'neutral reason' such as facilitating social harmony or communication, and not for any claim of intrinsic worth or truth value. But liberals, he says, have adopted a stronger principle when it comes to religion – 'benign neglect'. On this principle, the state 'should avoid promoting [religion] *at all*, even for neutral reasons of efficiency or harmony. There should be a firm 'separation of church and state' (Kymlicka 2002: 344, emphasis quoted).

What is puzzling about this account of the distinctiveness of the religion model is that the origins of so-called church–state separation were themselves largely rooted in a neutral or pragmatic response to the thorny problem of endemic religious conflict. Why would a model that is itself the product of pragmatic thinking rule out pragmatic reasons as a legitimate basis of political intervention? One might say the model inscribes a prediction, in this case, about the perils of political and religious entanglement based on past experience, which no one wishes to repeat. But meaningful predictions are open to empirical falsification. It is hard to see how various kinds of state recognition commonly extended to religious minorities – from conscientious objection to tax subsidies – compromise religious freedom or fan the flames of religious conflict.

Indeed, Kymlicka's own theory of minority cultural rights seems to violate his principle of 'benign neglect'. On his theory, members of cultural minorities are entitled to certain cultural rights wherever they are disadvantaged through no fault of their own in enjoying the good of membership in a societal culture. And he is alert to how religious minorities may be similarly disadvantaged to ethnic minorities. For example, he cites how Easter and Christmas public holidays symbolically and practically disadvantage Jewish and Muslim citizens, and suggests how the latter's festivals may also be publicly recognised (Kymlicka 1995: 114, 222 n. 9).[4] Similarly, he argues that while it would be better if Sunday closing laws were abolished altogether, Sabbatarians are entitled to exemptions where these laws apply

---

[4] Tariq Modood (2007: 26–7) observes how religious minorities tend to figure prominently in Kymlicka's discussion of isolationist groups (such as the Amish and Hutterites) and of exemptions from standing law, while scarcely rating a mention in his otherwise advocacy of group representation in the democratic process, public subsidisation and institutional inclusion for cultural minorities. The reluctance to address religious minorities in these latter respects may have something to do with Kymlicka's endorsement of strict church–state separation, as Modood suggests. That Kymlicka is willing to offer faith communities symbolic recognition and institutional representation in the case of public holidays is thus doubly interesting. For my own critique of Kymlicka's theory of cultural rights, see Levey (1997). I discuss the problem of symbolic recognition of public holidays in Levey (2006c).

(Kymlicka 2002: 374 n. 21). In particular cases, then, Kymlicka is compelled to override his strict account of benign neglect and church–state separation out of some sense both of justice and the force of circumstance. This is scarcely surprising. His account of benign neglect demands a near-impossible standard of separating religion and politics. It precludes a state from acting in the sphere of religion despite all manner of compelling state interests for so intervening.

Another approach to 'benign neglect' understands it contextually rather than as an abstract principle, yet is also problematic. Michael Walzer (2001: 150–3) believes that in immigrant societies like the United States benign neglect should apply equally to religious *and* ethnic minorities. Walzer grants that immigrant societies impose language and other nationalising cultural pressures on their citizens.[5] However, he argues that these national cultures are typically 'thin' and open to cultural difference. Under such conditions, state cultural provisions for religious and ethnic minorities are harder to justify. First, immigrants 'have to accept the cultural risks that immigration entails and sustain their own thick culture, if they can'. Second, because the national culture is thin, such minorities have less *need* of state support for their own ethnic or religious cultures, and so less entitlement.

'Thinness' is obviously a relative property. Walzer's main example of a thin national culture is the United States, with which he contrasts the much thicker and more imposing national cultures of Europe, and especially France. The other major immigrant democracies – Canada and Australia – arguably have thinner national cultures than the old nation-states of Europe, but also thicker ones than the United States. Walzer (1997) himself discusses Canada as a 'hard case'. And one of his proffered characteristics of a thin national culture – the openness to hyphenated or dual identities – doesn't much apply in Australia, where hyphenation is still frowned upon and cultural uniformity still championed, notwithstanding its thirty-year experiment with multiculturalism (Levey 2008b). The first limitation of Walzer's argument, then, is that it is unclear that it could apply to anywhere other than the United States.

---

[5] Previously, Walzer (1992: 100–1) has gone further to suggest that *non*-nation-states like the United States are 'neutral with reference to the language, history, literature, calendar, or even the minor mores of the majority'.

But does it apply *even* to the United States? In its favour, the obvious vestiges of Anglo-American or WASP dominance – such as Sunday as the nominal day of rest, Christmas as a public holiday, the office of Chaplain and the daily prayer recitation in both houses of Congress[6] – may not amount to much. In the abstract, thinness and equality might demand that the inscription of 'In God We Trust' on US legal tender be removed or, in the interests of polytheistic and atheistic inclusion, that 'In Gods We Trust' and 'Who is this God, anyway?' be added. Or one might simply say – along the lines of the Chaplain's Office of the US Senate – that 'the United States ... has honored the historic separation of Church and State, but not the separation of God and State'.[7] Either way, few people seriously worry that the current legal tender in the 'One nation, under God' meaningfully violates the rights and opportunities of non-monotheistic Americans.

It is also the case that American national culture has thinned out, in important respects, over the course of its history. Walzer (2001: 151) cites his own experience as an American Jew in appreciating just how thin and open American national culture is. Yet, American Jews had to battle hard against the entrenched idea of America as a Christian nation in the nineteenth and early twentieth centuries. Their renowned support today for a 'high wall of separation' between state and religion took root during their campaigns against Sunday closing laws and denominational trappings in public schools in the decades before and after the Civil War (Cohen 1992). At first petitioning for exemption against the 'blue laws', they progressively adopted the position that the laws themselves were a slight against their religious equality and should be abolished. From the 1940s, the American Jewish Congress and other secular Jewish organisations were at the forefront of developing the separationist position across a slew of issues before the courts (Pfeffer 1967; Wood 1985; Ivers 1995). In one sense, the Jews thus helped to transform American public culture. Yet, Walzer is right in that they could do so only because the national culture furnished

---

[6] However, guest chaplains from various faith communities are permitted to offer a customary prayer. This occasionally still provokes objection: when a Hindu recently led the Senate's morning prayer, members of a Christian group in the gallery shouted that 'this is an abomination' and had to be escorted out (*Guardian Weekly*, 20 July 2007).

[7] http://www.senate.gov/reference/office/chaplain.htm.

them the wherewithal to forge a separationist jurisprudence. It was the thickness of the First Amendment's Establishment clause, as it were, that enabled them to thin out the public space for themselves and others.

Walzer's account of benign neglect in the USA looks less compelling, I think, when one changes the angle and considers the plethora of exemptions allowed minority members from standing American law and policy. These bear on rules and regulations governing such things as dress codes, work time release, the preparation of food, medical and post-mortem procedures, and educational and employment provisions (US Commission on Civil Rights 1983; Curry 1989; Weisbrod 1989; Eisenberg 2002). Even if America's is the thinnest of all national cultures, it would appear to be not so thin – and minorities so un-needy of cultural consideration – that such adjustment of legal and other regulatory codes is deemed warranted. Neither, evidently, do immigrant minorities in the US entirely have to accept the cultural risks that immigration entails. Walzer's main concern is with public subsidies and group autonomy rather than exemptions for ethno-religious minorities, and so one could argue, I suppose, that American culture is thick enough to warrant various exemptions from general laws and regulations, but thin enough *not* to warrant public subsidies and autonomy for cultural minorities. Two points are worth making.

First, even if one judges that immigrant groups have little or no *just entitlement* to public subsidies or autonomous decision-making, there are other grounds upon which states may wish to extend such assistance or recognition. In an earlier essay, Walzer (1995 [1980]: 152–3) himself entertains the idea of 'ethnicity as a collective good'. Group membership often sustains a sense of identity and pride, yet there are many 'religious and cultural freeloaders', people who benefit from their group, but do not contribute their time or money to it. Hence, public subsidies to cultural minorities might help to sustain this kind of collective good. Another argument is that cultural diversity may be deemed a *public* good in the interests of *all* citizens and therefore deserving of some public support (Parekh 2000). This is a dominant theme, for example, in Australian multicultural policy (Levey 2008a). Thinness of a national culture, then, at best undercuts some, but not all, arguments for government support and recognition of cultural minorities. But secondly, Walzer's argument for benign neglect issues primarily from an assessment of need, and – as he concedes – community needs may change. One thing that may pre-empt such changes is benign neglect itself. Over time, a 'thinned-out' and benignly neglectful national culture can undermine thick minority cultures no less than 'thick' national cultures can. It is no accident, for example, that recent years have seen some secular American Jews join their more observant co-religionists in questioning their separationist fervour, as they wonder aloud whether its costs to their community now outweigh the benefits (Dalin 1993; Mittleman, Licht and Sarna 2002).

Whether framed in terms of abstract principle or national contexts, benign neglect is a 'blanket' concept that is ill-equipped to capture the complex, deep and multifarious relations between the liberal state, religion and ethnicity. The problem concerning religion extends beyond a particular concept, however. It goes to a deeply ingrained preconception about the *scope* of religion's distinctiveness in relation to the liberal state. Just how difficult it is to get beyond this preconception is well illustrated by a recent discussion of religious identity in democracies. Amy Gutmann (2003) offers what in many ways is a subtle and sophisticated analysis of the issue. She rejects the idea of a strict separation between church and state and between religion and politics. She argues instead for what she calls a 'moderate version of two-way protection', where 'church is protected from state and state from church, and neither protection is absolute ... because either protection taken to its extreme limits would undermine the other'. She also argues that the line dividing acceptable from unacceptable forms of religious accommodation is bound to be a 'permeable' one, since this will be decided by both 'ethical argument and democratic deliberation', and thus will vary across democratic contexts (Gutmann 2003: 154, 190).

And yet Gutmann quickly resorts to equating *significant* church–state separation with *strict* church–state separation. According to her, many democracies, 'such as Israel and England, are committed to something closer to a model of one-way protection, which accepts the first part of two-way protection – protecting religious freedom – but rejects the second part – separating church and state'. Similarly, she writes: 'Delegation to the most common organized religious groups of various political powers – often over publicly-funded education as well as family law – is another feature of one-way protection, illustrated by Israel, India, Canada, and Belgium' (Gutmann 2003:153).

This way of characterising these countries is too quick. It assumes that church–state separation means that government is totally divorced from any kind of engagement with religion or religious bodies. Historically, this was not the original meaning or format of church–state separation in the West, as Ian Hunter details in the next chapter; nor is it the pattern of most existing liberal democracies today. Indeed, as Veit Bader (2007: 334 n. 14) observes, the best exemplars of strict separation of state and religion are the 'Amish, Hutterites, Mennonites or Chassidism in the US, and ultra-Orthodox Jews in Israel', since they 'do not ask [for] or accept any public money and just want to be left alone and engage in politics only if this "splendid isolation" is threatened'.

Even on the 'divorced-from-religion' model, the cited countries qualify in an important sense. While they may each, in their own way, grant religious communities authority over certain areas of law or life, such as family law and education, they also deny these same communities jurisdiction over many *other* areas, such as criminal law and health. Israel is arguably the most problematic case of those mentioned. The ethno-religious character of the Jews for whom the state was created, the 'status-quo' concessions to the religious parties at the state's founding, the absence of any civil alternative to prescribed religious jurisdictions such as marriage and divorce – which sees many non-observant Israelis opting to marry abroad – and an electoral system that magnifies the influence of minor sectarian parties all combine to seriously entangle religion and politics. Still, Israel is no theocracy, and its laws ultimately remain subject to the civil courts (Jacobsohn 1993: 29). Of course, England has an established church, and this involves a religious test for a senior public office, namely, Sovereign of the Realm, along with some other formal privileges and duties. In truth, the significance of the established Church of England is, as Gutmann notes, largely symbolic. Indeed, even the symbolism rings hollow. In this day and age, most non-Anglicans in Britain are likely to consider their ineligibility to assume the monarchy to be a relief rather than a disability. Religious minorities do not much feel that establishment makes them second-class citizens (Modood 1994). The nativity qualification attached to the Presidency of the United States – which has frustrated Californian Governor Arnold Schwarzenegger's political ambitions – would appear to be a more significant handicap.

Strict church–state separation – such as the American 'high wall of separation' and France's *laïcité* – needs to be understood as occupying one end of a spectrum of church–state separation, not as the latter's very definition. Ostensibly the separation is not an end in itself but is designed to serve freedom of conscience, freedom of religion and civil coexistence. No less than Israel, the American and the French cases illustrate Gutmann's point that pursuing either church–state separation or religious freedom to the extreme will undermine the other. This much is obvious with the 2004 French law banning the wearing of conspicuous religious signs at state schools. Less obvious, though no less indicative, is the commonplace approach of liberals in the United States to want to exclude religious arguments from public debate, as Veit Bader discusses in Chapter 5.

Strict church–state separation also harbours a deep inconsistency in its ostensible concern for protecting freedom of conscience. Gutmann, for example, argues both that the consciences of non-religious and religious people should be respected and treated alike by democratic governments, and that 'publicly funded programs not be controlled by religious authorities or used for religious purposes' (Gutmann 2003: 154, 190–1). Why state subsidisation of religious groups threatens that which is important about church–state separation is not self-evident. Perhaps the most powerful explanation is Thomas Jefferson's (1982: 260): 'that to compel a man to furnish contributions of money for the propagation of opinions which he disbelieves *and abhors*, is sinful and tyrannical'. Maybe so. But it is also the case that democratic citizens routinely endure governments spending their money on all sorts of public policies that they may abhor. Some have to watch campaign funds go to parties or candidates whose policies they reject on the most profound moral grounds. Sometimes this situation is called the tyranny of the majority. More commonly, the acceptance of this situation as part and parcel of democratic life is said to be a democratic virtue.

I return to my initial observation. Religion is uniquely situated in relation to the liberal state at the same time that religious identity is akin to other forms of cultural identity. Negotiating these twin features of religion in liberal societies is not helped by overstating the scope or firmness of religion's unique situation. Some entanglements between religion and politics are manifestly contrary to a secular state

and liberal society: notably, the enforcement of religious doctrine or
laws, religious tests for public offices and opportunities, and the denial
of freedom of worship. Otherwise, the line demarcating church–state
separation is highly 'permeable', in Gutmann's phrase, or a 'floating
threshold', as Ian Hunter nicely puts it (Chapter 2, p. 0). Within a
'strict' separationist context like the USA, the anomalies in how
establishment clause cases are decided are legion.[8] Between contexts,
the anomalies are even more impressive. Thus, Britain's High Court
denies a schoolgirl's wish to wear a chastity ring as an expression of
her Christian faith on the grounds that the ring is not a Christian
symbol or requirement and so doesn't meet her school's uniform
exemption policy, while the American Civil Liberties Union (ACLU)
forces the US government to cease funding the Silver Ring Thing
chastity programme precisely because of its religious associations
(*BBC News* 2007; *BBC News* 2005).[9]

Clearly national contexts are important. It is not difficult to see why
the extraordinary religiosity of American society may warrant a
higher wall of separation between state and religion than elsewhere.[10]
But within particular contexts as across them, it turns out that our
images of secularism are often more fixed than our practice of it.

---

[8] As Michael McConnell (1992: 119–20) puts it:

> Thus, as of today, it is constitutional for a state to hire a Presbyterian minister
> to lead the legislature in daily prayers, but unconstitutional for a state to set
> aside a moment of silence in the schools for children to pray if they want to. It
> is unconstitutional for a state to require employers to accommodate their
> employees' work schedules to their sabbath observances, but constitutionally
> mandatory for a state to require employers to pay workers compensation when
> the resulting inconsistency between work and sabbath leads to discharge. It is
> constitutional for the government to give money to religiously-affiliated
> organizations to teach adolescents about proper sexual behavior, but not to
> teach them science or history. It is constitutional for the government to provide
> religious school pupils with books, but not with maps; with bus rides to
> religious schools, but not from school to a museum on a field trip; with cash to
> pay for state-mandated standardized tests, but not to pay for safety-related
> maintenance. It is a mess.

[9] In the latter case, after filing a lawsuit against the US government, the ACLU
reached a settlement agreement with the Department of Health and Human
Services that saw funding of the programme cease until the Silver Ring Thing
could clearly distance itself from religious activities. See: www.aclu.org/
reproductiverights/sexed/24246prs20060223.html

[10] Although it might also be the case that building high walls only encourages
people to try to get over them.

Is Islam different?

If poll results, editorials and a growing chorus of commentators are to be believed, however, the main problem today is not religion in general. Most faith communities in the West have long accommodated themselves to democratic norms and institutions. Rather, the problem is said to reside expressly with Muslims or in Islam. Certainly, it is unlikely that western democracies would suddenly be so concerned with secularism and its protection were it not for the Muslim presence and perceived challenge posed by Islam. Is Islam different from other religions vis-à-vis integration into western societies?

Whatever else may be said of Samuel Huntington's (1996) thesis of a clash of civilisations, his analysis had the virtue of addressing issues of potential conflict in broader terms than those slotted under the usual confines of religion. Often the points of friction between Muslim immigrants and their western host societies have as much to do with sensibilities and general cultural orientation as they do with specific Islamic precepts (a matter that Tariq Modood and I explore further in discussing the Danish cartoon affair: Chapter 10). The arrival in recent times of Muslim immigrants in numbers to Europe – and, to a lesser extent, North America and the antipodes – serves to remind us just how culturally laden are western institutions. Suddenly the patterns of our behaviour, the rhythms of our days and weeks and – as S. Sayyid points out (Chapter 8) – even the concepts through which we view and organise our world look, at turns, conspicuously Judeo-Christian (to use that often misleading phrase) or, more commonly, secular and cosmopolitan. Thin national cultures begin to feel a bit thicker in these circumstances.

Suggestions of a fundamental incompatibility between Islam and western societies nevertheless face the problem of the empirical evidence. The overwhelming majority of Muslims living in western countries have successfully integrated or seek to do so (Klausen 2005; Casanova, Chapter 6). Still, recurring controversies such as those over gender equality and freedom of expression do raise questions regarding the situation of Islam in the West.

One reason popularly cited for the distinctiveness or problematic nature of Islam is that it is a transnational religion. This suggestion is clearly inadequate. Catholicism and Judaism – to cite just two examples – are also transnational faiths that are, at the same time, well integrated into their national societies. To be sure, this was not always the case. However, this history only underscores the *similarities* between Islam today and the experience of other minority faiths. Locke (1963) baulked at tolerating Catholics (whom he considered loyal to Rome), and equivocated over tolerating 'Mohametism' (which he thought looked to Constantinople). And in the New World, Catholics were often reviled as disloyal and anti-modern, especially in nineteenth-century America (Casanova 2001, and Chapter 6) and in nineteenth- and early twentieth-century Australia (Rickard 1996). Similarly, the reservations and prejudices popularly aired today about the integration of Muslims are strikingly reminiscent of the impassioned debates over the incorporation of Jews as equal citizens in late eighteenth-century Europe (Levey and Moses forthcoming). Then the claims were that Jews were disloyal, clannish and separationist, adhered to an obscurantist religion and would not make good soldiers (since, it was presumed, they could not fight on the Sabbath or eat with their comrades, and were too short) or productive citizens (since they had too many holidays) (e.g. Michaelis 1995). Today the claims are that Muslims are separationist and disloyal, adhere to an anti-modern, sexist and violent religion, and are rather too soldierly in defending their faith. In any case, transnational religious allegiance scarcely seems the problem. In today's globalised world, where diasporic communities are increasingly common and where dual and multiple citizenships are legally recognised in many countries, transnational allegiances are quite at home.

Another popular impression is that Islam's difficulties in the West flow from Muslims being particularly pious. Meaningful comparison of levels of religiosity across different faith communities is a fraught exercise. However, clearly, there are many highly religious/observant/ practising faith communities, in their own terms, extant in western societies. More promising are observations that highlight particular features of Islam. One is that religions of ritual and law such as Islam and traditional forms of Judaism have a harder time 'accepting pluralism' than faiths that stress inner conviction and belief, such as Christianity, since these 'ask little of politics beyond being left alone' (Galston 2003: 73–4). This way of putting the point seems a bit askew; historically, both Islam and Judaism have had little trouble accepting pluralism in the form of other faith communities, as, shown, for example, by the Ottoman millet system. Both Bayle in his

Dictionnaire (1697) and Voltaire in his *Traité sur la tolérance* (1762) thought Islam far more tolerant than Christianity in practice.[11] More to the point is whether Islam and Judaism are challenged by *liberal* pluralism, with its emphasis on the freedom of the individual and common citizenship rights and obligations. The assumption that 'religions of law' are more likely than 'religions of belief' to clash with liberal law is understandable. Interestingly, exactly the opposite argument was made by the observant Jew and philosopher Moses Mendelssohn on the cusp of Jewish emancipation in modern Europe. Writing in the same year that Jefferson penned his *Notes on Virginia* – 1782 – Mendelssohn (1986) argued that because Judaism rejects dogmas and has no interest in the coercion of belief, it is more compatible with the new regime of civil laws than are Christian denominations. 'Let everyone be permitted to speak as he thinks' – Mendelssohn (1986: 139) counselled – 'to invoke God after his own manner or that of his fathers, and to seek eternal salvation where he thinks he may find it, as long as he does not disturb public felicity and acts honestly towards the civil laws ... and his fellow citizens'.

A related view to the 'religions of law' contention is that Islam has no notion of the separation of religion and state that might ease its adaptation to life in liberal democracies. Christianity has always had Jesus' admonition: 'Then give to Caesar what is Caesar's and to God what is God's' (Luke 20:25). And from the time of the Jews' Babylonian exile (586 BCE), their sages propounded the principle of *dina d'mulkhuta dina* – 'the law of the land is the law' – which recognised the political authority of non-Jewish rulers alongside the authority of Jewish law (Landman 1968). In fact, classical Islam did fashion something of a distinction between religion and state (Lapidus 1975; Hanafi 2002; Kelsay 2002). The religious scholars or *'ulama* had the task of interpreting the Qur'an and of defining who was a true Muslim, and served, to some extent, as a check on the power of government officials. The state, on the other hand, comprised a separate set of institutions, the caliphate foremost among them. Nevertheless, it is true that the caliphs ruled in the name of Islam and, indeed, were considered just rulers insofar as they upheld *shari'a* or Islamic law

---

[11] As Israel (2006: 618) paraphrases Bayle's position: the 'Muslims slaughtered far fewer people in the name of their religion than the Christians massacred during the St Bartholomew's Day Massacre in 1572 in Paris alone'.

(Kazemi 2002: 41). Muhammad – their model – was both prophet and statesman. Hence, in a common phrase, Muslims speak of religion and politics as *din wa dunya* or twins (Kelsay 2002: 7).

There is both an important similarity and difference between Islam and Judaism here. Like the Jewish principle of 'the law of the land is the law', the Islamic recognition of religious and political spheres was itself incorporated into the religious law. It did not follow the Christian notion of there being two distinct realms or jurisdictions – religious and civil (or four distinct realms, if we follow Charles Taylor's point in the preceding Foreword about the separate Christological distinction between the immanent and transcendent worlds). The Jewish sages ceded authority to non-Jewish rulers over some matters, such as taxes, but this recognition was itself posited as a religious injunction, and rabbinic authority was reserved over a considerably more extensive range of issues. The key difference is that the Islamic differentiation of religion and politics applied in a context where Muslims ruled themselves, whereas the Jewish version developed beyond the sovereign Jewish biblical commonwealths in a context of exile and of being subject to foreign rule (Galston 2003).[12] Muslims also have lived under foreign rule for many centuries, including in significant numbers in the wake of the Christian reconquest of Spain (*c.* 800–1492). However, as Abdullah Saeed notes (Chapter 9, p. 207), the 'natural state of affairs, from the point of the view of the jurists, was Muslim rule over Muslims'. Until relatively recently, the defining Muslim experience has been mainly one of self-government rather than of diaspora.

This historical dimension brings us to what is perhaps the most normatively significant point about the situation of Islam in contemporary democracies. Muslims were not a party to the religious-cum-liberal settlements that they are now expected to abide. For all their bitter experience, Catholics were a key party to the negotiations that resulted in the treaties of Augsburg (1555) and Westphalia (1648), which first institutionalised religious toleration and church–state separation (in the sense of divorcing politics from religious truth claims) in the modern West. While the Jews were outsiders to this

---

[12] Much classical, exilic Jewish thought nevertheless *imagines* the continued existence of Jewish self-government and sovereignty in the Land of Israel. See, for example, Levey (2006b).

process, later they were expressly asked by Napoleon I, in 1806 and 1807, where they stood on respecting the civil laws, their loyalty to France and their attitude towards their fellow citizens. Their generally agreeable answers changed Jewish life forever.[13] Muslims were neither a party to the religious settlements nor asked for their acceptance of liberal arrangements in this fashion.

For this reason, the significance of immigration looms especially large in the Muslim case. Does the act of immigrating imply an acceptance of all the norms and institutions of the host society? Or does a host society's willingness to admit people of culturally diverse backgrounds imply an acceptance to accommodate, at least to some extent, the immigrants' cultural difference? Such questions animate a good deal of public debate today over multiculturalism and cultural diversity in many countries. The recent introduction or flagging of so-called 'citizenship tests' in places such as the Netherlands, Germany, Britain and Australia – all mainly in response to Muslim immigration – seem to be attempts to provide some mechanism of contract or informed consent for would-be members of a society where it may have been absent. So, for example, the Netherlands now shows prospective immigrants from non-western backgrounds videos of couples kissing and homosexuals holding hands to better prepare them for life among the Dutch. Meanwhile, in Britain and Australia, the tests require English language proficiency as well as some familiarity with the history, institutions and 'core values' of these countries.[14]

These tests may or may not be effective in advancing the integration of newcomers; they certainly have been criticised on a variety of grounds. However, despite the inflammatory public debates they have sometimes occasioned, it is a mistake, I think, to view these tests as a return to the public-loyalty tests of old. In fact, citizenship tests do not

---

[13] It is probable that Judaism and the Jews would have been changed forever regardless of Napoleon's twelve questions to the Jewish Notables of Paris and their ratifying body, the Sanhedrin, a year later. The origins of Reform Judaism, for example, lie in the Jewish Enlightenment of the latter eighteenth century (Meyer 1967). The point is that the Jews were presented with an official opportunity to accede to the new terms of civic equality in Europe, and formally accepted them.

[14] On the Dutch and proposed German tests, see 'Testing the limits of tolerance', *Deutsche Welle*, 16 March 2006: http://www.dw-world.de/dw/article/ 0,2144,1935900,00.html. On the British and Australian tests, see respectively: www.lifeintheuktest.gov.uk/htmlsite/index.html and www.australiantest.com/.

really even test citizenship. Where it is not a formal legal status,
citizenship is a practice, usually mastered over the course of a life.
Citizenship tests at best test information and skills that are presumed
to be relevant to the practice of citizenship. Canada has had a written
test since 1994, and the US version dates back to the late 1980s. What
citizenship tests do not do is absolve liberal-democratic states from
grappling with how they might otherwise best respond to the cultural
diversity of their population. For one thing, the social, political and
economic factors that affect why people immigrate can often qualify
the sense of voluntarism implied by their departure for another
country (Levey 1997: 218). For another, and as noted earlier, even
where immigration is voluntary, needs and circumstances will often
change both on the part of immigrant groups and the host society.
Questions will perforce persist about how best to respond to particular
cultural claims in light of present conditions.

Have the original religious settlements outlived their usefulness?

When people say that Muslims fail to abide by western practices, they
forget that the western practice was just to reach an accommodation
between contending religious groups. Does this mean that the liberal
settlements of the religion question have now outlived their relevance?
Should we be thinking instead about a new settlement or pact?

The notion of 'settlement' in this context can be misleading. Our
so-called religious settlements mostly are and always have been
dynamic and evolving arrangements. In this book, for example, Ian
Hunter (Chapter 2) discusses the Brandenburg-Prussia case and its
implications for political thinking and practice today. For him, the
problem is that the original religious settlements based on modus
vivendi pragmatism that aimed to secure civil peace have been variously supplanted by post-Kantian rationalist, post-Thomist communitarian and critical-theoretical approaches. On this view, the original
settlements haven't been allowed to prove their contemporary worth;
we need to retrieve them. In contrast, for David Saunders (Chapter 3,
pp. 73, 79) discussing the French case, the challenge is in seeing how
the Separation of Churches and the State settlement of 1905 was not
then 'a transcendent principle ... fixed and constituted once and for
all', but rather a 'revisable *pacte laïque* for the peaceful coexistence of

different communities of faith'. This is not to say that, beyond France, there is no substance any more to the idea of religious settlements in liberal democracies. Clearly, there are traditions of thinking and practice – some inscribed formally in constitutions and some not – that set the boundaries of what may be institutionally possible and perhaps even of the imaginable in particular countries. There are also cases of religious 'settlements' being established in novel and instructive ways, as Rajeev Bhargava explains in relation to India (Chapter 4, pp. 82–109). Nevertheless, the terms of such settlements always require interpretation. So there is great latitude and, at times, call for reinterpretation and adjustment.

Liberal practice tends to be in advance of liberal theory here. Tariq Modood (Chapter 7) notes how liberals invoke secularism today to quarantine religious groups from participation in the public life and activity of Britain. So, it is worth recalling that long before anyone had heard of multiculturalism, Britain (like many other liberal states) was routinely extending to religious minorities various forms of accommodation. For example, Jews and Quakers have been entitled to solemnise a state-recognised marriage according to their own customs from the time of Lord Hardwicke's Marriage Act of 1753, while Catholics and Protestant non-conformists have been able to do so since the Marriage Act of 1836 (Hamilton 1995: 43–4). Under the 1944 Education Act, Roman Catholic, Methodist and Jewish schools were funded by the state (Modood 1994: 65), while a parent could demand that the education authority make arrangements to provide his/her child with a particular religious instruction where a county or voluntary school did not offer that form of instruction (Poulter 1986: 166) – similarly regarding legal exemptions. Mention has already been made of American Jews' (generally successful) quest to secure relief from Sunday closing laws in the late nineteenth century. In the state of New South Wales in Australia, Jews have been exempt from some laws governing animal slaughtering since the 1920s.[15] And so on.

Multiculturalism can mean many things and be defended on a variety of grounds, including identity and recognition, equality and

[15] *Prevention of Cruelty to Animals Act 1901–1953* (NSW). As I write, the New South Wales government has flagged its intention to again review the present exemptions available to Jewish and Muslim ritual slaughtering. Several countries in Europe have already outlawed or qualified these ritual practices.

justice, autonomy and liberty, civil peace and inclusion, and economic and public goods. The point worth making here, is that whichever interpretation one prefers (or none), there is a very real sense in which multicultural accommodation was foreshadowed in relation to religion long before it was applied to other identity groups. That practice should be in advance of theory is, perhaps, as it should be given Hegel's point that the owl of Minerva flies at dusk. Regarding secularism and religion, however, the question might be asked: how many dusks does it take before our theory aligns with what we think it right to do in practice?

The inverse problem also occurs, of course. Today there is a lot of talk about reaffirming 'core' liberal values in light of the perceived challenges to them from cultural minorities. Yet, many people confuse these values with the sentiment, 'this is how we do things here' (Levey forthcoming). A good example is the current debate in many places over Muslim girls and women wearing various forms of modest clothing, such as the *hijab*, *niqab* and *burka*. To be sure, sometimes the concern is framed in terms of gender equality, and this is a legitimate question, albeit one that recommends sifting cases rather than blanket prescriptions. Commonly, however, the objection is simply that such apparel is a 'visible statement of separation and of difference', as former British Foreign Secretary Jack Straw put it. Straw explained that it was essential to have 'face-to-face' conversations with his constituents, where one could 'see what the other person means, and not just hear what they say' (*BBC News* 2006c). This would likely be news to his colleague and the former Home Secretary, David Blunkett, blind since birth. Doubtless many people do find threatening the head coverings some Muslim women wear. But perception of threat is in the eye of the beholder; another way of dealing with confronting clothing is to get used to it. In many liberal democracies today, it would seem, 'you can take it off, but you can't put it on'; you can strip down, but you can't cover up. That is an odd way of honouring the core values of liberty and equality.

Inclusion and a sense of belonging are surely also important values for a cohesive society. As Bhikhu Parekh (2006: 200) observes, it is vitally important that 'Muslims in Europe' become 'Muslims of Europe and hopefully over time even Europeanized Muslims'. Europe may be able to learn from the major immigration democracies in this respect. In exploring the differences in the European and the American contexts regarding Muslims, José Casanova (Chapter 6, pp. 160–3) finds grounds for hope in the ability of successive immigrant generations in the USA to both adjust to and adjust established institutions in the effort to be 'at home'. As he puts it, 'Islam is becoming not just a fast growing religion *in* America, but an American religion'. Australia, too, has seen positive signs of accommodating Muslims despite a conformist culture and the Christmas 2005 Cronulla Beach riots. While Europe was debating headscarves and France was banning them at state schools, the Victorian Police Academy was supporting a specially designed *hijab* that allowed Australia's first Muslim policewoman to graduate wearing the traditional headpiece (*The Australian* 2004). In similar fashion, the *burka* has been modified to fit Australian lifestyle, with a 'burkini' now available to Muslim women training to be surf lifesavers (*Sydney Morning Herald* 2007). Some Australian Muslims have even begun to refer to themselves as 'Aussie Mossies'.[16] These are good examples of what Parekh means by 'neglected identities' being brought 'into creative interplay with the religious identity', and of individuals being encouraged 'freely to define and relate them'.

Earlier I noted how religious categories and arguments were the idiom in which 'secular' and liberal positions were originally cast, since this was the dominant mode of thinking at the time. Today, in the places with which we are concerned, the shoe is on the other foot: the dominant categories and idiom tend to be those of secularised or Enlightenment liberalism, and so questions of accommodating religion and cultural minorities are typically approached in these terms. Most religious traditions harbour diverse interpretations of the tradition's key beliefs and values, whether contemporaneously or over time, and usually both. This is as true of Islam as it is of Christianity and Judaism. Those who complain, for example, that what Islam needs most is its own Reformation need to get out more; this process of reinterpretation and readjustment in the face of contemporary circumstances is well underway, as Abdullah Saeed reports in Chapter 9, and to which process he himself is a contributor (e.g. Saeed 2006; see also Kurzman 1998).

If interpretive diversity applies to religious traditions, then it would be surprising if it weren't true of the liberal tradition as well. The history of liberalism is nothing if not the reinterpretation – and

---

[16] http://aussiemossie.blogspot.com/.

typically extension – of what its principles mean in light of prevailing circumstances. The original religious settlements have been, in this sense, modified and renegotiated ever since their inception. Core liberal values are vessels into which we pour our preferred meaning. John Rawls (1985: 242) noted how some people may 'regard it as simply unthinkable to view themselves apart from certain religious, philosophical, and moral convictions', even where 'our conceptions of the good may and often do change over time, usually slowly but sometimes rather suddenly'. Liberals are no less susceptible to such dynamics. The liberal approach most honoured in practice is a kind of 'principled pragmatism'. It is pragmatic insofar as it is responsive to contingency and changing needs. It is principled because exponents typically seek to show how new thinking respects what are taken to be the foundational values. This flexibility is doubtless one of the reasons why liberalism has proved so resilient. Multiculturalism is best understood as just the latest instalment of this principled pragmatism in responding to new groups and conditions. Even our current predicament, with all its fear and anxiety and associated retreat from multiculturalism in various ways, may be seen as a tweaking of the liberal reformation that is multiculturalism rather than a return to the hard assimilationism of old (Brubaker 2001).

In his posthumously published book, *In the Beginning Was the Deed*, Bernard Williams (2005) cautions liberals that they should never suppose that they have conclusively answered Hobbes's question of how to live together in mutual security. This applies to pragmatic no less than it does to rational-cum-universalistic approaches. It is an interesting question whether it is possible to return to purely pragmatic arrangements given the advanced, world-historical entrenchment of the Enlightenment project, reason and values such as individual autonomy.[17] What is clear is that today more than ever we can benefit from probing again the original religious settlements, recovering their 'pragmatic temper' where appropriate, and considering possible readjustments in the light of our multicultural condition.

---

[17] Early liberal ideas and arrangements have been increasingly promoted in recent years (e.g. Gray 2000, Kukathas 2003). In Levey (2006a), I question whether liberal critics of liberal autonomy fully let go of this normative tradition.

PART I

Debating secularism

2 The shallow legitimacy of secular liberal orders: the case of early modern Brandenburg-Prussia

IAN HUNTER

This chapter offers a brief discussion of the historical legitimacy of secular liberal political orders, taking early modern Brandenburg-Prussia as its main example.[1] The point of the exercise is to show that liberal government – together with the associated phenomena of political secularism and the distinction between public and private domains – arose in response to particular historical circumstances to which it remains tied. Proto-liberal political orders and styles of thought arose first in sixteenth- and seventeenth-century Europe in circumstances dominated by widespread religious civil wars, taking shape in the national religious settlements designed to bring these wars to an end.[2] Modern liberalism continues to bear the marks of its historical emergence not because of the purity of its origins or the

---

[1] As it is argued that the particular forms assumed by historical liberal orders depend on the character of nationally specific religious settlements, the German case is not offered as normative for all the others. Rather, it is used to exemplify the kinds of circumstance under which proto-liberal government emerged and the kinds of constraint this imposes on our understanding of their legitimacy.

[2] To characterise seventeenth-century Brandenburg-Prussia as 'proto-liberal' is certainly not immediately perspicuous, given the absolutist character of its government and considering that liberalism is normally associated with anti-monarchical democratic parliamentary groupings that arose during the nineteenth century. But neither is it revealing to characterise the forms of toleration and religious freedom that emerged in Brandenburg-Prussia as 'absolutist' in the usual sense, because they were products of complex developments in the jurisprudence and institutions of imperial *Staatskirchenrecht* rather than arising from unaccountable princely rule as such. And it is important to register the fact that it was indeed these juridical forms of toleration and religious freedom that passed into the nineteenth century, where they were rebaptised 'liberal' and entered into a marriage of convenience with democratic parliamentary platforms. Until a better term emerges, then, it seems that capturing this real continuity between seventeenth- and nineteenth-century

universality of its foundations, but because the exigency to which it was an improvised solution – that of governing rival religious, ideological or moral communities – remains a problem.[3] I shall argue that not only the legitimacy of liberal orders but also the ways in which we can think about this legitimacy remains tied to their role in managing this problem. This does not mean that liberal orders understood in this way are incapable of normative defence, although it does mean that this defence is characterised by a certain philosophical shallowness (Geuss 2002). The main philosophical discussions of liberalism have always regarded this shallowness as a fundamental weakness, giving rise to competing programs to provide liberalism with philosophical foundations or, in the case of communitarian critique, to do away with it altogether. I shall argue, though, that the philosophical shallowness of liberal orders is a direct outcome of their historical emergence and is a key condition of their (relative) success in handling the problem of governing antagonistic moral communities.

A good deal of the argument over the secular character of liberal orders takes place between those who think that Rawlsian political philosophy has provided a proper secular or public foundation for liberalism – in some construction of reason – and those who deny this. Those who deny it do so by arguing that Rawls's construction of reason is itself ideological and thus not properly secular and public in the required sense (of universally accessible or affirmable). This means that Rawls's attempt to exclude 'private' religious beliefs from the sphere of political decision must be regarded as one ideology's illegitimate attempt to exclude others. By silently identifying his philosophical liberalism with the liberal order itself, Rawls's critics prematurely

---

Staatskirchenrecht outweighs the risk of anachronism attending the use of 'proto-liberal'.

[3] In 1993, in the course of arguing against the continuing need for the religious neutrality of the modern state, Michael Perry could indicate his agreement with the statement that 'the risk of major instability generated by religious conflict is minimal. Conditions in modern democracies may be so far from the conditions that gave rise to the religious wars of the sixteenth century that we no longer need worry about religious divisiveness as a source of substantial social conflict' (Perry 1993: 714). The fact that this was written in the same year as the first Islamist attack on the World Trade Center in New York indicates a degree of historical prematurity in consigning religious divisiveness and state religious neutrality to the past, even if secular ideologies are equally capable of fomenting social conflict.

conclude that in exposing the ideological character of his constructions of reason they have shown that liberal orders – French Republican *laïcité*, German state pluralism, English broad-church liberalism – are themselves founded on an illegitimate secularist ideology. With the transformation of multiculturalism into multi-religionist apologetics, the demand to readmit diverse cultures into the political sphere – from which they have been (supposedly) illegitimately excluded – mutates into a demand to readmit diverse religions. It is by no means clear, though, what this demand amounts to in practice, given the uncertainty as to whether academic anti-liberalism is engaged in repudiating an American political philosopher or the liberal political order itself.

In the following I argue that this entire field of argument and counter-argument – secularist versus anti-secularist, liberal versus multicultural or communitarian – is redundant with regard to the historical existence and political legitimacy of secular liberal orders. Secular liberal orders are based neither on a universally accessible (secular) rationality nor on a particularistic (ideological) rationality, hence they are not open to philosophical defence or attack in the usually envisaged ways. The legitimacy of liberal political orders should rather be understood in terms of the goal of enforcing civil peace between mutually hostile religious or ideological communities, including, on occasion, between communities of secularists and anti-secularists. As we shall see, the political jurists who helped forge such orders did not regard civil peace as simply one norm among others – including justice, natural good, holiness, salvation – about which one might argue and among which one might choose on the basis of free reason, natural law or divine command. Rather, they regarded the unconditional acceptance of this norm as the only means of entry into the civil state. Further, they regarded the maintenance of civil peace as the key source of the state's legitimacy, rather than as an entitlement of states whose legitimacy rests on such supposedly higher sources as divine right or natural law, popular will or democratic deliberation. We shall see that such states were secular only in making civil peace (rather than holiness) into the objective of coercive political authority, thereby removing churches from the exercise of such authority, which the political jurists could do while remaining devout members of these churches.

Seen in this light, the demand to readmit religious (moral, ideological) communities to the public sphere is either a relatively harmless mistake or a less innocent attempt to erode the state's religious neutrality and pluralism. The demand is relatively harmless when it arises from the notion that the 'public sphere' is a domain of irenic debate from which the liberal order has unfairly excluded religions so that it can enforce its own secular ideology. Once it becomes clear, though, that the public sphere in liberal states is actually formed through the exercise of political-juridical coercion for the purposes of social peace, this demand loses its innocence. It becomes in effect a demand to allow religions and ideologies access to the state's coercive instrumentalities, as happens in confessional and party states. If anti-secularists are unsure about what they want in demanding the political recognition of religion, it is because they are unclear about where they stand in the political twilight between philosophical criticism and ideological subversion of the secular liberal order.

In developing this line of argument I shall be diverging from three main modern philosophical discussions of liberalism: post-Kantian discussions associated with Rawlsian philosophical liberalism, post-Thomist accounts focused on culture and community, and critical-theoretical discussions arising from the metaphysics of transcendental phenomenology. Despite their vociferous (and real) differences, these three broad traditions agree in ascribing the shallowness or normative weakness of historical liberalism to its lack of a grounding in popular sovereignty. Of course, each of the philosophical ideologies construes popular sovereignty in its own way: philosophical liberalism in terms of a consensus reached by individuals possessing universal reason; communitarianism in terms of a consensus arising from culturally perfectible goods; and critical theory in terms of inter-subjective agreement reached through discursive exchanges in a suitably idealised public sphere. This, I shall argue, gives rise to a fundamental misunderstanding of historical liberal orders, in part because it gives too much weight to a subsidiary historical development – the emergence of electoral democracies during the nineteenth century – and in part because the sovereignty of liberal states is not popular in any of the above philosophical senses. The sovereignty of early liberal states was conceived not in terms of a moral consensus that it had to express, but in terms of a political end that it had to achieve – namely, bringing peace to confessionally divided territories (Seidler 2002; Hunter 2004b). The basic idea was not that confessionally divided communities could reach a political consensus on the basis of universal reason or a common culture or, indeed, agonistic debate. Rather, it was that the inter-communal conflict resulting from the absence of such a consensus could be contained, if only states could develop a unified and unchallengeable form of political authority that was neutral between rival religious communities (Gray 2000).

The mismatch between philosophical discussions of liberalism and historical liberal orders has given rise to a series of related problems in contemporary debates. In the first place it has led to misunderstandings regarding the degree to which liberal orders are in need of justification and the kind of justification or legitimacy to which they are susceptible. Next, the mismatch has produced an inappropriate all-or-nothing argument regarding the neutrality or secularity of liberal states. Third, it has led to a similarly absolutist debate around the character and defensibility of liberal constructions of the public–private threshold, quite at odds with the historical and variable character of this separation. Finally, it has led to some basic misunderstandings concerning the sense in which historical liberal orders can be characterised as democratic. In the following remarks I say a few things about each of these problems, using the form of proto-liberalism that emerged in early modern Brandenburg-Prussia as my example of an historical liberal order.

Justification and legitimacy

If we are to understand the ineluctable shallowness of early modern justifications of proto-liberal government, then two initial observations are required. First, it must be recalled that the political thinkers who developed these justifications – in France, L'Hospital and Bodin; Hobbes and Locke in England; in Protestant Germany, Conring, Pufendorf and Thomasius – were not pure academics dedicated to philosophy for its own sake. Rather, they were jurists and political advisers who combined academic work with practical advice to rulers and governments, and who did so under the shared pressure of providing a rationale for government under conditions of religious civil war. Second, unlike today's Kantians, communitarians and critical theorists, in developing these rationales their prime concern was not to base politics on an independent theory of right or justice. Rather, it was to show how a politics whose prime objective was civil peace could itself be seen as just or legitimate (Geuss 2002). Their aim was not to show the political authority of morality, but the morality of political authority (Hunter 2004b).

It thus may be true yet beside the point to argue that early liberal rationales for political authority are not based on fundamental principles of justice, such as those developed in the name of rational individuals bent on respecting each other's freedom, or those derived from fundamental human goods supposedly embedded in human community or culture. Hobbes and Pufendorf were well aware of these deeper philosophical justifications for political authority, not least because of their hostile encounters with them in the contemporary Christian natural law and Aristotelian political philosophy that dominated the universities (Schneider 2001; Dreitzel 2003). They self-consciously rejected these deep justifications, however. This was in part because the justifications were ideological doctrines advanced by rival confessional parties and gave rise to irresolvable controversies over the true nature of the right or the good – as indeed they continue to do.[4] More importantly, though, it was because in their very depth these justifications threatened to undermine the grounding of civil authority in social peace. By pushing the ground of civil authority onto the specifically philosophical level of rational right or natural good, these justifications delivered it to the churches and their academic theologians and philosophers who, speaking in the name of these higher principles, could claim to legitimate civil authority and thus of course to de-legitimate it (Dreitzel 2001b: esp. 841–5). This was quite undesirable for thinkers whose prime task was to separate churches from the state and then to subordinate them to it, in order to render the state capable of governing confessionally divided communities.

In reworking the natural law tradition to provide an appropriately shallow justification for civil authority in sociability and civil peace, Samuel Pufendorf thus insisted that he was elaborating norms that would remain 'within the Compass of this Life only', that set aside the incendiary issue of salvation, that applied only to 'external' conduct regardless of inner beliefs, and that could be derived through observation and sound reason (Pufendorf 2003: 18–24). The net effect was to exclude salvational theology from the domain of political ethics. Pufendorf indeed made the political pact central to his grounding of

---

[4] For a modern instance of this kind of controversy, see the exchange between Robert Audi and Paul Weithman (Audi 1989; Weithman 1991; Audi 1991).

civil authority, yet, despite attempts to treat him as a representative of Aristotelian contractarianism (Denzer 1972; Behme 2002) or as a forerunner of the Kantian variety (Schneewind 1987; 1996), his construction of political authority is of a quite different kind. On the basis of a quasi-Hobbesian (Epicurean) political anthropology – according to which man is a creature driven by destructive passions and incapable of rational self-governance – Pufendorf establishes two conjoint bases for political authority: first, in the capacity of an authority to establish political subjection through coercion; and second, in this authority's 'just cause' for doing so (Pufendorf 1934: 87–112). This just cause is understood not in terms of a rational or communitarian consensus among the compacting parties, but in terms of the mutual fear that drives them to transfer their capacities for political decision and political coercion to the state, in exchange for mutual protection (pp. 949–66). Rather than arguing that might is right, Pufendorf's aim was thus to include might as a component of a reconfigured conception of right (Hunter 2004b).

Despite, or rather because of, its philosophical shallowness, Pufendorf's justification for obligation and authority is neither weak nor lacking in political salience and clarity. In making the state's concrete capacity for unchallengeable political coercion into a *condition* of its legitimacy – rather than treating coercion as a merely ancillary or instrumental capacity of a state that is already legitimate on other 'higher' grounds – Pufendorf avoids the dichotomies between the ideal and the real, rational principles and their 'non-ideal' contexts etc., that both disable political philosophy and render it incapable of facing up to the realities of rule. A state lacking the power to coerce also lacks the capacity to obligate its citizens. Further, by tying the citizens' recognition of their obligation to their fear-driven exchange of obedience for protection, Pufendorf makes the state's legitimacy independent of other or subsequent judgements concerning, for example, whether this exchange is truly just or fair, in accordance with the moral law or man's natural moral dispositions, and so on. For men have entered the state not on the basis of considered judgements regarding the fairness of its principles, or because these principles accord with natural goods or natural rights revealed by God or human reason, but simply out of fear of each other and for the mutual protection that the state offers. This means that the citizens' duty of obedience to the state should not be conditional on their judgements as to whether the state fosters such goods or respects such rights. Instead, obedience remains unconditional up to the limit case of the state failing to protect its citizens or becoming their enemy, at which point the pact dissolves into social war (Seidler 1996; Wyduckel 1996).

Pufendorf's reconstruction of political authority and obligation should be seen as a transposition of the fact of religious civil war into the register of ethical thought. Its basic premise is that rational agreement on fundamental norms is impossible and dangerous to pursue. It was the fracturing of Christendom into rival churches encased in mutually hostile confessional states and estates that had precipitated the series of wars of annihilation known collectively as the Thirty Years War (1618–48) (Heckel 1983; Schilling 1988; 1995). Pufendorf took this fracturing to be permanent and, unlike Leibniz, he was never tempted by a 'common ground strategy' according to which a synthetic or syncretistic 'philosophical religion' might yet provide the state with a broadly acceptable religious or moral foundation. Instead, drawing on the labours of anonymous public-law jurists responsible for the religious settlements of 1555 (Peace of Augsburg) and 1648 (Peace of Westphalia), as well as on such political scientists as Conring and Hobbes, Pufendorf argued that the survival of states (hence too of churches) requires that political authority be made immune from the 'private' religious aspirations and judgements of citizens. Owing to their grounding in rival theological conceptions of law, right and good, deep philosophical–theological justifications for political authority – in divine law or Christian natural law, in rational right or natural good, in the will of God or will of the community – are a liability in times of religious civil war, serving only to sharpen and intensify inter-communal religious conflict. Pufendorf's shallow rationale for political authority and obligation is thus more closely aligned with the political architecture of historical liberal orders than are those of his philosophical rivals, not least because his rationale was designed to defend such orders against de-legitimating philosophical and theological critique.

The pre-eminence of civil peace over the right and the good as the founding norm of political authority is thus not the result of its philosophical superiority. After all, it has always been child's play for philosophers to ask whether Pufendorf's construction of authority's 'just cause' – in terms of the exchange of obedience for protection – is itself just or good, thereby ostensibly bringing it into question.[5] Rather, the pre-eminence of the norm of civil peace is political, in the sense that the condition of entrance into the civil state is that those seeking its protection must leave all judgements regarding the best way to provide this peace to the state itself. In particular, to the extent that they might impact on the 'public' maintenance of peace, citizens must suspend philosophical and theological judgements regarding the right and the good, pursuing them only in a 'private' sphere defined (by the state) in terms of the absence of such impact. The question of whether it is right or good to exchange obedience for civil peace is thus either inconsequential (to the extent that it remains in the 'private' space of the academic seminar) or illicit (to the extent that it results in actions that breach a civil peace deemed to be unjust or wrong).

Pufendorf's radical reconstruction of the character and legitimacy of political authority has two main consequences for modern discussions of the liberal state and for questions of secularity and multiculturalism in particular. In the first place, by conceiving entrance into the civil state in terms of the fear-driven exchange of obedience for protection, Pufendorf refuses to treat the citizen as an extension or expression of a pre-existing moral personality, such as that of the Christian ruled by divine law or the 'man' bound by natural law.[6] Instead, he regards the citizen as a *sui generis* moral persona created by the political pact and subject to the duty of political obedience arising from it (Pufendorf 2002: 67–9, 92–3). To the extent that Pufendorf's construction captures a basic element of the liberal state, then it is impossible for such a state to 'recognise' cultural or religious personae (communal identities) in the political domain *stricto sensu*; that is, to accept these personae as the source and object of the state's unchallengeable exercise of political coercion, or sovereignty. Indeed, the whole point of Pufendorf's architecture is to ensure that political coercion will not be exercised on behalf of cultural or religious

---

[5] Leibniz initiated this philosophical critique of Pufendorf, but one finds a similar critique of the attempt to ground political ethics in social peace in Kant and his followers, including Rawls. For further discussion see Hunter (2004a).

[6] It is not difficult to extrapolate this separation of civil and religious persona to other religious identities, for example, Jews and Muslims living inside modern liberal states. But it should also apply to ideological identities – for example, to Marxists and even Thomist communitarians and Kantian liberals – in the sense that the ideals of the person envisaged in these ideologies should not be coercively enforced by the state.

personae – the prime source of religious civil war – and will instead
be exercised on behalf the newly autonomous persona of the citizen,
understood as instituted through the exchange of obedience for civil
peace.

At the same time and for the same reason, however, it is impossible
for the exercise of political coercion to be based on the persona of the
rational individual, whether this persona is construed in terms of the
capacity to enter into a rational consensus (Rawls 1971), to adopt an
impersonal truth-based 'view from nowhere' (Nagel 1987), or to have
rationally justified knowledge of the 'objectively' good life (Raz
1990). Pufendorf's individuals have just enough reason to know that
their insecurity and fear can be alleviated through the appointment of
a sovereign, but not enough to make the sovereign's commands into
the embodiment of their collective rational will. Rather than freely
entering the sovereignty pact in order to co-ordinate their rational
judgements – as in Rawls's 'original position' or Habermas's 'ideal
speech situation' – Pufendorf's individuals are driven into the pact
by fear, and find themselves transformed by an agreement that is
neither rational nor free. Through the pact they acquire a new persona: not that of the individual capable of some form of rational self-
governance, but that of the citizen capable of being governed by a
sovereign to whom he has delegated his capacity for political reason.
In short, neither communitarian nor liberal forms of political philosophy can engage the architecture of historical liberal orders because
both assume a continuity of identity between 'man' – as a rational and
moral being – and 'citizen', the model for which is the unified persona
of the philosopher himself. Historical liberal orders, however, are
premised on the separation of these personae. It is for this reason that
Pufendorf rejects all conceptions of popular sovereignty.

The significance of this minimalist or shallow architecture for the
liberal state is that it does not require individuals to have a substantive
moral personality in order to qualify as citizens. Citizens of the liberal
state do not have to be the *vir bonus* of the Aristotelian *polis*; the
orthodox Christian of the early modern confessional state; the good
party member of the Marxist party state; or, indeed, the good public
reasoner of a Rawlsian rational republic, or the active citizen of a
'deliberative democracy'. This is because in early liberal orders the
state is seen not as the expression of its citizens' moral personalities
but as the organised means of ensuring that they will not harm each

other, particularly when they disagree over the best kind of moral personality. Such a state makes no deeper moral demands on its citizens than that they be law-abiding in their external behaviour. As individuals whose vocation often involves cultivating and defending a unified and substantive moral personality, theologians and moral philosophers are uniquely ill equipped to understand the moral minimalism of liberal citizenship.

The second broad consequence of Pufendorf's reconstruction of political authority is that while it vastly increased the power of the state in the domain of the political, it simultaneously drastically reduced the scope of such power, by restricting it to just this domain (Holmes 1995; Schmitt 1996). As a result of their separation from the persona of the citizen, the 'man' and the Christian could no longer seek to influence the governing powers of the state. For the same reason, however, the state could no longer claim to govern the personae of the 'man' and the Christian; that is, individuals in the course of their familial, commercial and religious lives, to the extent that these lives entailed no breach of civil peace. As we shall now see, the secularisation of the state achieved by restricting it to the end of maintaining civil peace was not one that had to extend to all domains of society, precisely because it was not based on a secularist philosophy or a universalising conception of reason.

Neutrality and secularisation

It is not difficult to see the marks of a certain kind of secularisation in Pufendorf's construction of political authority. This is clear enough in his use of the goal of civil peace to exclude salvationist theology from the justification of sovereignty, with a view to precluding the exercise of sovereignty on behalf of mutually hostile Christian confessions (Döring 1993). Moreover, this secularisation is connected to the proto-liberal character of Pufendorf's conception of government. In restricting the exercise of political authority to the achievement of civil peace, secularisation confined legal coercion to 'external' actions, thereby supplying an important rationale for toleration and religious freedom (Seidler 2003). The state should have no business in policing how citizens found their way to God or, indeed, whether they did.

Understanding the relation between early modern secularisation and proto-liberalism turns out to be unexpectedly difficult, however,

mainly because modern discussions rely on categories that arose
during the nineteenth century and reflect concerns quite unlike those
held by the early moderns. On the one hand, modern philosophical
liberalism has tied the state's religious neutrality to secularisation by
identifying the latter with reason. Here reason is understood as a
general human capacity to grasp norms that are in principle capable of
being freely affirmed by everyone, thereby excluding the particularistic norms associated with religious belief as principles for state
action (Audi 1989). Despite the fact that philosophical liberals like
Rawls and Nagel shy away from calling this conception of reason
'secular', preferring instead such adjectives as 'public' (Rawls 1993:
212–54) or 'impersonal' (Nagel 1987; 1991), it seems reasonably clear
that these are indeed synonyms for secular. This is not least because
the key contrast-class is 'comprehensive religious and philosophical
doctrines', whose incapacity for universal assent is due to their ori-
ginating in beliefs lying outside generally accepted and scientific forms
of reasoning (Rawls 1993: 224–5). These philosophical liberals refuse
to countenance the Hobbesian and Pufendorfian construction of the
state's religious neutrality – in which the state declares itself confessionally indifferent in order to secure civil peace – because such a
settlement is not something freely affirmed by everyone and is therefore neither reasonable nor legitimate according to their philosophico-
democratic conception of legitimacy. Rawls rejects this path to civil
peace because it is not 'stability for the right reasons', thereby indi-
cating his prioritisation of right reason over stability, or philosophy
over civil peace (Rawls 1993: xxxix, 142–4). The philosophical
(Kantian) conception of neutrality or secularity (in terms of rational
universalisability of norms) and the democratic conception of political
legitimacy (in terms of free universal affirmation) are thus mutually
reinforcing. In making the neutrality and legitimacy of the state
depend upon the citizenry's general acceptance of a particular conception of reason, however, philosophical liberalism can scarcely
avoid having to impose this conception of reason on the citizenry,
thereby jeopardising the state's neutrality towards 'comprehensive
religious and philosophical doctrines'.[7]

---

[7] Benhabib (1986: 316–27) treats this problem as a dilemma arising from the
universalisability principle, and Baynes (1992: 72–3) refers to it as the
'paradox of democratic legitimation'. They are not interested in the fact that

On the other hand, communitarian and Catholic (Thomist-Aristotelian) philosophers have developed their negative view of the neutrality or secularity of the liberal state by attacking the philosophical liberals from the standpoint of a rival philosophical (or theological) anthropology. Beginning with the premise that all norms are embedded in ideas of the good life held by particular cultural and ideological communities, they apply this to the norms of Rawlsian rationality and neutrality, understandably treating them as symptomatic of a (Kantian) rationalistic of philosophical culture and conception of the person (MacIntyre 1988; Kymlicka 1989; Sandel 1998). Underlying this critique, however, is a specifically Thomist-Aristotelian conception of the person, understood as a repository of dispositional goods – benevolence, justice, reason – whose realisation awaits participation in the community that transmits their perfected forms (Douglass 1994; Hollenbach 1994; Reames 1998). Given that the state is not the only community in which this might occur and, indeed, that religious communities might well be better placed to perfect such goods, then it is illegitimate to exclude religions from the public sphere (Taylor 1992) or to separate church and state (Weithman 1991). We can note in passing that the communitarian exposé of the ideological dimension of Rawlsian (Kantian) reason is easily matched by the Rawlsian critique of the particularistic character of communitarian (Thomist) conceptions of the good, leading to a stalemate whose roots are almost certainly to be found in nineteenth-century battles between Protestant and Catholic metaphysicians. It is more important to observe, though, that in attacking Rawls's rationalist-secularist conception of neutrality, the communitarians purport to be attacking the religious neutrality of historical liberal orders themselves. This of course is a convenient presumption for anti-secularists, for it makes it look as if the religious neutrality of actual liberal states is an expression of a comprehensive secularist doctrine, and hence can be licitly opposed in the name of an anti-secularist doctrine. But this turns out to be wrong, on both counts.

---

this problem does not affect historical liberal orders – that is, liberal orders not grounded in ideologies of popular sovereignty – as their concern is with showing how the paradox can be resolved within the parameters of this ideology by, for example, the 'utopian' transformation of citizens into democratic dialogue partners.

To the extent that they are based on historical argument, both sides of the debate over secularisation misunderstand the sense in which an early liberal state like Brandenburg-Prussia was secular, and the kind of religious neutrality it developed. In early modern Germany, secularisation was not the stake in an all-or-nothing philosophical–theological struggle over the foundations of state and society. Rather, as Martin Heckel has shown, it was a relatively little-used term within the apparatus of imperial public law, emerging in the context of public-law settlements to religious civil conflict.[8] The first recorded modern use of the Latinate word 'secularisation' is dated at 1646. Here, significantly, it was the term chosen by the French ambassador to the treaty negotiations for the Peace of Westphalia, the Duc d'Longueville, to refer to the abolition of religious principalities and the expropriation of church property by Protestant states (Heckel 1989a: 773). This first usage is a pointer to the political-juridical setting in which secularisation emerged, and to the limited array of historical developments that it covered in the early modern period. During the seventeenth and eighteenth centuries secularisation centrally referred to the state's withdrawal from the enforcement of religious (canon) laws, particularly in the areas of heresy and witchcraft; the establishment of judicial parity of treatment for the Catholic, Lutheran and (eventually) Calvinist churches in imperial legal and political institutions; and the establishment of 'political toleration' of the three main confessions as mandated by the complex provisions of the Peace of Westphalia, which was secular in the sense of having divorced peace from the question of the truth of the rival confessions (Heckel 1989a: 789–96).

Pufendorf characterised these developments in terms of the separation of state from church and, indeed, they can be said to have resulted in the secularisation of the state in the sense that it now sought to govern churches as civil associations, remaining neutral between their rival truth claims (Pufendorf 2002). These developments, however, did not issue in a wholesale secularisation or

---

[8] Heckel is the pre-eminent German historian of church–state relations and of public church law (*Staatskirchenrecht*). His papers have recently been collected as *Martin Heckel, Gesammelte Schriften: Staat, Kirche, Rechte, Geschichte*, ed. K. Schlaich (Tübingen: J. C. B. Mohr, 1989–97), 4 vols. In this section I rely on his remarkable yet under-used treatise, 'Säkularisierung: staatskirchenrechtliche Aspekte einer umstrittenen Kategorie' (Heckel 1989a).

'rationalisation' of society, still less in an evacuation of religion from a 'disenchanted' world. Neither did they result in the state adopting a secularist ideology to be used as an instrument of general social transformation. Such ideas belong to the nineteenth and twentieth centuries, and are associated not with public-law peace treaties but with the academic disciplines of philosophical history (Hegel, Marx, Habermas) and sociology (Durkheim, Weber, Habermas), which purport to track social and intellectual processes whereby a de-Christianised scientific view of the world arises from social modernisation and rationalisation (Heckel 1984). These ideas are radically anachronistic in relation to the early modern secularisation of the state, which refers not to some wholesale transformation of society and the person, but to a specific reconfiguration of the relations between political, juridical and ecclesial institutions and their associated moral personae. Far from being undertaken by atheistic philosophers seeking to *écrase[r] l'infame*, this reconfiguration was the work of devout jurists, seeking above all to protect their own confession from annihilation by its rivals, and finding this protection in a system of state-regulated churches.

In Pufendorf's summary recapitulation of this complex state of affairs, there were now two kingdoms: a civil or political kingdom, and a 'Kingdom of Truth' (Pufendorf 2002: 32–6, 56–9). The Kingdom of Truth is inhabited by teachers and learners where, as in the relation between Christ and his disciples, the truth would be conveyed through love and emulation to the exclusion of all coercive power. The civil kingdom, though, is inhabited by the sovereign and his subjects, and here civil peace would be maintained through the exercise of coercive power, but only if the sovereign relinquishes all claims to teach the truth and refrains from all religious compulsion. Defined by the coercive maintenance of social peace, the persona of the prince or state has no role in the pursuit of religious or philosophical truth. Defined by the pursuit of theological and philosophical truth, the persona of the teacher or church has no role in the exercise political authority (pp. 69–73, 91–94). Churches would thus become 'colleges' or voluntary associations within the state, while the state would become the security envelope within which civil associations are to be contained (Schlaich 1997). As Heckel shows, the results of this secularisation are limited and ambivalent, as it is only the political-juridical framework of the state that is secularised, leaving churches and

other associations free to pursue rival absolute truths within the parameters of social peace (Heckel 1989a: 893–5).

The religious neutrality of an early modern liberal state like
Brandenburg-Prussia was thus not based on a universalisable reason,
impersonal standpoint or 'view from nowhere'. The notion that this
neutrality must be based on rational truths that all parties could
affirm – including the rival churches – is something that its architects
would have regarded as absurd at best and dangerous at worst. The
gradual secularisation of juridical and political institutions was not
the result of insights into objective truths – whether those of common
sense or scientific reason – governed by the principles of rational
universalisation and democratic affirmation. It was instead the outcome of piecemeal political-juridical changes. These were governed by
the end of establishing peace between the fratricidal confessions
regardless of ultimate truth, and were executed by an echelon of
political jurists (*Staatskirchenrechtler*) who had mastered the new art
of separating their personae as Christians and citizens, giving rise to a
view from somewhere very particular indeed. Of course, modern
philosophical liberals can say that even if this neutrality of the early
liberal state results in civil peace, it is not 'stability for the right reasons', and is illegitimate to the extent that political coercion is not
based in reasons that can be democratically affirmed. Proto-liberals
like Pufendorf would not have cared in the slightest, however, as they
had their own conception of legitimate coercion, based solely on the
exchange of obedience for protection.

At the same time and for the same historical reasons, however, the
religious neutrality of early liberal states was not, as the communitarians and associationalists claim, the expression of a secularist
doctrine or ideology lacking pre-eminence over the theological doctrines of the churches. As we have observed, neutrality was rather the
result of the historical removal of theological doctrines from a complex of political and juridical institutions: from legal systems and legal
training, systems of political representation and legislation, and the
institutions for negotiating and concluding peace treaties. In the
context of the growing military and economic power of emergent
territorial states, these changes were intended to transform churches
from the status of estates participating in political authority to that
of voluntary associations under the tutelage of sovereign territorial
states. The religious neutrality of early liberal states was thus not the

result of a philosophical or theological theory that might be proved false, but of a set of changes that rendered law and politics indifferent to the truth and falsity of such theories.

Pufendorf and Thomasius were quite familiar with the communitarian conception of the state, as Aristotelian and Thomist versions of this doctrine continued to dominate the teaching of politics and natural law in seventeenth-century universities, Protestant as well as Catholic (Dreitzel 1988; 2001a, 2001b). As a result of the changes just mentioned, however, the Thomist-Aristotelian conception of the state – as the means of perfecting man's natural moral disposition or good – was gradually rendered redundant. The emerging liberal state was one in which 'it is discipline, not nature, that fits a man for such a society' (Pufendorf 1934: 952), and in which 'it is not necessary that subjects give their whole hearts to the cultivation of virtue … as … it is enough that they refrain from external vices to the extent that they disturb external peace' (Thomasius and Brenneisen 1696: 28). From this point on, the Aristotelian conception of the polity as the community in which man perfects his inner moral disposition would find its concrete correlate only in the church, which nonetheless continued to function as a model for society as such. This state of affairs is most evident in the Catholic-Thomist conceptions of 'civil society' as the church writ large (Colas 1997), but is also manifest in Protestant-Kantian conceptions of the 'kingdom of ends' and the 'ideal republic', which are conceptions of a morally improving society or church (Hunter 2001: 353–63). Despite their vociferous internecine disputation – so characteristic of rival ecclesiologies – Rawlsian defences of secular neutrality and communitarian attacks on this in the name of a repressed community are both defences of an ecclesial conception of society against the reality of a state long since indifferent to the moral perfection of its citizens.

The secularisation that permitted early modern German states – specifically, Brandenburg-Prussia – to establish neutral parity of treatment for rival religions was thus not based on the (supposed) universal freedom and autonomy of secular reason. It was too strongly tied to a particular historical problem (that of governing conflicting confessional communities) and was too deeply indebted to particular styles of thought (public-law jurisprudence and the political sciences associated with it) for this to be the case. At the same time, the secularised neutrality of proto-liberal states was not an expression of a secularist culture – at moral par with the rival religious cultures – or an ideological mask for the imposition of secular values on autochthonous moral communities or associations. We can see this from the fact – discussed below – that this same neutrality would later be used to protect religious orders and religious schools when radical secularist parties sought their abolition through democratic mandate. Even if it emerged from the purging of theocratic imperatives from political and juridical institutions, the neutrality of the liberal state could be and indeed has been used to prevent secularist ideologies from capturing these institutions. To repeat the point, this is because this neutrality is not based on a secularist philosophy but on the imperative to pacify conflicting ideological groupings, which can be secular or religious. It is thus quite misleading of those seeking to divorce liberalism from secularisation to characterise such *secularist* ideological states as Nazi Germany and the Soviet Union as *secular* in the historical sense. On the contrary, these were states whose political and juridical institutions were indeed captured by ideological parties, destroying the neutrality derived from their historical secularisation, and turning them in effect into modern avatars of the millenarian confessional state (Caplan 1988).

The public–private threshold

The tendency of opposed philosophical positions to result in all-or-nothing contests, so characteristic of the secularism debate, is no less marked when it comes to discussions of the public–private threshold. Pufendorf's construction of political authority leads to a demarcation of a public political domain along two convergent axes. In the first place, the public domain is equated with the sphere of politics, where politics is understood in terms of the state's exercise of coercive power restricted to ('external') actions capable of infringing civil peace. Second, this requires excluding from the domain of the political those forms of discourse incapable of observing this restriction or that serve other ends. For Pufendorf, this exclusion applied pre-eminently to theology, whose objective is not civil peace but salvation, and which targets man's inner moral condition (Pufendorf 2003: 17–21). Thomasius, though, extended it to metaphysical philosophy and Christian natural law, to the extent that these too promised man some kind of moral regeneration through contact with transcendent truths (Thomasius 1950).

In converging on the idea of a state restricted to maintaining public (external) peace as delimited through public (non-theological, political-juridical) discourse, Pufendorf's construction was in fact recapitulating a fundamental historical transformation: the gradual de-theologisation and juridification of political discourse that had taken place during the sixteenth and seventeenth centuries as a result of the pressure to find political and juridical solutions to religious conflicts (Hammerstein 1986; Heckel 1989b). 'Public' in this context took its bearings from *jus publicum* or public law: the juridical ordering of the state's field of action as it had emerged from the great imperial religious settlements; the laws and decrees of territorial princes; and the political jurisprudence of figures like Conring, Pufendorf and Thomasius (Stolleis 1995). Here the concept of public had nothing to do with the metaphysical notion of unfettered communication between intellectual beings (Hunter 2005: 23–6). This metaphysical idea of public, however, would be merged with the political in Kant's conception of popular sovereignty, and transmitted to modern debates via Habermas's doctrine of the public sphere and Rawls's concept of public reason (Kant 1970a; 1970b; Habermas 1989; Rawls 1993: 212–54). A good deal of the confusion in modern discussions of the public–private demarcation comes from the anachronistic projection of the latter metaphysical conception of the public onto the former public-law conception. This is a confusion that debilitates the discussions undertaken by both Rawlsian philosophical liberalism and Habermasian critical theory.

John Rawls seeks to elide the particularity of the political-juridical construction by merging it with the notion of public reason. If public reason wins the right to filter the doctrines and norms entering the public political domain – that is, to determine the doctrines and norms suited to coercive enforcement – this is in part because it employs common-sense forms of reasoning and generally accepted scientific knowledge (Rawls 1993: 223–7). But it is also because it applies this common reason to constitutional ideas and values understood as 'implicit in the public political culture of a democratic society' (p. 223), rather than to the values or doctrines of particular (religious, ideological) associations, which would result in a 'non-public' use of reason. In a clear pointer to the presence of the metaphysical conception of public, however, Rawls refuses to deem non-public uses of reason 'private', preferring instead to see them as 'social' and arguing

that they can still 'converge' in the public domain if everyone respects 'the fundamental concepts and principles of reason' (pp. 220–1).
This precludes any recourse to the public-law understanding of public:
namely, as the space of compulsory tranquillity maintained by political-
juridical institutions whose constitutive premise is that opposed ideological groups do not share fundamental principles of reason and
therefore must be governed independently of such principles. On the
contrary, Rawls treats the paramount juridical institution – the United
States Supreme Court – as itself the 'exemplar of public reason'. The
court can have this role because Rawls views it as the custodian of both
common public reason and a Lockean 'higher law' whose role is to set
constitutional limits for political authority, thereby turning the court
into the instrument and interpreter of popular sovereignty (pp. 231–4).
In short, Rawls seeks to overcome the historical (political-juridical)
particularity of the liberal public domain by identifying the constitutional court with both common reason and a higher (natural) law. In
doing so, he forgets the role of the state in establishing the pacified
society in which courts can operate. He also risks turning the constitutional court into a kind of Kantian church or secularist Vatican, by
treating it as the organ of a perfected community of public reasoners.

In opposing Rawls's philosophical liberalism, critical theorists seek
to solve the problem by challenging the normative credentials of the
public–private threshold as such. This is in part because critical theory
establishes an array of illegitimate public–private dyads, in which the
liberal separation of state and church is aligned with the capitalist
separation of state and market, and with the patriarchalist separation
of the male domain of work and the female domain of family, sexuality and domesticity – all of which entail repression and exclusion of
the private side of the dyads (Benhabib 1992, 2002). But the ultimate
source of this delegitimation of the secular state lies in critical theory's
background metaphysics, transcendental phenomenology, which
regards any regulatory formalisation of a given domain as an occlusion
or instrumentalisation of the 'life-world'. The life-world is understood
as the domain of pure inter-subjective meaning-creation and is thus a
variant form of the metaphysical conception of the public as the
community of rational (spiritual) beings (Husserl 1970: 161–4). Like
Rawls, critical theorists thus have a doctrinal commitment to the belief
that 'private' differences will be overcome through the purification
and convergence of formalised doctrines in a space of free rational

exchange, except that they ascribe this overcoming to the long-term evolution of democratic institutions rather than short-term reconciliation of personal viewpoints (Baynes 1992). In this intellectual setting, the early modern juridical construction of a public political domain loses its defining rationale in the pacification of fratricidal religious associations. It passes through the looking-glass of metaphysics and appears instead as a formalistic occlusion of life-world contexts destined to be overcome with the return of the true public sphere: the unfettered dialogue of the members of an 'ideal speech community' (Habermas 1996). Similarly, it has been argued that the political-juridical privatisation of religion is destined to be overcome through an historical process of 'deprivatisation'. This will see religions lose their own formalistic and repressive aspect, thereby re-entering the 'public sphere' to participate in democratic will-formation on behalf of the life-world (Casanova 1994: 40–66). Again, the metaphysical conception of public is being retrospectively projected onto the actual political-juridical construction of public as the state-maintained space of compulsory civil tranquillity.

Despite all that can be learned from this rich debate, it should already be clear that both sides of it are inimical to the proto-liberal construction of a political public sphere. Two broad points will have to stand for a much longer discussion. In the first place, neither philosophical liberalism nor critical theory can comprehend the specific language in which politics was separated from religion, and the highly ambivalent cultural-political context in which this language was formulated. A central discourse in this regard was that concerning the *adiaphora* or 'indifferent things': things neither prescribed nor forbidden by God, hence unnecessary for salvation. In deeming to be *adiaphora* the vast bulk of matters over which the rival confessions had spilt blood – everything from public holy days and liturgical forms through to the sacramental rites and the incendiary theological doctrines of the Trinity and Christ's 'two persons and one nature' – Pufendorf's follower Christian Thomasius sought to consign them to two adjacent realms. Either the *adiaphora* belong in the domain of 'Christian freedom', where individuals can choose to observe these indifferent matters or not, without suffering religious coercion; or, should they give rise to public tumult, then they fall within the sphere of state supervision, where they become matters of sovereign command and legal regulation (Thomasius 1994). The *adiaphora* are thus not matters on which religious associations currently disagree but from which they might be led to a politically enforceable overlapping consensus through Rawlsian public reason. Neither are they matters whose contentiousness might be overcome through a process of historical evolution that will transmute their fractious adherents into irenic participants in the state's dialogical foundations. Rather, they are matters in relation to which the state employs a studied indifference to the extent that they do not lead to breaches of civil peace, and a calibrated coercion to the extent that they do. Here we can see the historical separation of private and public domains.

The proto-liberal distinction between matters of free private observance and public matters subject to political coercion was thus not a principled one, based on the philosophical distinctions between non-public and public reason, or 'personal' and 'impersonal' viewpoints. But neither was there no such distinction, as if the private were merely a voice that had been arbitrarily excluded from a public sphere to which it must return in free communication with all other voices. Rather, what emerged was a shifting threshold in which forms of religious worship could be either public or private – open to political coercion or not – depending on political-juridical assessment of their capacity to threaten social peace. In a typical actual case, Thomasius considers the question whether under the terms of the Treaty of Westphalia – guaranteeing toleration to the three main confessions – a Catholic prince may ban his Lutheran subjects from singing a popular hymn that reviles the 'pope's murderous ways', or whether this is a private religious matter. As *adiaphora*, hymns in general might fall into either category yet, given its capacity to threaten civil peace, this hymn is properly carried across the threshold of public suppression by the prince's assessment that it does indeed threaten civil peace (Thomasius 1994: 121–4). Similarly, modern liberal states face no fundamental political, juridical or ethical obstacles when banning 'hate speech' that emanates from Christian churches or Islamic mosques. Once it is seen that the liberal state is not an expression of the rights or beliefs of its citizens, and is only a means of ensuring that they will not harm each other, then it is redundant to claim that such action infringes civil and religious liberties.

The discourse on *adiaphora* contributed to the formation of a public political domain principally through its use to secularise the legal system. In his campaign against the canon and civil laws used in heresy prosecutions, Thomasius could thus declare all of the doctrines over which dissidents were accused of heresy to be *adiaphora*, which meant that they lay outside both religious and juridical coercion (Hunter 2004a). The law itself had to be reconfigured such that it ceased to enforce 'true faith' and dealt only with the civil disturbances arising from heresy disputes, which the sovereign settled without regard to the question of theological truth (Thomasius and Brenneisen 1696). The 'public sphere' that emerged from this and a host of similar changes was public in the sense of forming a sphere of state action demarcated by a system of public law from which theological imperatives were gradually being removed. This sphere was not public in the sense of being grounded in Rawlsian public reason – that is in 'fundamental concepts and principles of reason' that all might share – as it was too deeply indebted to such highly specialised public-law constructions as the *adiaphora*, placed at the disposition of the state. But neither is it plausible to treat the secularisation of the state's juridical framework as a repressive exclusion of the churches from the public sphere of intersubjective meaning-creation. In fact, it was the exclusion of the churches that created the public domain – as the domain of religiously neutral legitimate coercion – and even were a (metaphysical) 'public sphere' of free meaning-creation to exist, then doctrinaire proselytising churches would not belong to it.

Second, if the liberal public–private distinction emerged as a floating threshold pegged to civil disorder, then the associated relation between state and 'society' emerged with a similarly floating form. Once again the main forms of modern political philosophy are of little help in understanding this relation, largely because they treat the ordering of society as if it were governed by the end of preparing citizens to participate in popular sovereignty, however this is envisaged. Rawls thus treats the domain of social administration – education, health, welfare – as if its forms ('primary goods') and limits were determined by the goal of forming citizens capable of the equal exercise of autonomous reason, who then legitimate the liberal state by choosing to found it in the principle of reciprocal freedom of rights (Rawls 1971: 42–4, 150–2; Gutmann 1987; Rawls 1993: 199–200, 299–331). Meanwhile, Thomist and communitarian philosophers treat society as the space in which humanity's dispositional goods will be perfected, allowing them to dissolve the state into the larger concept of 'civil society' understood as the sum of all socio-moral associations (Hollenbach 1993; Perry 1993; Elshtain 1994). Finally, critical theorists envisage the state–society relation as one in which the state – whose juridification and instrumentalisation have alienated it from the communicational associations of civil society – will be reabsorbed into society through the gradual democratisation of the institutions of social administration themselves (Cohen and Arato 1992: 492–563; Habermas 1996: 359–87).

What these accounts fail to capture is the constitutive ambivalence of the proto-liberal relation between state and society. On the one hand, it is the withdrawal of the state from the governance of religious life (later also familial and commercial life) that creates the sphere of 'free civil associations' whose first inhabitants are the churches, together with their universities and schools. On the other hand, this withdrawal is neither an alienation of state from society nor a pure functionalisation of civil associations for the needs of the state. This is in part because the state maintains oversight of such associations only at the limit-threshold of threats to civil peace, and in part because, having confined itself to the domain of security, the state must rely on these associations to provide social governance in such areas as health, education and welfare. The relation between state and social governance that emerges in this ambivalent space is thus not the transparent one in which social governance provides the rational beings required for a just state. Neither is it the dialectical one in which the social associations alienated from the state as a result of its juridification are destined to return as the state's democratic communicational link to the life-world. Rather it is one in which, having monopolised the authority to preserve the envelope of security regardless of popular will, the liberal state allows a high degree of autonomy to the associations that emerge inside this envelope, such that government takes shape as a process of managing these relatively autonomous forms of corporate expertise.[9] This is not least because (as already noted) the demarcation of the public-political domain took

---

[9] In focusing on the manner in which social administration became tied to these relatively autonomous forms of discipline and expertise, Foucault's discussion of 'governmentality' offers an important insight into this development, albeit one vitiated by Foucault's anti-statist tendency to treat 'disciplinary' government as displacing state sovereignty, and by the associated tendency to ignore the historical problem of governing religious communities (Foucault 1991; 2003).

place as a limited secularisation of the juridical framework of political authority, not as an attempt to secularise society as a whole. As a result, while the liberal state had to establish public institutions that were indifferent towards absolute religious and moral truths – in order to forestall its moral capture and the return of the confessional state – it nonetheless made no attempt to exclude such truths from these institutions or to use the latter to inculcate an exclusive state religion or ideology.

The character of this ambivalent relation between state and society or sovereignty and social governance can be seen in the crucial instance of public schooling. On the one hand, during the eighteenth and nineteenth centuries European states established public school systems intended to form citizens possessing common basic moral and literary abilities, and this indeed entailed the exclusion of sectarian teachings to the extent that they threatened shared citizenship. On the other hand, states did not pursue this goal by building school systems designed to inculcate a secularist state ideology – as would be attempted in the Soviet Union and Nazi Germany – or a national civil religion. Instead, states began to fund existing religious schools, requiring them in return to submit to governmental inspection (Laqueur 1976; Melton 1988). Further, where states built their own schools, these were organised around a deconfessionalised version of the Christian pastoral pedagogy and monastic disciplines of the religious schools, as pedagogy is a highly culturally specific institution that states cannot reinvent, only adapt and manage (Hinrichs 1971; Foucault 1977: 135–69; Hunter 1994). The result was the emergence of state school systems that were public in the sense of being organised around a deconfessionalised moral pedagogy oriented to common citizenship, yet permitted significant scope for religious instruction through the pluralistic representation of the various confessions within the curriculum and through the funding of religious schools.

The maintenance of this delicate balance between the secularised framework of the school system and its relatively autonomous religious and moral pedagogies is a matter of constant adjustment and management, rather than the drawing of a principled line. It is significant that such management became more difficult with the democratisation of liberal states during the later nineteenth and early twentieth centuries, when secularist and anti-secularist political parties sought to bend public schooling to their rival agendas. In the

German case, *pace* Rawls, the Constitutional Court would indeed be called on to manage the threshold between the public and private dimensions of the newly established common school system. This occurred during the 1920s when the court was compelled to adjudicate between those who wished to secularise society by purging religious instruction from the school system and using it to inculcate a secularist ideology, and their opponents who sought to use schooling to inculcate the Christian religion as a bulwark against godless secularism (Heckel 1989a: 782–6, 844–8). The Court moved in neither direction. Instead, in keeping with its role in maintaining the juridical secularisation of the framework (but not the contents) of civil society, it provided rulings that required public schools to refrain from endorsing any particular religion or ideology, while allowing them to conduct religious instruction via a pluralistic representation of all the public confessions. This meant that state schools in effect supported the Christian religion, while simultaneously fostering a relativised concept of religion and a non-proselytising 'cultural Christianity'.

As long as we keep in mind that here secular refers to the religious neutrality of the juridical framework and not to a totalising ideological imperative, then it is appropriate to view the Constitutional Court as acting to maintain the secular character of state schooling. One might also say that it was acting on the basis of deeply embedded constitutional arrangements, as long as one accepts that these embody the state-regulated religious pluralism of the German settlement, rather than Rawlsian public reason or a Lockean 'higher law' supposed to limit political authority on behalf of popular sovereignty. In maintaining the educational conditions for common citizenship, the Court was not attempting to ensure that the school system would produce autonomous rational beings capable of choosing fair principles of justice. Rather, it was attempting to set parameters for a schooling that would allow future citizens to be educated in the religion of their parents while respecting or at least tolerating other religions.

At the same time and for the same reasons, however, it would be quite misleading to argue that by setting limits to unfettered religious inculcation the Court was excluding religious-cultural groups from the public sphere, hence that such groups are destined to return to this sphere as irenic dialogue partners in a space of free democratic intersubjectivity. If we use 'public' *strictu senso* – referring to the domain in which the state exercises coercive force to maintain peace – then the school system does not exist in the public domain, unless and until it harbours threats to civil peace, as we saw in the case of Thomasius's treatment of the Lutheran hate hymn. But if we are using the notion of public sphere more broadly, to refer to social exchanges between diverse religious or ideological associations, then we are talking about the domain of social governance rather than that of state sovereignty. Here, though, it seems clear that the governance of the school system is designed to *include* the churches in such exchanges, albeit by requiring them to accept toleration and religious pluralism as a permanent feature of the social landscape. Given that the Catholic church resisted making this accommodation until the second half of the twentieth century, it is hardly plausible to see the churches as irenic partners in a dialogical civil society unless one recalls the role of the state in their initial pacification and the role of government in managing their mutual interaction. In this regard, Dominique Colas offers a timely reminder: 'Still, is there not cause to believe that the only reason the Church does not impose its choices, particularly in the matter of moral custom, on all persons, Catholic or not, living in the same political community is that it does not have the political means to do so?' (Colas 1997: 87). There is little reason to think that 'new' immigrant religions would be any different in this regard.

Finally, we can observe that like multi-confessionalism, multiculturalism also occupies this ambivalent space created when state sovereignty withdraws to the edges of a pacified social domain whose management it delegates to relatively autonomous governmental institutions. Multiculturalism is thus not a threat to the cultural or religious homogeneity of the liberal state, because this state was forged to cope with the absence of such homogeneity, finding its legitimacy not in the rational consensus of its citizens but in its capacity to deliver them from mutual fear through the exercise of political coercion. For the same reason, however, it is meaningless for advocates of multiculturalism to press for the 'recognition' of particular cultural or religious communities at the level of the state, as the state exists only to pacify such communities, leaving their recognition and 'perfection' to the domain of social governance. Canada provides the apposite illustration of the ambivalent place of multiculturalism in a liberal state. On the one hand, Canada is the liberal state with the most developed system of multicultural rights and entitlements at the level of social governance, in such areas as schools, language policy, regional autonomy, welfare rights and native title. On the other hand, Canada is also one of the few liberal states to have used its full coercive powers against a particular cultural-political group. It did so in 1970, when it invoked its War Measures Act to suspend the Bill of Rights, increase police powers and deploy its armed forces in order to crush the secessionist Quebec Liberation Front, which had indeed threatened civil peace by kidnapping and murdering a Quebec cabinet minister. Both sets of actions are entirely characteristic of the shallow legitimacy of the secular liberal state.

Concluding remarks on popular sovereignty

At the beginning of this chapter I suggested that by mortgaging their accounts of liberalism to deep notions of popular sovereignty – whether in the form of Rawls's account of a democratic will arising from public reason, or of his opponents' account of a will arising from cultural identity or an inter-subjective public sphere – philosophical accounts tend to overshoot the ineluctable shallowness of historical liberal orders. In the rationales that the proto-liberals elaborated for political authority, sovereignty cannot be popular, because it is uncoupled from the expression of a common moral will – whether God's, the people's or reason's – and is tied instead to the achievement of a particular end, civil peace, for which the state is brought into existence. The fact that sovereignty cannot be popular, however, does not mean that governments exercising it cannot be democratic. Indeed, Pufendorf goes out of his way to argue that once there is state sovereignty – that is, a political authority possessing sole legislative power and the monopoly of armed force required to enforce laws – it does not matter too much which form of government is chosen to exercise sovereignty (Pufendorf 2003: 192–207). Of the three stand-ard forms – monarchy, aristocracy and democracy – each has its characteristic strengths and weaknesses, yet none is inherently more legitimate than the others, because legitimacy resides not in the form of government but in the sovereignty that it exercises.

It might seem that the emergence of democratic forms of liberal government during the nineteenth century has relegated the proto-liberal conception of sovereignty to the past; if, that is, the emergence of democratic will-formation makes the political-juridical separation of sovereign and subjects untenable. Despite the magnitude of the changes accompanying the emergence of democratic electoral systems, however, it would be rash to identify these with the arrival of popular sovereignty. In the first place, Pufendorf was well aware that in democracies the same individuals may be both governors and governed; yet he sought to preserve the distance between sovereignty and moral communities by denying that these individuals have the same duties in these different offices. The duties of the members of a democratically elected government thus should not be derived from their 'personal' (religious, moral, ideological) beliefs but from the end of sovereignty itself – the security and welfare of the territorial population and its protection from external threats – which must be implicit in the platform of all democratic parties. Second, there is a sense in which this gap between the ends of sovereignty and the moral commitments of those who exercise it is built into the constitutional architecture of the liberal state. As a result of the secularisation of sovereignty's juridical framework, those exercising it are compelled to adopt a relativistic and pluralistic outlook towards the commitments of the different moral communities, including their own; although it goes without saying that this compulsion will meet with varying degrees of resistance, sometimes organised, as in the case of Christian democratic parties. Third, if electoral democracy is understood as a way of appointing those who are to exercise sovereignty – rather than as a means of expressing a rationally, culturally or discursively based popular will – then there is no necessity for entire populations to acquire this demanding relativistic and pluralistic outlook. Finally, if this is true, then we will need to reassess the public role of philosophical defences of popular sovereignty, whether these come in the form of metaphysical conceptions of rational agreement, communitarian conceptions of cultural identity, or critical-theoretical conceptions of inter-subjective dialogue. Is it possible that these represent the persistence of an 'ecclesial' anti-statism that has never forgiven the liberal state for removing the means of political-juridical authority from those who wish to use society to perfect humanity?

3 France on the knife-edge of religion: commemorating the centenary of the law of 9 December 1905 on the separation of church and state

DAVID SAUNDERS

Pursuit of a general theory of secularisation did not stop David Martin capturing a chilling sense of historical contingency: 'Had the Reformation triumphed in France, as it nearly did, the sociological and historical consequences for European history and development would have been fantastically different. Few knife-edges have carried such a burden of multiple and vast alternatives' (Martin 1978: 38). One could not ask for a more dramatic trailer to discussions of the government of religion in today's world than this suggestion that our present arrangements could, so nearly, have been quite other than they happen to be now. The further implication is that particular 450-year-old circumstances – the end of Catholic unity and the fortunes of *la Réforme* in France – might have an enduring cultural imprint. The eight French 'Wars of Religion' raged for thirty-six years from 1562. The St Bartholomew's Day Massacre of Huguenots by Catholics was in 1572. The Edict of Nantes, under which the French Crown – Henri IV – recognised the administration of religious plurality as a fact of government, was promulgated in 1598. Nancy Roelker (1996: 228) terms sixteenth-century France the 'crucible of Europe', reiterating the metaphor that John Salmon (1975: 13) had previously adopted to characterise the French religious wars as 'the crucible in which some of the competing forces from an earlier age were consumed in the fire and others blended and transmuted into new compounds'.

In this crucible, though, it was less the case that the base matter of religious conflict was transmuted into eternal truth. Rather, unprecedented political devices had to be improvised and novel legal moves had to be devised to counter inter-communal violence consequent on the Christian fracture.[1] It is the political and legal heritage of this early modern history of religious settlement that I want to invoke in the course of this chapter.

The aim is to consider the government of religious difference historically, at the level of particular institutional arrangements, not at the level of universal moral reason or transcendent truth. I shall therefore avoid endorsing any sectarian programme, secularist or anti-secularist. This posture might seem inappropriate, given the controversial nature of my principal focus: the first centenary of the 9 December 1905 French law on the Separation of the Churches and the State, a Republican law habitually viewed as having instituted *laïcité* as the distinctively absolutist principle of French secularism. In fact the term *laïcité* does not appear in the legislative text. Nor does the phrase, 'on the Separation of the Churches and the State', which has come to name the law. But let there be no question: this was a fundamental law of institutional disconnection and non-establishment whereby, a century ago, after fifty stormy years of political strife and religious confrontation, the National Assembly legislated the separation of churches and the state. Nevertheless, while normative-minded secularists and anti-secularists alike might assess the 1905 law as an exemplary instance of anti-religious legislation, a more descriptive and contextual account of the French legislator's work might lead us to relativise so uniform an assessment. The point will be to lessen the risk of obscuring the historical contingency of the nineteenth-century political-legal scene and to avoid reducing *laïcité* – and the 1905 law – to an uncompromising anti-religious posture. In the interest of a more nuanced view, then, this chapter will treat the 1905 legislation as part of a religious settlement or modus vivendi achieved by a religiously neutralised liberal state order.

This is not to deny the law its own normative and constitutional dimension. The principle of *laïcité* has its current expression in Article 1 of the French Constitution: 'France is an indivisible, secular, democratic and social Republic.'[2] Article 1 continues: '[The Republic] shall guarantee equality before the law of all citizens without distinction

---

[1] On the French wars and fundamental law, see Thompson (1986).
[2] The original text of the 1958 Constitution placed these words as Article 2. It was amended to the current form by Constitutional Law 95–880 of 4 August 1995. See www.conseil-constitutionnel.fr/textes/modif.htm.

according to origin, race or religion. It shall respect all beliefs.' It is a
classic statement of liberal neutrality towards the plurality of religious
beliefs, the freedom of which the state will respect, on condition that
these beliefs are kept private.[3] Yet, what happens to the principle, now
that the state that achieved the 1905 religious settlement finds itself
governing a religious community that was not party to the settlement?
Arriving at its first centenary, then, the 1905 law separating church and
state was not guaranteed celebration as the embodiment of a transcendent Republican principle. To the contrary, the issue was its possible future reform.

The controversy reopened old lines of fracture. The French Catholic
bishops favoured preserving the law; a century ago, at the behest of an
intransigent papacy, they resisted its passage and disobeyed its conditions. The Protestant Federation announced that it favoured reform;
early last century the Protestants embraced the original statute.

Other fractures were political and contemporary. The then President,
Jacques Chirac, favoured preservation of the law as an unshakeable
'pillar of the [Republican] temple'. Addressing a meeting of Prefects on
7 December 2004, Jean-Pierre Raffarin, Chirac's Prime Minister, cut
to the quick: 'La République rassemble; le communautarisme divise' –
The Republic brings us together; communitarianism divides. Raffarin,
like Chirac, would have celebrated the centenary of the 1905 law by
declaring it and *laïcité* off-limits to reform. Nicolas Sarkozy, though
head of Chirac's own party, the centre-right *Union pour une mou-
vement populaire* (UMP), noisily favoured reform. He wanted to
'modernise' the law to meet today's circumstances: Islam is now
France's second religion and – Sarkozy argued – unless the French
state provided public funds for Muslim activities, foreign sources
hostile to France would fund Islamist elements. Sarkozy published his
views in 2004, in *La République, les religions, l'espérance*: in essence,
where a century ago the political order of the day was 'separation' of
religion and politics, today it should be 'complementarity'. With his
election to the office of President on 6 May 2007, Nicolas Sarkozy is
now in a position to pursue revision of the traditional schema and
implement his 'modernisation' plan.

---

[3] 'Private' does not of course equate to 'inside your head'. Its primary referent
is private associations as distinct from public or state institutions.

Nor were the intellectual press slack. At least three books published in 2005 address the 1905 law. Jacqueline Lalouette's *La séparation des églises et de l'Etat* offers an intellectual history of the 'idea' of separation and its nineteenth-century evolution, from 1789 to 1905. Jean-Paul Scot's *'L'Etat chez lui, l'Eglise chez elle'* – a title borrowed from Victor Hugo – offers an account of what was at stake in the confrontation of Catholics and secularists. Third, Yves-Charles Zarka has edited a collection of four views – two for and two against reform – under the title *Faut-il réviser la loi de 1905?* (Lalouette 2005; Scot 2005; Zarka 2005).

In turning to legislative history – rather than to notions of universal rights or cultural identity – I shall consider three major points of historical focus on the emergence of state neutrality and *laïcité*: the nineteenth-century battles that preceded the 1905 legislation; the early twentieth-century making of that law; and, finally and most specula-tively, the political-legal responses to religious civil war in sixteenth-century France. This third focus on 'the crucible' is not merely archival. Rather, it is introduced in order to ask whether the twentieth-century law – considered as a pacification measure – might find some inherit-ance in the early modern attempt at religious peace in France.

Immediately, an omission is evident: the Revolution of 1789 is missing! In fact, there will be some mentions of 1789, but *en passant*. There is a pedagogic point to this omission. It is to resist the temp-tation to discuss secularisation and the historical relations among law, morality and religion by taking up a position for or against the so-called 'Enlightenment subject' or self-determining rational individ-ual. For all its currency in critical discourse on religion and so much else, the striking of a programmatic attitude towards this allegedly atomistic rational individual is no way to respect the real complexity of the topic. We are, after all, dealing with a historical 'knife-edge', one that has carried a 'burden of multiple and vast alternatives'.

Nineteenth-century battleground: secularists and anti-secularists

The political history of nineteenth-century France has something for most every taste: monarchical, imperial and Republican reg-imes; reactionary, reformist and revolutionary moments (these last in 1848 and, in 1871, when in the heady days of the Paris commune, anti-clerical *communards* executed as hostages the Catholic Archbishop of Paris and three Jesuit fathers). The century unleashed forceful clericalising and secularising programs. Despite 1789 and the Declaration of the Rights of Man and the Citizen, Catholicism remained for many a plausible political doctrine. Under the 1801 Concordat between Napoleon and Pius VII, Rome kept its 'ultramontane' grip on French internal affairs and external relations. There were consequences for everyday life. Civil marriages were possible, but from 1816 there was no divorce.[4] For a decade from April 1825, capital punishment was applied to acts of sacrilege, such as profaning a consecrated host. Only slowly and unevenly were medicine and death detached from religious observances, with the medicalisation of health care and the possibility of civil burial. Yet, there was no inevitable movement towards secularisation. In June 1873, in Lyon (and subsequently in other cities), civil burials were restricted to the early morning hours, with attendance limited to three hundred! Meanwhile, the Minister for War suppressed military honours awarded to persons having a civil burial (Lalouette 2005: 317–18). These were the years of a clericalised army, real or imagined, and of mass pilgrimages to Catholic shrines.

The Revolution, then, had neither exterminated the French clergy nor extirpated all religion. True, by requiring clergy to swear allegiance to the Constitution, the 12 July 1790 *Constitution civile du clergé* had clamped their operations into the framework of the temporal laws. Yet, the memory of this embrace of church by state – the 'church garrotted by the tyrannical state' – would later be exploited by Catholic apologetics, into the polemics of the twentieth century, as an awful warning against secularisation. It is the case, also, that the Revolution saw France break with Rome: the Revolutionary Constitution of 3 September 1791 annulled the Concordat of 1516 between François I and Leo X. Yet, as just noted, the Napoleonic regime would soon restore the bridge to Rome and Pope Pius VII with a new Concordat in 1801.[5]

Against this backdrop, intellectual and visceral splits between Republican anti-clericals and Catholic pro-clericals fuelled multiple

---

[4] The right of divorce was restored by the Naquet Law of 27 July 1884.
[5] The 1801 Concordat recognised Catholicism as the majoritarian religion of the French people. It also allowed a measure of recognition to Protestant and Jewish confessions.

confrontations. Civil war – *la guerre des deux France* – remained a present danger in the fraught first decades of the Third Republic (1870–1940).[6] The battle was nowhere fiercer than in respect of public education. The antagonists squared off in vitriolic campaigns fought to capture the minds and allegiance of the next generation … or at least to save them from falling into the adversary's hands. Under the Ancien Régime, education had consisted in a religious instruction that prepared you for a Christian life and death. Now, at mid century, the school became a key vector of civil power and controversy, whether for the secularists' historical cause of social transformation and Republican integration, or for the Catholics' divine cause of spiritual salvation and participation in eternal life. As legislative landmarks, it is usual to cite the law of 28 June 1833 (*loi Guizot*), which established state primary education while retaining religious instruction, and the law of 15 March 1850 (*loi Falloux*), which extended education to a secondary level while allowing the Catholic Church to run primary schools. The principal landmark, though, is the law of 28 March 1882 (*loi Ferry*), establishing a school that was 'free, secular and compulsory'. In Jules Ferry's hopeful words, this was 'not a law of combat'.[7] It was, rather, 'one of those great organic laws destined to live in harmony with the country, and to enter our way of life'.[8] As Minister of Public Instruction, Ferry dealt prudently with contentious issues such as crucifixes in schools. He recognised that 'the place of a crucifix is in the church, not in the school', yet he refrained from ordering their immediate removal. Ferry was a politician of the middle ground: 'my struggle is the anti-clerical struggle, but the anti-religious struggle, never, never'.[9]

This slow quarantine of public life from clerical interventions – in provisions for civil marriage, civil death, public medicine and public education – served as preliminary to the 1905 Law of Separation.

[6] Founded on 4 September 1870, the Third Republic was dissolved by the Pétain regime on 10 July 1940.

[7] Jules Ferry served in the office of Minister of Public Instruction and Cults from 1879 to 1883. He died in 1893. The *loi Ferry* made primary schooling compulsory for ages 6 to 13. It also replaced religious instruction with civic and moral instruction.

[8] '[U]ne de ces grandes lois organiques destinées à vivre avec le pays, à entrer dans les moeurs'. In Baubérot (2000: 56).

[9] '[M]a lutte est la lutte anticléricale, mais la lutte anti-religieuse … jamais, jamais'. In Baubérot (2000: 52).

Other legislative moves in the 1880s saw the abolition of Sunday observance as an official day of rest and the abolition of public prayers at the opening of Parliament.

Incremental legislative work proceeded. Yet, the French state remained entwined – under the 1801 Concordat – with the intrusive theocratic disposition of a Pope who, in 1854, propounded the dogma of the immaculate conception of the Virgin Mary and, in 1870, advanced the dogma of pontifical infallibility as a divinely revealed truth. But Pius IX did more than this. In 1864, he issued the *Syllabus errorum*. Directed at the French state, the *Syllabus* catalogued the eighty 'principal errors' of modern times, errors that the Church now anathematised. The principles of any public law that failed to recognise Rome's ultimate supremacy, spiritual and therefore temporal, were thus condemned. The Sovereign Pontiff claimed a divine right of intervention, by force if needed, in any matter relating to French 'law and manners'. Rationalism and indifference were rejected; miracles, spiritual mystery and revealed truth were promoted. The eightieth proposition of the *Syllabus* precluded – forever – any accommodation between the Supreme Pontiff and 'liberalism'.

For this imperial theocracy and its total religion, the place of the French state lay within the spiritual and temporal jurisdiction of the Church of Rome. French temporal law was to be kept subordinate to the divinely grounded canons of the church. In political terms, Rome would exercise control over civil matters ranging from the appointment of French bishops to the content of the school curriculum in France. Rome would seek the end of civil marriage and eliminate persistent Gallican-conciliarist tendencies among French bishops. Conversely, such clerical interventions in the public life of French citizens radicalised anti-clerical rage and provoked deeply anti-religious dispositions. The scene was set for a long exchange of violences and mutual demonisations.

The 1905 Law of Separation

As the century turned, 'doctrines of hatred' – anti-semitic, anti-protestant, anti-clerical – filled the air of France (Baubérot 2000: 65). The Dreyfus affair of 1894 continued to inflame French passions. The cemeteries might be no longer defined by the confessional identities of the dead and clerical teachers might no longer have the dominant role in public schools; yet, was anything really settled? Was the role of religion in the polity now defined? Was the capacity of the Catholic Church and the Pope to intervene in French domestic and external matters at last delimited?[10] Who really represented France and the French?

The years 1901 to 1904 were a time of Republican ascendancy. For radical secularists, the final extirpation of religion from public life seemed at hand, thanks to secular reason's enduring aggression – *la guerre à toujours* – against superstition and religious darkness; that is, against the alleged obscurantism of the Catholic Church. This radical line is identified with the neo-Jacobin figure of Emile Combes. Under his militant premiership, the law of 7 July 1904 on associations was passed, closing access to the teaching profession – including in the previously authorised religious schools – for any members of the religious orders or *congrégations*.[11] The legislation led to an expulsion of some 30,000 clergy, no longer salaried by the state, from the ranks of teachers. No less seismic was the law of 25 July 1904, by which the French Republic unilaterally broke off diplomatic relations with the Holy See.

To explain the rise and persistence of such intractable conflict over the government of religion in public life, Jean Baubérot (2000: 76–7) identifies two principal factors. The first is demographic: in France in 1870, there were 37 million Catholics, 580,000 Protestants and 50,000 Jews. Given this uneven distribution of confessional weight, 'the pluralism of recognised religions [*cultes reconnus*] does not correspond to a truly pluralist situation'. In short, 'pluralism is therefore above all a production of politics'. This was pluralism's strength, but also its weakness. The second factor is ideological: conflict was fuelled by the two irreducibly sectarian minorities. Pro-clerical Catholic and anti-clerical Republican each advanced a non-negotiable claim to political supremacy. For the former, there was no salvation outside the

---

[10] The conflict of clericalism and anti-clericalism would not die, despite Leo XIII's 1892 direction to French Catholics to accept the Republican government as a legitimate political authority. The Pope also undertook not to intervene, via the pulpit, in French electoral politics.

[11] Among its other anti-clerical provisions, the Law of 7 July 1904 ordered the closure, within ten years, of schools where students were taught under the auspices of the *congrégations*. It is worth noting that – at the turn of the century – there were more than 3,000 Catholic religious orders in France, marshalling some 200,000 women and men.

universal Catholic Church. For the latter, there was no escaping the historically inevitable completion of secular reason.

Was there space and will for a middle ground? In fact, between 1901 and 1904, there was a retreat from the brink of civil conflicts over church–state separation and the Concordat, the former being rejected but the latter being endorsed by Rome, positions diametrically reversed by the anti-clerical Republicans. In Parliament, the tabling of multiple proposals for a law on separation led to the establishment of a *Commission de séparation* – the 'Commission of 33' members – on 11 June 1903. An independent socialist, Aristide Briand, was elected as *rapporteur*. In the twenty-one months preceding parliamentary debate, Briand compiled a 268-page *rapport*. This made the case for a 'liberal' separation, whereby the interests of the French state would be protected while the freedoms of conscience and religious worship would be fully respected. Carriage of the law then occupied the *Chambre des députés* – the lower house – over forty-six sessions between March and July of 1905. In these months of debate on the Bill, the parliamentarians of the Third Republic rehearsed the battle cries of forty years of combat over the relations of church and state. Each side – Catholic and Republican – demonised the other as an evil threat. For Catholics, the prospect of separation presaged a dark future of religious persecution and an expectation of the wrath of God. For Republicans, the prospect of separation promised a bright tomorrow and an expectation of the rule of reason.

Some Catholic members feared persecution by a future state.[12] Others were willing to set a date on this dark eventuality, convinced that separation would entail the imminent destruction of all religion.[13] This, of course, was precisely what radical Republican advocates of separation enthusiastically envisaged, equally convinced that the long-delayed 'de-Christianising' of France was now at hand ... and to be assisted by inducing Catholics to split themselves schismatically

---

[12] Thus M. l'Abbé Gayraud: 'I know you do not wish to go as far as violent persecution ... yet ... you cannot know if the next majority government will want to take this to its conclusion and press ahead with these measures that are menacing us now.' See *Annales de la Chambre des députés*, Item 5, 21 March 1905: 1248.

[13] Thus M. Georges Berry: 'If this chamber adopts the proposed separation, in twelve years' time the priests will be ... reduced to begging for their bread ... the churches will be closed.' See *ibid.*, Item 5, 21 March 1905: 1241.

between a more patriotic adherence to a Gallican tradition and a less patriotic allegiance to ultramontane Rome. The colour of militant secularist discourse can be gauged by listening to the address of the 'free-thinker', Maurice Allard, radical socialist Deputy for the Var, recommending his alternative to the Commission's Bill:

> Why do we Republicans, and above all we Socialists, want to de-christianise this country? Why do we fight religions? We fight religions because they are a permanent impediment to the progress of civilisation ... The day when the anthropomorphic God of the Jews left the banks of the Jordan to conquer the Mediterranean world, civilisation disappeared from the Mediterranean basin. And later when Christianity left Rome and Greece where it had entirely choked civilisation and where it left only ruins and rubble and arrived in France, there was no longer in our country any Art, Literature or Science. It needed the Revolution to restore to our race its true strength and its chance of progress. Under the influence of Judeo-Christianity, all enlightenment had been extinguished, leaving only the shadows. Even today, how many potential advances have not been realised because we drag behind us the heavy ball and chain of Judeo-Christianity, with its cortège of prejudices and conventional lies?[14]

Other republicans, though, were less strident, suspecting that a 'separated' Catholic Church, released from its traditional Concordat-bond to the Gallican state, might be all the more free to engage in future political interventions. In 1905 – more than now – a grassroots anti-clericalism promised a serious anti-religious vote.

---

[14] Thus M. Maurice Allard:

> Pourquoi nous républicains, et surtout nous socialistes, voulons-nous déchristianiser ce pays? Pourquoi combattons-nous les religions? Nous combattons les religions parce qu'elles sont un obstacle permanent au progrès de la civilisation ... Le jour où le Dieu anthropomorphe des Juifs quitta les bords du Jourdain pour conquérir le monde méditerranéen, la civilisation disparut du bassin de la Méditerranée. Et plus tard quand le christianisme quitta Rome et la Grèce où il avait étouffé toute la civilisation et où il n'avait laissé que ruines et décombres et arriva en France, il n'y eut plus dans notre pays, ni Art, ni Lettres, ni Science. Il fallut la Révolution pour redonner à notre race sa véritable puissance et sa possibilité de progrès. Sous l'influence du judéo-christianisme, toute lumière avait disparu, il n'y avait plus que ténèbres. Aujourd'hui encore combien de progrès ne sont pas realisés parce que nous traînons derrière nous ce lourd boulet du judéo-christianisme, avec son cortège de préjugés et de mensonges conventionnels?

> See *ibid.*, 10 April 1905: 1628. On Allard's contributions to the deliberations on the Separation Bill, see Scot 2005: 226–28.

For Briand, opening the debate in the Chamber on 21 March 1905, the urgent task was less to right the wrong of history than to locate a political exit from this 'constant conflict over the essential questions of independence and dignity'.[15] Rejecting Allard's *contre-projet* as a Bill aimed at 'the suppression of churches by the state', Briand stressed instead that 'for the Commission, freedom of conscience is inseparable from the capacity and the right of the faithful to express their religious feelings freely, in their chosen form of worship'.[16] His driving motivation was the liberal imperative of civil peace:

I have a horror of religious war. The success of my ideas and their real-isation depend too much on the pacification of spirits for me not to desire to see the church accommodate itself to the new regime. Then we can move on to address other questions that might be more elevated or, at any rate, more practical. Yet we are obliged to anticipate what tomorrow might bring, and we would be truly imprudent if we did not think about how to provide the state with the arms it will need tomorrow to resist the militias of the church. It is in this spirit that the Commission's Bill has been set down. I repeat that the Bill is broad-based and liberal, sufficiently liberal.[17]

For Briand, then, a middle ground of civil peace was to be mapped out in terms of a new and liberal accommodation between state and church. Only in this way could there be a 'pacification of spirits'.

Yet, from their respective extremes, Catholic and Republican antagonists appealed each to their favoured transcendental standards, be it the eternal wisdom of God in the cosmos or the irresistible advance

---

[15] See *ibid.*, Item 5, 21 March 1905: 1242.

[16] Thus Aristide Briand: 'Mais pour la commission, la liberté de conscience est inséparable de la faculté, du droit pour les religieux d'exprimer librement leurs sentiments religieux sous la forme du culte.' See *ibid.*, 10 April 1905: 1635. Allard's motion was lost by 480 votes to 59.

[17] Thus Aristide Briand:

J'ai horreur de la guerre religieuse. Le succès de mes idées, leur réalisation dépend trop de la pacification des esprits pour que je ne désire pas voir l'Eglise s'accommoder du regime nouveau et nous permettre de tourner nos efforts vers des questions peut-être plus hautes, en tout cas plus pratiques. Mais nous sommes obligés de prévoir ce que demain pourra nous apporter, et nous serions véritablement bien imprudents si nous ne pensions pas à donner à l'Etat les armes dont il pourra avoir besoin pour résister demain aux milices de l'Eglise. C'est dans cet esprit que le projet de la Commission a été arrêté. Je répète qu'il est large, libéral, suffisamment libéral.

See *ibid.*, 6 April 1905: 1559.

of human reason in the history of France. The former made separation absolutely resistible; the latter made separation absolutely inevitable. After all, for Catholics, a century-old ghost – the 1790 *Constitution civile du clergé* – had not been laid to rest. In these circumstances, the capacity to inflame civil violence remained real.[18] Re-reading these debates a century later, their sheer tensions underscore David Martin's (1978: 71) observation: 'The Latin [Catholic] pattern contains enormous pressures towards the separation of church and state ... simply on account of the immense splits over religion per se.'

The Law of Separation was finally adopted by the lower Chamber (by 341 votes to 233) and the Senate, signed on 9 December and promulgated on 11 December 1905. Unsurprisingly, this legislation did not mark the end, once and for all, of the matter of religion. So, should we understand the 1905 law as an immutable threshold in French political history, where the Republic recognised its own grounding principle? If so, in 2005 the Law of Separation can be commemorated in its timeless integrity. Or was the 1905 law an expedient political and prudential measure, designed to deal with a problem of its times? If so, the law is now open to revision, to deal with problems of today, such as the provision of state funding for mosques and imams.

Before addressing these issues, though, a look at certain articles of the Law of Separation and a brief consideration of contemporary responses to the 1905 law are appropriate.

The Law of Separation comprises forty-four articles under six headings, the guiding principles being set down in Articles 1 and 2 (followed by a further forty-two articles giving the technical modalities of the law, such as the arrangements for transferring properties and funds between church and state).[19] Article 1 concerns citizens' 'freedom of conscience':

---

[18] Other arguments were more concrete. Should the issue be put to a national referendum? Briand opposed the notion of a referendum, recommending instead a vote by the Deputies as the elected representatives of the people. See *ibid.*, Item 5, 21 March 1905: 1243.

[19] The six headings (*Titres* I–VI) are as follows: I – *Principes* (Articles 1–2); II – *Attributions des biens: pensions* (Articles 3–11); III – *Des édifices des cultes* (Articles 12–17); IV – *Des associations pour l'exercice des cultes* (Articles 18–24); V – *Police des cultes* (Articles 25–36); VI – *Dispositions générales* (Articles 37–44). It is notable that the term *laïcité* appears in none of the forty-four articles.

The Republic ensures freedom of conscience. It guarantees the free exercise of religions with the sole restrictions decreed hereafter in the interest of public order.

[La République assure la liberté de conscience. Elle garantit le libre exercice des cultes sous les seules restrictions édictées ci-après dans l'intérêt de l'ordre public.]

Article 2 inscribes the principle of 'non-recognition' or state neutrality towards all religions:

The Republic does not recognise, fund or subsidise any religion. In consequence, as from 1 January following the promulgation of the present law, state, departmental and commune budgets, together with all expenses relating to the exercise of religions, will be abolished. This notwithstanding, expenses relating to almoners' services and intended to ensure the free exercise of religions in public establishments such as *lycées*, *collèges*, schools, hospices, asylums and prisons may be included in the said budgets. Public establishments of religion are abolished, in compliance with the provisions set out in Article 3.

[La République ne reconnaît, ne salarie ni ne subventionne aucun culte. En conséquence, à partir du 1er janvier qui suivra la promulgation de la présente loi, seront supprimées des budgets de l' État, des départements et des communes, toutes dépenses relatives à l'exercice des cultes. Pourront toutefois être inscrites auxdits budgets les dépenses relatives à des services d'aumônerie et destinées à assurer le libre exercice des cultes dans les établissements publics tels que lycées, collèges, écoles, hospices, asiles et prisons. Les établissements publics du culte sont supprimés, sous réserve des dispositions énoncées à l'article 3.]

In debate, battle was joined over Article 4, which proposed replacing the established public law notion of churches as 'recognised cults' with the notion of churches as private associations (*associations cultuelles*) to which the state would now transfer stewardship of church properties and incomes.[20]

Rome dismissed this new administrative entity. Pius X issued the encyclical *Gravissimo officii*, ordering French Catholics to reject all *associations cultuelles*.[21] Catholics might thus legitimately resist the

---

[20] See Title IV, Articles 18–24, relating to the establishment of 'associations' to manage the affairs of the churches.

[21] The Pope described the 1905 statute as 'law not of separation but of oppression'.

law and block the audits (*inventaires*) of church properties that the new law proposed.[22] Auditing began, even as Rome used the prospect of the *inventaires* to fire up fears of illegal expropriation of Catholic wealth and to justify total non-compliance.[23] In the event, in the face of civil violence, the government curtailed the audits.

So much for the making of the 1905 law, now closely identified with the Republican principle of *laïcité*. By way of an assessment of the law and this principle, it is worth noting two propositions advanced by one of the anti-reform voices in the Zarka collection, the historical sociologist, Jean Baubérot (2005), on the 1905 law and the notion of *laïcité*: first, that *laïcité* is best understood as a political and legal 'pact'; second, that this *pacte laïque* – instanced by the 1905 law – does not represent a consensus.[24] Each is a significant point.

First, *laïcité* is best understood not as a transcendent principle but as a political and legal pact. Those who ground religious freedom in something deeper – in universal rights or in cultural identity – will treat the legal pact as a second best. So, the 'pacting' view of *laïcité* poses a broader challenge: can we see juridical and political settlements – contingent accommodations, arrangements, modi vivendi, containments, rules for living together – as cultural achievements of the first order?

---

[22] See Title 2, Article 3:

> Les établissements dont la suppression est ordonnée par l'article 2 continueront provisoirement de fonctionner, conformément aux dispositions qui les régissent actuellement, jusqu'à l'attribution de leurs biens aux associations prévues par le titre IV et au plus tard jusqu'à l'expiration du délai ci-après.
>
> Dès la promulgation de la présente loi, il sera procédé par les agents de l'administration des domaines à l'inventaire descriptif et estimatif:
>
> 1° Des biens mobiliers et immobiliers desdits établissements;
>
> 2° Des biens de l'État, des départements et des communes dont les mêmes établissements ont la jouissance.
>
> Ce double inventaire sera dressé contradictoirement avec les représentants légaux des établissements ecclésiastiques ou eux dûment appelés par une notification faite en la forme administrative.
>
> Les agents chargés de l'inventaire auront le droit de se faire communiquer tous titres et documents utiles à leurs opérations.

[23] The same fears were exploited by the *Action française*, the right-wing literary-political movement, for the purposes of its national-Catholic propaganda.

[24] Baubérot (2000: 96) underscores the second proposition: 'The pact, in fact, creates no new consensus. A juridical and political production, it assumes that the ideological extremisms are contained ... without ever achieving, for all that, a common perspective.'

Second, the pact creates no new consensual reality. Were the pact to lay claim to consensus, it would risk entering the lists in combat with the very 'ideological extremisms' that must be contained. As the instrument for a modus vivendi, the pact is precisely not an 'overlapping consensus' of convergent reasonings. The 1905 law did not converge on a higher-order perspective that transcended the two particularisms: Catholic supernaturalism or Republican civil religion.

Such was the political achievement of *la laïcité comme règle du vivre ensemble* (*laïcité* as a rule of coexistence) (Baubérot 2000: 99). In the face of sectarian extremes, religious and secular, a political-legal middle ground was not only emerging. It was also proving quite resilient, both to Catholic intransigents and to the zealots of a secular civil religion.

The Law of Separation: a happy hundredth anniversary?

The 1905 *inventaires* – a 'profanation' for Catholics but evidence of the 'march of reason against superstition' for Republicans – were not the last affair to inflame passions and threaten civil war. True, under the subsequent Clemenceau regime, the law of 28 March 1907 calmed Catholics by permitting religious gatherings without prior notice and by allowing church bells once again to be rung to summon the faithful. And in 1923, relations between the French state and the Holy See under Benedict XV were restored, while in France the 1905 law on *associations cultuelles* – so resented by the Catholic Church – was amended to grant diocesan organisations under the bishops the associational status. But then, in May 1924, the elections returned power to a Socialist/Radical government. Secularist attacks on the *fantasmes* of religion resurfaced. A return to the 1905 arrangements was demanded and, once again, a war of French against French threatened.

Nevertheless, in the heated inter-war atmosphere, the state demonstrated its capacity for neutrality in a further way. Now, when political ideology threatened the civil order as religious ideology had previously done, the state took action – within the 'secular' legal framework established by the 1905 law – to curtail political proselytising in the public schools. Such was the burden of directives issued by the Minister of Public Instruction on 28 April 1924 and 12 April 1934, the latter prohibiting 'the wearing of political insignia, the distribution of tracts or brochures, whether inside or in proximity to the school establishment, and generally any demonstration of political association' (Le Tourneau 1997: 279–80). This manifestation of the state's neutrality towards 'all beliefs' – political no less than religious – confirms its occupancy of the middle ground. In 1940, though, the pro-Catholic Vichy regime of Marshall Pétain abolished the Third Republic and, with it, the principle of separation between state and church.

Of course, with the liberation of France, the wheel would turn again in the protracted history of conflict between the religious and the secular. Where does the wheel point now? Is the constitutional principle of state neutrality a principle constituted, once and for all, as the timeless bedrock of a Republican order? The 1905 Law of Separation concerned the four confessions then recognised in France: Catholic, Lutheran (Protestants of the Augsburg Confession), Reformed (Calvinist) and Jewish. Today, Islam is the second religion in France.

This new circumstance raises no end of questions. Can the 1905 law be commemorated as the embodiment of a transcendent principle, in circumstances that were unforeseen a century ago? What happens to the principle, when the state that achieved the 1905 religious settlement finds itself governing a religious community that was not party to the settlement from which the state itself arose? Is such a community free – on the grounds of its professed religion – not to belong to the juridical order of the state? In a modern liberal state, should the laws reflect the religious norms that define the distinctive self-identification of its member communities? Is the respect for cultural pluralism and religious freedom that has characterised liberal states compatible with security measures necessary to protect against external and internal threats to public order by militant religionists? And, as always, what do today's anti-secularists actually want?

In France, this debate has at least three dimensions: empirical, jurisprudential and historical. Empirically speaking, should the French state now break with its own prohibition on funding a religion? Should public funding contribute to the construction of mosques and offer imams studies in French language, law and institutions? But would the provision of aid to French Muslim organisations breach Article 2 of the 1905 law (*La République ne reconnaît, ne salarie ni ne subventionne aucun culte*)?[25] In practical terms, would state aid to

---

[25] The question assumes an answer as to who – or what – should represent the Muslim community of France in its dealings with the state.

one religion lead to demands for state aid to all? Would state recognition of a religion return France to the condition of an 1801 Concordat? And – looking from the other side in the 'war of the two Frances' – would subsidisation risk reinflaming the wrath of radical secularists? Civil peace might be more rare and delicate – but less reliable – than we have come to assume.

Jurisprudentially speaking, the presence of the Muslim community raises at least two further issues. These concern the status of rights. A creature of its times, the 1905 law properly addressed the government of religion in terms of churches or *cultes*, that is, at the collective level. When Article 1 spoke of the 'free exercise of religions' (*le libre exercice des cultes*), it was not treating religion at the level of individual conduct or belief. A century later – as the 'Muslim headscarf' controversy has made manifest – it is a question of the individual believer's human right to express their religious identity, in public if they so wish. No matter how old that identity, to conceive its public expression as an inalienable individual right to be different is very new. This novelty – and the current deployment of rights discourse more generally – underscores the historicity of the legal thought in the 1905 French law. That legislation makes no explicit reference to 'rights'.

Implied or explicit, the conflict between the provisions of the 1905 law and the respect now demanded for individuals' rights signals a second jurisprudential issue: a clash of norms. In the 'headscarf' controversy, official reluctance to recognise displays of religious difference – in accord with the state's obligation of neutrality towards the religions of its citizens – risked construal as 'discrimination'.[26] What is happening? Is one transcendent principle under siege from another? In a France so long exposed to the clash of rival sectarian identities, the law of 1905 staked out a constitutional common ground for peace. What can be said is that an attack on this constitutional

---

[26] 'Discrimination' here becomes the name for neutrality. An equal treatment for all finds itself depicted as blindly indifferent to the individual's sense of their own religious difference. As of this writing, the United Kingdom Parliament has passed into law the Racial and Religious Hatred Act 2006. The Act creates a new crime: incitement to religious hatred. It has the support of the Muslim Council, who – with some reason – recognised that the proposed law would grant the Muslim community legal equality with the Christian and the Jewish. In the British context, it appears, a right of equality is still seen as a means of eradicating a problematic instance of religious difference.

common ground is underway, conducted in the joint names of religious difference as a fundamental right inhering in the individual and the primordial power of one's religion as an identity whose authenticity cannot be questioned.[27]

It is too soon to know whether this attack will seriously prejudice civil peace by undermining the notion of political unity. True, the campaign for a religious right of difference is directed against the 'indifference' of the religiously neutral state, rather than against a rival confession or creed. And no doubt the campaign can serve to register individuals' hard-won autonomy from an obligation to believe and belong, the sort that was historically imposed by confessional states.

Historically speaking, the 1905 law poses a challenge. Should it be considered as the expression of a transcendent principle, a truth revealed, fixed and constituted once and for all a century ago? Seen in this light, though, the law loses its visibility as the mechanism of a *pacte laïque*, an adaptable instrument for creating a legal middle ground on which to build a modus vivendi among otherwise mutually hostile communities of faith. Yet, it is not wholly implausible to see the 1905 law as the unambiguous outcome of a long-term attempt to recast the French state within a secularist ideology. Its radical defenders do just this.

A sixteenth-century lineage for the 1905 law?

Does the 1905 law have a political-legal lineage that goes back to the sixteenth-century peace-making in the face of France's serial religious civil wars? As far as I know, no scholars of *laïcité* identify such an early modern lineage. I want to do so, to set the issue within the history of France as a constitutional liberal state possessed of a religiously neutralised juridical order. Stephen Holmes (1988: 5) points the way: 'liberal beliefs about the proper relations among law, morality and religion first acquired distinct contours during the wars of religion that ravaged France between 1562 and 1598'. Perhaps, by looking back to pre-democratic and pre-Enlightenment developments in politics and law, we might better understand the limited scope of action imposed on modern liberal regimes by their political histories.

---

[27] On moves in international law to establish universal guarantees of a 'right to be different', see Evans (2001).

At this point, then, I drop the usual periodisation for the 1905 law. Rather than the militant anti-clericalism of 1789, the sixteenth-century attempt at religious settlement becomes the backdrop for the construction of *laïcité* and the twentieth-century juridical accommodation-by-separation of church and state. In this way, we begin to mute the image of French *laïcité* as an intransigent, all-or-nothing expression of the Parisian philosophical Enlightenment and Revolutionary Jacobin zeal.

With the sixteenth-century fracture of Christianity into rival confessions, Catholic communities clashed savagely with their Protestant rivals.[28] Faced with the contagions of popular religious violence, officers of the French state began to imagine – and attempted to create – a political and legal framework for peace that was novel, in the sense of being neutral towards the religious plurality. The aim was a stable civil order in a multi-confessional society.

Already, in the encroaching shadow of the religious wars, Charles IX's Chancellor, Michel de L'Hospital, put the Crown's case for civil peace. Speaking on 26 August 1561 to the assembly of the States-General at St-Germain-en-Laye, L'Hospital started by recognising the fact of the 'diversity of religions'. He regretted the strife now flowing from such division. Next, he indicated his wish to address 'not the controversies of religion ... but only what pertains to police, in order to contain the people in rest and tranquillity'.[29] Then, L'Hospital identified a logic that might govern religious plurality peacefully:

The King does not want you to engage in dispute over which [religious] opinion is the best; for here it is not a question of establishing the faith, but of regulating the state. It is possible to be a citizen without being a Christian. Even the excommunicate does not cease to be a citizen. We can live in peace with those who hold to different opinions.[30]

---

[28] Crouzet (1991) is the benchmark study of popular religious violence and the actions of 'God's warriors' in early modern France.

[29] 'Je ne veux mettre en dispute les controverses de la religion ... mais seulement ce qui appartient à la police, pour contenir le peuple en repos et tranquillité.' (L'Hospital 2001: 59).

[30] 'Le roi ne veut point que vous entriez en dispute quelle opinion est la meilleure; car il n'est pas ici question *de constituendâ religione, sed de constituendâ republicâ*; et plusieurs peuvent être *cives, qui non erunt christiani*: même l'excommunié ne laisse pas d'être citoyen. Et peut-on vivre en repos avec ceux, qui sont de diverses opinions ...' (L'Hospital 2001: 62).

The striking precept that 'even the excommunicate does not cease to be a citizen' required the listeners to conceive the community of citizenship as a neutral space of political government and peace, to one side of the contested ecclesiastical domain.

To create such a space, legal expedients were explored. Acts of 'oblivion' were incorporated into the edicts of pacification. Bi-confessional tribunals with parity of confessional representation – *chambres mi-parties* – were instituted, marking an attempt at legal neutrality.[31] To be effectively implemented, however, the precept of neutrality presumed sufficient disengagement by legal officers – legislators and judges – from the 'controversies of religion'. It also presumed a measure of religious neutralisation – a de-sacralisation – on the part of law. These were tall orders in the midst of confessional civil war. As religious animosities sharpened, L'Hospital's moves to manage religious plurality could not override confessional interests that proved beyond negotiation. Religious identities trumped civil peace. The majority of Paris *parlementaires* – the principal French judicial estate – held firm to their status as *pars principis* with its jurisdictional prerogatives and ancient sacral duty: the protection of the French nation's universal Catholic mission.

If L'Hospital envisaged a neutral civility of law and political citizenship, this was not a 'secularisation' in any usual sense of the term. Rather, it was an interim measure, pending a future reunification of the faith. That there was no question of a general eclipsing of religion, as is demonstrated in Denis Crouzet's (1997) study of L'Hospital's complex *christocentrisme*, an elevated evangelical faith that rose above the war of confessional truths, borne aloft by neo-Platonic and Stoic currents.[32] This was anything but an ideology of secularism. Unlike three centuries later, there was no question of a general attack on the foundations of Christian faith. There was no question of expelling the religious orders or curtailing the existing ecclesiastical

[31] Olivier Christin (1997) argues for the 'autonomisation of political reason' arising from the political work, legal developments and local community initiatives for peace deployed in the quest for religious pacification in sixteenth-century France and Germany.

[32] As Crouzet (1997) shows, L'Hospital's religious-metaphysical faith remained almost completely opaque to his contemporaries. It gained him hostility and deep suspicion – indeed vicious hatreds – from both the Catholic and the Protestant sides.

regimes governing marriage and burial. Indeed, such actions would have made civil peace less, not more, likely.

Yet – in terms of a secularisation of the political and legal order – L'Hospital's initiatives in the 1560s showed how a state might seek civil peace and a stable political order by temporarily sidelining the dispute between confessional communities fashioned around rival religious identities. This meant subjecting external conduct – the public order of worldly life – to a rule of law, not a rule of religion. By envisaging the political state's strategic capacity for neutrality towards religious plurality, L'Hospital provided the concrete political-legal instance and a framework subsequently theorised in Jean Bodin's *De la République*, among whose future relayers would be Thomas Hobbes.[33] Appearing in 1576, four years after the St Bartholomew's Day Massacre, Bodin's great treatise conceptualised sovereignty as absolute, indivisible and secular in a manner that aligned its author with the Chancellor's peace-brokering initiatives. If, as Bodin now argued, the sovereign state was the sole legitimate source of the civil law, a plurality of faiths could be recognised and need not mean catastrophe ... provided that the will of the unified sovereign retained the power of final determination as the civil law. This proto-*politique* theory found expression in the Edict of Nantes.[34]

Further work is needed on setting an early modern 'absolutist' state into the context of its historical emergence and – a taller order – on correlating the political and legal arrangements in an early modern 'absolutist' state with those in a modern liberal constitutional state.[35]

[33] Translated into English and published by Richard Knolles in 1606, Bodin's *De la République* was one of the most read books in early seventeenth-century English political circles.

[34] Bettinson (1989) warns against reifying a diverse set of ideas, a variety of initiatives (such as L'Hospital's) and a number of political episodes into a unified *politique* ideology with something like an epochal transformative power. As he reminds us, *politique* was the preferred term of censure deployed by Catholic Leaguers to besmirch all those who would abandon religious truth and seek accommodation with known heretics and proven schismatics.

[35] The traditional connotations of 'absolutist' – totalitarian, secularising – are being reviewed in revisionist scholarship on the history of absolutism. For Marcel Gauchet (1994: 212): 'We still need a precise historical characterisation of that religious revolution of politics or that political revolution of religion which intervene at the end of the sixteenth century and which are going not only to condition the transfer of the attributes and prerogatives of spiritual authority to the temporal authority, but also to furnish this inherited

Yet, it is plausible to recognise Michel de L'Hospital's attempted religious settlement as an improvised solution to a problem that has returned to our twenty-first-century agenda: how to govern religious difference and ensure peaceful coexistence of rival religious communities.

Conclusion: historical, not prophetic

It is too soon to know how the 1905 Law of Separation will be reformed – if, indeed, it is reformed – in the Sarkozy presidency, although the new President's will to act on this and many other 'reforms' cannot be doubted. But the point of this chapter is not to guess the future. To the contrary, the aim has been to show how one liberal state – in whose political history religious and constitutional issues have had a particular salience – has dealt with the clash of sectarianisms, religious and secular.[36]

sovereignty with its definitive and specifically modern meaning.' Carl Schmitt's celebrated aphorism to the effect that European political concepts are derivations from theological concepts has a certain resonance here, as it does in Martin's (2003) suggestion 'that – classical sources apart – ideas like liberty, equality and fraternity are secular translations of Biblical texts, such as our oneness (irrespective of all adventitious characteristics) in Christ, the unity of humanity "under God", and the way in which every human being is a king and a priest "unto God"'. Yet, there is quite another side to the story. In his secularising revision of the natural law tradition, Samuel Pufendorf aimed precisely in the reverse direction: it was essential, for the sake of civil peace, not to transfer the attributes of spiritual authority to the temporal authority. For Pufendorf, if religious peace was to be achieved, theology could not furnish the model for the civil sovereign, whose office called for new and secularised forms of thought.

[36] To contextualise the Law of Separation as an arrangement peculiar to French political and legal history, a comparative note is useful. Bauberot (2000: 121) compares the process of *laïcisation* in France, of which the 1905 law was a key manifestation, with the process of *sécularisation* in the Anglican and other northern European settings. The latter process has been slow, incremental and almost organic, without external intervention by the state. By contrast,

in a process of French style *laïcisation*, we are dealing above all with an external state regulation having a tendency towards conflict, which finishes – through a pacification of the conflict – with a distancing of the church–state links (first threshold of *laïcité*) and then with a formal equality of the separated churches (second threshold of *laïcité*). Conversely, in the process of *sécularisation*, we find above all an internal modality of state intervention having a tendency towards conciliation.

In this account of the 1905 French Law of Separation, I have made a case for a more nuanced and less ideologically pure view of *laïcité*, in part by stressing the contingencies that marked the legislative struggle to establish a juridical middle way between militant secularists and intransigent Catholics. To give this middle way a measure of historical gravity, I have also suggested a possible lineage from Michel de L'Hospital's 'excommunicate [who] does not cease to be a citizen' to Aristide Briand's legislative work, a century ago, that established for all French citizens a non-confessional constitutional order. Each of these legal initiatives – although more than three centuries apart – aimed in its own way at a political neutralisation of religious-sectarian conflict. Each thus posed a challenge to the divisive forces of religious – and, in the 1905 case, secular – collectivism. Each, in its particular historical setting, envisaged a plural space of neutral civility for all citizens where – otherwise – a confessional monopoly or ideological uniformity might have ruled.

True, the 1905 law marked a legal inroad into ecclesiastical authority. Yet, as a religious pacification measure and therefore quite unlike the spirit of 1789, it was not an anti-religious legislation. Michel de L'Hospital would surely recognise the point of words written in 1906, some three centuries after his death: 'The state has neither to deny nor to affirm it [the authority of the clergy over the faithful]. The state does not know about this, and has no need to know about this. All the state knows [and recognises] are groups of French citizens'.[37]

Without an appropriate regime of implementation, any legislation may be no better than chimerical. A full account of the 1905 law would therefore survey the workings of the *Conseil d'Etat*, the *Cour de cassation* and the administrative tribunals in matters arising under the new legislation. Their task was an equitable case-by-case balancing of the principle of *laïcité* and the freedom of religion. For instance, the *Conseil d'Etat* had to rule on a case arising in the *Pas-de-Calais*, where an *association* had been established in accordance with the provisions of the 1905 law.[38] The incumbent Catholic priest

---

[37] Ferdinand Buisson, 'L'ultimatum romain', cited in Scot (2005: 286). Buisson was the President of the *Commission de séparation*.

[38] This case is cited in Baubérot (2005: 118–19). For Baubérot, though, the decision is symptomatic of an enduring problem. By not endorsing the 'law-abiding' but irregular and 'out-of-communion' priest, the *Conseil d'Etat* underscored the unspoken prejudice of the 1905 law in favour of the Catholic Church and against the plurality of faiths, then and now.

would continue in office and in occupation of his two churches, but redefined as a civil association under the new legal rules. However, the local bishop intervened, on the grounds that the papal interdiction against *associations* meant the priest was no longer in communion with the Church of Rome. The bishop therefore named as replacement a priest who, in rejecting the *association*, remained competent to provide for Catholic worshippers. At first glimpse, we may be surprised, even shocked, to learn that in adjudicating the conflict, the *Conseil d'Etat* found in favour of the replacement priest, despite the latter's rejection of the law. How could this be? In fact, the *Conseil d'Etat* based its decision on legal and pragmatic grounds. Only a priest who was in communion with the Church could effectively meet the law's liberal purpose: to ensure a continuing freedom of worship according to the rules of the church in question.

The more muted and liberal view of *laïcité* and the Law of Separation adopted in this chapter is not the norm. For Jean-Paul Scot (2005: 254), 'Separation is indeed the institutional accomplishment of the long and conflictual process of secularisation of state and society, of which the years 1789 to 1799 were the first real instance', For David Martin, modern France and the French law represent the paradigm instance of Enlightenment secularism and 'secularist indoctrination by the state':

[T]he rigorous state monopoly exercised by the Catholic Church in France after the Revocation of the Edict of Nantes in 1685 was transposed into the monopoly eventually exercised during the Third Republic by the omnicompetent secular state. Just as for the Catholic Church error had no rights, so for the sacred Republic Catholic error had no right to acknowledgement in the public realm. (Martin 2003)

Depicted in this anti-statist light, the 1905 French Law of Separation displays an almost 'totalitarian' character. Conversely, it loses its visibility as a revisable *pacte laïque* for the peaceful coexistence of different communities of faith. If we adopt this latter view, we might better see the 1905 law in a more nuanced and historical light: as a liberal middle way between rival sectarianisms – one religious, the other secular – not as an illiberal (or totalitarian) imposition of a secularist ideology in pure Enlightenment style.

There is reason to adopt this liberal view. Just a century ago, this was the view that offered a chance of civil peace in the face of an incipient religious civil war. Responding in the *Chambre des députés* on 7 March 1907 to Catholic voices that had denounced the 1905 law as *une loi de meurtre* and demanded its abrogation, Briand maintained a liberal cool:

As for ourselves, gentlemen, in spite of you, in spite of all these exaggerations, we know how to remain calm [*conserver notre sang-froid*]: we shall desist from any act that could have as a consequence what many, unfortunately, desire, even invoke with their most ardent vows of service to some wretched political designs, namely, that blood be shed on the law of the Republic. No, that will not come to pass. The law will remain what it is ... It will be implemented with moderation and prudence but without weakness, with circumspection but without fail.[39]

Nor was it only French Catholic deputies who provocatively voiced 'these exaggerations'. There was always the Roman dimension. In February 1906, Pius X published the encyclical *Vehementor nos* as a frontal attack on the principle of the church–state separation, an attack mounted to defend 'the inalienable and sacred rights of the Church'. Citing the 'supreme authority that God had conferred' upon him, the Supreme Pontiff proceeded to condemn the French legislation as

violating natural law, the law of peoples and the public faith owed to treaties, as contrary to the divine constitution of the Church, to its essential rights and liberty ... We reprove and condemn [this law] as a grave attempt on the dignity of this apostolic see, on our person, on the clergy and on all the Catholics of France' (quoted in Scot 2005: 275).

Emboldened by the pontifical *raison d'église*, the Catholic press in France called on its readers to restart 'the admirable wars of religion': 'Would not Christian France applaud if, in the space of a single night, all the sectarians and free-masons were exterminated? The Saint-Bartholomew was a splendid night for France and the Fatherland' (quoted in Scot 2005: 276).

Just a hundred years ago, in France, these things were being said by those for whom eternal issues were at stake. Worse, they were being heard. Does recalling this history not invite a measure of caution towards today's increasingly audible 'anti-secularist' calls for a readmission of religion to the public sphere as a partner in the democratic

---

[39] Aristide Briand, *Annales de la Chambre des députés*, 7 March 1906, 1260–1.

process?[40] Is the work of the religiously neutral state now over and done with? Are religious threats to civil peace in multi-religious societies just a relic of the past? Are the relations of church and state now definitively softened and safe, once and for all? Whether or not these historical controversies are at an end, it remains true that the French law of 1905 achieved a durable measure of law-based civil peace, in the face of religious passion and secularist zealotry. That peace is an achievement to be commemorated in our hate-filled European history, now or at any time.

[40] See, for instance, on this *nouvelle vague religieuse*, Casanova's (1994) 'post-Catholic' case for readmitting a 'de-privatised' religion – no longer just a matter of the private inner world of belief – to full participation as a civil force in public life.

4 Political secularism: why it is needed and what can be learnt from its Indian version

RAJEEV BHARGAVA

Secularism appears to be under siege everywhere. The predicted decline or privatisation has failed to occur not only in non-western but in western societies (Casanova 1994). In hindsight it seems the ascendance of secular-humanism was episodic and temporary, restricted anyway to a few highly visible European societies. Moreover, political secularism, the doctrine of the separation of state and religion, was jolted with the establishment of the first modern theocracy in Khomeini's Iran. Soon other religious voices began to be heard and then to aggressively occupy the public domain. In Egypt, people were urged to free themselves of the last vestiges of a colonial past and to establish a Muslim state. In 1989, an Islamic state was established in Sudan. In 1991, the Islamic Salvation Front won the election in Algeria. Islamic movements emerged in Tunisia, Ethiopia, Nigeria, Chad, Senegal, Turkey and Afghanistan (Kepel 1994; Westerlund 1996). The states of Pakistan and Bangladesh increasingly acquired theocratic and Islamicist overtones (Ahmed 1987; Mohsin 1999).

Movements that challenged the seemingly undisputed reign of secularism were not restricted to Muslim societies. Singhalese Buddhist nationalists in Sri Lanka, Hindu nationalists in India, religious ultra-orthodoxy in Israel and Sikh nationalists who demanded a separate state partly on the ground that Sikhism does not recognise the separation of religion and state, all reflect a deep crisis of secularism (Juergensmeyer 1994).

Protestant movements decrying secularism emerged in Kenya, Guatemala and the Philippines. Protestant fundamentalism became a force in American politics. Religiously grounded political movements arose in Poland. In western Europe where religion for many is still largely a private response to divinity rather than an organised system of practices, migrant workers of former colonies and an intensified globalisation began to bring into question the existing, rather marginal place of religion in society. A privatised Christianity has been thrown together with Islam, Sikhism and pre-Christian South Asian religions, that draw a boundary between the private and the public differently. These strange bedfellows have created a deep religious diversity the like of which has not been known in the West for centuries (Turner 2001: 134). As the public spaces of western societies are claimed by these other religions, the weak but distinct monopoly of any one religion is beginning to be challenged by the very norms governing these societies. This is evident in Germany and Britain but was highlighted most dramatically by the headscarf issue in France (Freedman 2004). The suppressed religious past of these societies is now foregrounded in a way that questions any claim about the robust secular character of these states.

The secular state is contested not only by politicians, civil society groups and clerics; it is questioned even by academics. Indian academics were among the first to voice their opposition to secularism (Chatterjee 1998; Madan 1998; Nandy 1998). By the 1990s, this criticism was also voiced by several scholars in the West. Initially, critical academic writing in the West accepted the framework of liberal democracy and sought to fine-tune it. It argued (a) that the public justification of a policy by secular reason should not preclude actual decision-making to be grounded solely on a religious rationale (Greenawalt 1988); or (b) that not only political decisions, but their justification too, could in certain contexts rely exclusively on religious reasons (Perry 1991); or (c) that by demanding the exclusion of religious convictions from public life, liberal democrats violated their own principle of equal respect (Eberle 2002, 188–9).

Critiques of western secularism have since become sharper and gone much further. Several western scholars claim that by trivialising faith, secularism is hostile to religious believers. By enjoining believers to leave behind religious convictions when they step into public life, secularism, it is argued, inhibits diversity and homogenises the public domain. Some claim that modern political secularism is a child of single-religion societies, and that while it may be suited to Protestantism and religions that are weakly protestantised, it excludes or is actively inimical to other religions (Connolly 1999: 23–5; Keane 2000: 14–18; Asad 2003). Some say that secularism has failed to accommodate community-specific rights and therefore is unable to protect religious minorities from discrimination and exclusion. Others argue that secularism has become immodest, demanding from others what it dare not expect from itself – blind to its own assumptions and presuppositions, it denies dependence on a visceral register that it publicly denounces as irrational. Besides, how can it fight religious hegemony and in the same breath try to establish itself as the sole basis of adjudication in public life? Secularism is a deeply parochial doctrine with universalist pretensions (Connolly 1999: 38–9). Critics even argue that its peace-talk is mere sham because deep down it is a conflict-generating ideology that threatens pluralist democracies.

However, critical writing on secularism is deeply ambiguous between two claims. First, that the deep crisis of secular states signifies that we must look for alternatives to them, and second, that we look not for an alternative to secular states but rather for their alternative conceptions, and by implication, for alternative conceptions of political secularism. It is important then to begin this enquiry by asking what distinguishes secular states from their competitors and – this remains largely unclear – what precise alternatives critics have in mind when they seek to replace secular states. More importantly, we must ask what the merits and demerits of secular and non-secular states are. This is a sensible question, given that any sound, ethically sensitive, practical reasoning must be comparative in nature, and must tell what ethical gains or losses might ensue if we are to transit from a secular state to some other kind of state that presumably grants more importance to religion. If secular states are indeed more worthy, we must also ask if this is true of all secular states or of only some. And if only some, which exactly? This issue cannot be addressed unless we ask another important question: what are the different forms of secular states? Which of them are better and why? In what follows, I deal with these questions by elaborating what in my view is the proper conceptual and normative structure of secularism. This I hope will not only distinguish secular from non-secular states but also help individuate different types of secular states. I do this not because I have an interest in classification per se, but rather because there is a need to identify a version of secularism that meets the most important religious objections mentioned above, and because of my belief that an indifference to this objection and the consequent smugness that ensues from this neglect bolster otherwise indefensible anti-secular states. Finally, I explore whether a search for alternative conceptions of secularism leads us towards conceptual resources that cut through the division between a modern West and a traditional East. For example, I ask if the Indian version of secularism is a mere specification of an idea with western origins and imprint or if it is a genuine alternative to its western counterpart, one from which everyone, including the West, may benefit in the future.[1]

Theocracy and states with established religions

To identify the conceptual structure of secularism, it is best to begin by contrasting it with doctrines to which it is both related and opposed. Such anti-secular doctrines favour not separation but a union or alliance between church/religion and state. A state that has union with a particular religious order is a theocratic state, governed by divine laws directly administered by a priestly order claiming divine commission.[2] Historical examples of celebrated theocracies are ancient Israel, some Buddhist regimes of Japan and China, the Geneva of John Calvin, and the Papal states. The Islamic republic of Iran as Khomeini aspired to run it is an obvious example. A theocratic state must be distinguished from a state that establishes religion. Here religion is granted official, legal recognition by the state, and while both benefit from a formal alliance with one another, the sacerdotal order does not govern a state where religion is established.

Because they do not identify or unify church and state but install only an alliance between them, states with an established church are in some ways disconnected from it. The disconnection operates in different ways. For a start, these are political orders where there is a sufficient degree of institutional differentiation between the two social entities. Both the church and the state are distinct enough to have separate identities. This difference in identity may be due partly to role differentiation. Each is to perform a role different from the other: the function of one is to maintain peace and order, a primarily temporal matter; the function of the other is to secure salvation, primarily a

[1] I have yet to take into account the important and increasingly voluminous work of Veit Bader on the relationship of religion and politics.
[2] *The Catholic Encyclopedia* (Herbermann *et al.* 1913) defines theocracy as a form of political government in which the deity directly rules the people or the rule of the priestly caste. The rule of Brahmin in India is in accordance with the Dharma Shastras and would be theocratic.

Table 4.1 *Church–state relations: theocracies and state religions*

	Levels of connection (C) or disconnection (D)	
	Theocracy	State with established religion
Ends: first order C/D	C	C
Institutions and personnel: second order C/D	C	D
Law and public policy: third order C/D	C	C

spiritual concern. In a theocracy the same personnel perform both roles. In states with established religions, there may even be personnel differentiation. State functionaries and church functionaries are largely different from one another. Thus, disconnection between church and state can go sufficiently deep. Yet, there is a more significant sense in which the state and the church are connected to one another: they share a common end largely defined by religion. By virtue of a more primary connection of ends, the two share a special relationship. Both benefit from this mutual alliance. There is finally another level of connection between church and state at the level of policy and law. Such policies and laws flow from and are justified in terms of the union or alliance that exists between the state and the church. The institutional *disconnection* of church and state – at the level of roles, functions and powers – goes hand in hand with the first- and third-level *connection* of ends and policies. So this is what differentiates a state with established church-based religion from a theocracy: the second-order disconnection of church and state. Table 4.1 above clarifies these distinctions.

Just as a theocracy is not always distinguished from the establishment of religion, just so a distinction is not always drawn between the establishment of religion and the establishment of the church of a religion (a religious institution with its own distinct rules, function and social roles, personnel, jurisdiction, power, hierarchy (ecclesiastical levels), and a distinct and authoritative interpretation of a religion).[3]

---

[3] The whole question of church–state separation, I would claim, emerges forcefully in what are predominantly church-based, single-religion societies. The issue of religion–state separation arises, however, in societies without churches or/and with multiple religions, or when the hold of religion in societies

But clearly not all religions have churches. Yet, a state may establish such a church-free religion, i.e. grant it formal, legal recognition and privilege. Put differently, the establishment of a church is always the establishment of a particular religion, but the converse is not always true. The establishment of a particular religion does not always mean the establishment of a church. A majority of Hindu nationalists in India may wish to establish Hinduism as the state religion, but they have no church to establish. Such an establishment may be expressed in the symbols of the state as well, in the form of state policies that support a particular religion.[4] Early Protestants may have wanted to disestablish the Roman Catholic Church without wishing the state to cease recognising Christianity as the favoured religion. Alternatively, they tried to maintain the establishment of their preferred religion by the establishment of not one, but two, or even more churches. The establishment of a single religion is consistent therefore with the dis-establishment or non-establishment of church, with the establishment of a single church or with the establishment of multiple churches. This issue is obscured because in church-based religions the establishment of religion *is* the establishment of the church and the establishment of Christianity is so much a part of background understanding of several western societies that this fact does not even need to be foregrounded and discussed.

Finally, it is possible that there is establishment of multiple religions, with or without church. Possibly the emperor Ashoka in India came closest to it. It was also an aspiration of the Mughal emperor Akbar. Perhaps another example is the fourteenth-century Vijayanagar kingdom, which granted official recognition not only to Shaivites and the Vaishnavites but even the Jains.

We can see then that there are five types of regimes in which a close relationship exists between state and religion.[5] First, a theocracy

---

has considerably declined, when religion is considered by the majority to be largely insignificant.

[4] It is frequently said that secularism cannot exist in India because Hinduism lacks a church and therefore that there is no church to separate from the state. The hidden assumption underlying this assertion is that secularism means church–state separation. This is both false and misleading.

[5] I stress that the three types of state–church regimes discussed above are all ideal-typical.

where no institutional separation exists between church and state, and
the priestly order is also the direct political ruler. Second, states with
the establishment of a single religion. These are of three types: (a)
without the establishment of a church, (b) with the establishment of a
single church, and (c) with the establishment of multiple churches.
Third, states with establishment of multiple religions.

Secular states

Secular states are different from each of these five kinds of states. To
further understand this issue and distinguish different forms of secular
states, allow me to unfold the structure of the secular state. For a start,
we must recognise that a secular state is to be distinguished not only
from a theocracy (Feature *a*) but also from a state where religion is
established. But a non-theocratic state is not automatically secular
because it is entirely consistent for a state to be neither inspired by
divine laws nor run by a priestly order, but instead have a formal
alliance with one religion: exactly the sort of thing desired, it seems to
me, by the Bhartiya Janata Party in India. Second, because it is also a
feature of states with established churches, the mere institutional
separation of the two is not and cannot be the distinguishing mark of
secular states. This second-level disconnection should not be conflated
with the separation embedded in secular states, because though necessary it is not a sufficient condition for their individuation. A secular
state goes beyond church–state separation, refusing to establish religion; or, if religion is already established, it disestablishes it. It withdraws privileges that established religion had previously taken for
granted. Therefore, a secular state follows what can be called principle
of non-establishment (Feature *b*). Furthermore, the non-establishment
of religion means that the state is separated not merely from one but
from all religions. Thus, in a secular state, a formal or legal union or
alliance between state and religion is impermissible. Official status is
not given to religion. No religious community in such a state can say
that the state belongs exclusively to it. Nor can all of them together
say that it belongs collectively to them and them alone.

To grasp this point at a more general theoretical level, let me distinguish three levels of disconnection to correspond with the three
levels of connection already identified. A state may be disconnected
from religion at the level of ends (first-level), at the level of institutions

Table 4.2 *Church–state relations: theocracies, state religions, and secular states*

	Levels of connection (C) or disconnection (D)		
	Theocracy	State with established religion	Secular (mainstream)
Ends: first order C/D	C	C	D
Institutions and personnel: second order C/D	C	D	D
Law and public policy: third order C/D	C	C	D

(second-level), and the level of law and public policy (third-level).[6] A secular state is distinguished from theocracies and states with established religions by a primary, first-level disconnection. A secular state has freestanding ends, substantially, if not always completely, disconnected from the ends of religion or conceivable without a connection with them. Finally, a state may be disconnected from religion even at the level of law and public policy. Table 4.2 clarifies these distinctions.

Amoral and value-based secular states

I return to this third-level disconnection below. At this stage, it is particularly important to emphasise that the disconnection at each of the three levels may serve different ends. At the very least such ends are of two kinds. The first kind is amoral. Amoral secular states are so called because their entire purpose is to maximise power, wealth or both. They may have moral pretensions but really no commitment to values such as peace, liberty or equality. Usually, they are imperial and autocratic. A good example of such a predominantly secular state – despite the not infrequent allegation of its biased, Christian character – is the British colonial state in India, which was motivated almost exclusively by power, wealth and social order, and generally had a policy of tolerance and neutrality towards different religious

---

[6] As we shall see, this would also open up the possibility of distinguishing forms of secular states.

communities. This is not surprising, given that empires are interested in the labour or tribute of their subjects, not in their religion. Such self-aggrandising, amoral states may or may not disconnect with religion at the third level, that is, at the level of law and policy. They may have a hands-off approach to all religions, purely for instrumental reasons. However, if it serves their instrumental purpose, they may also connect with religion.

More on value-based secular states

Distinct from amoral states are value-based secular states. A fuller discussion of such states requires a better articulation of their connection with several important and substantive values, which I have summarised in Table 4.3. The first of these is peace, or rather the prevention of a society from its regression into barbarism, not an uncommon tendency where there exist two or more incompatible visions of the good life (Feature *c*). The second is toleration, i.e. the state does not persecute or allow the persecution of anyone on grounds of religion (Feature *d*). This value may be seen by some to be superseded by the discourse of rights, but in certain contexts it has continuing relevance. Why so? Because there are areas of society that remain beyond the reach of the legal regime of rights. For example, we know that courts are ineffective when overburdened with claims. To check this rot, out-of-court settlements are encouraged. In the same way, it is sometimes better to waive one's rights and rely instead on a policy of live-and-let-live. A secular state must have room for this. Third, a secular state is constitutively tied to religious liberty, a value with at least three dimensions. The first refers to the liberty of members of any one religious group (Feature *e*). It is a brute fact that in most religious communities, one or two interpretations of its core beliefs and practices come to dominate. Given this dominance, it is important that every individual or sect within the group be given the right to criticise, revise or challenge these dominant interpretations. The second aspect of this important liberty (Feature *f*) is that it be granted non-preferentially to all members of every religious community. The third dimension of religion-related liberty (Feature *g*) is that individuals be free not only to criticise the religion into which they are born, but to reject it and, further, given ideal conditions of deliberation, to freely embrace another religion or to remain without one.

Table 4.3 *Features of a secular state*

(*a*)	Non-theocratic
(*b*)	The principle of non-establishment of religion
(*c*)	Peace between communities
(*d*)	Toleration
(*e*)	Religious liberty to any one religious group
(*f*)	Religious liberty granted non-preferentially to members of every religious group
(*g*)	The liberty to embrace a religion other than the one into which a person is born, and to reject all religions
(*h*)	No discrimination by the state on grounds of religion to entitlements provided by the state
(*i*)	No discrimination in admission to educational institutions on grounds of religion
(*j*)	Equality of active citizenship: no discrimination on grounds of religion in the right to vote, to deliberate on public matters and to stand for public office

Religious liberty, when understood broadly, is one important value of a secular state. To understand another crucial ingredient, it is necessary to grasp the point that liberty and equality in the religious sphere are all of a piece with liberty and equality in other spheres. It is not a coincidence that the disestablishment clause in the First Amendment to the American Constitution institutes not only religious freedom but also the more general freedom of speech, of peaceful assembly and political dissent. It is entirely possible that a state permits *religious* liberty and equality but forbids other forms of freedom and equality. For instance, a person may challenge the authority of the religious head of his own denomination but not be free to challenge the authority of the state. This is impossible in a secular state that is committed to a more general freedom and equality. Thus, another critical value to which a secular state is constitutively linked is the equality of free citizenship.

The value of equal citizenship has two dimensions, one active, the other passive. To be a passive citizen is to be entitled to physical security, a minimum of material well-being and a sphere of one's own in which others ought not to interfere. The benefits of citizenship – resources that enable a dignified ordinary life – must be available to everyone and there is no room here for discrimination on grounds of

Table 4.4 *Church–state relations in three types of secular state*

	Levels of connection (C) or disconnection (D)		
	Amoral secular	Anti-religious secular	Mainstream value-based secular
Ends: first order C/D	D	D	D
Institutions and personnel: second order C/D	D	D	D
Law and public policy: third order C/D	Opportunistic C or D	One-sided C or D	D

religion (Feature *h*). This equal treatment is the province of equal (passive) citizenship. State agencies and the entire system of law must not work in favour of one religious group. If the state works to protect the security and well-being of some individuals or groups but fails to secure these meagre but important benefits to others then the principle of equal (passive) citizenship is violated. Likewise, since citizenship is conditional upon education, no one must be denied admission to educational institutions, solely on grounds of religion (Feature *i*).

The active dimension of citizenship involves the recognition of citizens as equal participants in the public domain (Feature *j*). Active participation does not only mean the mere possession of the right to vote but also a right to participate in public deliberation and to stand for public office. In secular states, such active citizenship rights ought to be available to everyone, regardless of religion. I have claimed above that disconnection of religion from state serves different ends. I now want to stress that the third-level disconnection may also take diverse forms. This helps us to distinguish different kinds of value-based secular states, each with a different understanding of what precisely this disconnection means, as summarised in Table 4.4.

One type of secular state conceives connection or disconnection at the third level in a wholly one-sided manner. To disconnect is to exclude religion from its own affairs but to have no limits on its own interventionist powers in the affairs of religion. Such states exclude religion in order to control or regulate them and sometimes even to destroy them. They may justify exclusion by claiming that religion is false consciousness or obscurantist or superstition, or may they do so in the name of a single value such as equality. They may even support religion but only to control it. Such secular states are decidedly anti-religious. I have in mind some communist states, the secular state in Turkey and since the nineteenth century periodically, the French state.

A second type of value-based secular state conceives this third-level disconnection as mutual exclusion. Such a state maintains a policy of strict or absolute separation. In this incarnation it typifies a hysterical brahminical attitude: religion is untouchable, so any contact with it contaminates secularist purity. Secularism here becomes a doctrine of political taboo and prohibits contact with religious activities. Such a view proposes that religious and political institutions live as strangers to each other, at best with benign or respectful indifference. Thus, here religion is excluded from the affairs of the state but the state too is excluded from the affairs of the religion. The state has neither a positive relationship with religion – for example there is no policy of granting aid to religious institutions – nor a negative relationship with it; it is not within the scope of state activity to interfere in religious matters even when the values professed by the state are violated. This non-interference is justified on the ground that religion is a private matter, and if something is amiss within this private domain, it can be mended only by those who have a right to do so within that sphere. This, according to proponents of this view, is what religious freedom means. Mutual exclusion is justified on grounds of negative liberty and is identical with the privatisation of religion.

When a state is disconnected with religions at all three levels in this particular way, then we may say that a wall of separation has been erected between the two. In different ways, the American wall of separation model and the French model of one-sided exclusion disconnect the state from religion at this third level of law and policy, one predominantly for the sake of religious liberty and the other primarily for the sake of equality of citizenship. These are the liberal and republican conceptions of secularism. Since these are the most dominant and defensible western versions of secularism, I shall put them together and henceforth designate them as the *mainstream* conception of secularism.

Theocracy, states with establishment and secular states: a normative comparison

I think we can now better answer the comparative question we raised at the beginning. When anti-separationists imagine the replacement of a secular state with some other type of state, which of the five religious states do they have in mind? Undoubtedly, some religious activists fervently desire the installation of theocracy or a state that establishes its own religion or church. However, most anti-separationist academics neither endorse this position nor explicitly reject it. They attack separation but wish to distance themselves from a wholly religion-centred polity. It is not hard to understand why, if they thought hard on this issue, they would eschew religion-centred states. A cursory evaluation of these states shows that these are all deeply troublesome. Take first historical instances of states that establish a single church – the unreformed established Protestant churches of England, Scotland and Germany, and the Catholic churches in Italy and Spain – the state recognised a particular version of the religion enunciated by its church as the official religion, compelled individuals to congregate for only one church, punished them for failing to profess a particular set of religious beliefs, levied taxes in support of one particular church, paid the salaries of its clergy and made instruction of the favoured interpretation of the religion mandatory in educational institutions or in the media (Levy 1994: 5). In such cases, not only was there inequality among religions (Christians and Jews) but also among the churches of the same religion, and while members of the established church may have enjoyed a modicum of religious liberty, those belonging to other churches or religions did not enjoy any or the same degree of liberty. When members of other church or religious groups possessed strength or number, then such a multi-religious or multi-denominational society was invariably wrecked by inter-religious or inter-denominational wars. If they did not, then religious minorities were not even tolerated and faced persistent religious persecution (e.g. Jews in several European countries).[7]

States with substantive establishments have not changed colour with time. Wherever one religion is not only formally but also substantively established, the persecution of minorities and internal dissenters continues today.[8] One has only to cite the example of Saudi Arabia to

---

[7] One exception to this, however, was the millet system of the Ottoman Empire, which had Islam as the established religion, but treated three other religious communities – Greek Orthodox, Armenian Orthodox and Jewish – as equals and gave them a respectable degree of autonomy.

[8] The distinction between formal and substantive establishment is important. In Saudi Arabia, Islam is both formally and substantively established. Britain has a

prove this point (Ruthven 2002: 172–81). It is important to dwell on this because in so many recent critiques of secularism, a more accommodative stance towards religion is recommended with an alarming neglect of some very elementary facts about what such an alliance might entail. Consider the situation in Pakistan, where the virtual establishment of the dominant Sunni sect has proved to be disastrous to minorities, including to Muslim minorities. For example, under Article 260 of the constitution Ahmadis have been deemed as a non-Muslim minority and forbidden from using Islamic nomenclature in their religious and social lives (Malik 2002: 10; Bhargava 2004: 30). A whole community has thereby been formally excluded by the state, both symbolically and materially, from its own religion. For over three decades, citizenship in Pakistan is defined with reference to majoritarian and exclusionary Islamic parameters. Therefore, political exclusion is built into the basic law of the land. By making adherence to Islam mandatory for anyone aspiring to the two highest offices in the country – that of the President and the Prime Minister – the Constitution ensures the exclusion of religious minorities from high political office (Malik 2002: 16).

I have taken Pakistan only as an illustration. Surely, after the pogrom in Gujarat in India, there is no doubt how disastrous the establishment of a Hindu *Rashtra* would be for Muslim minorities. Or consider the democratic state of Israel. Can any one reasonably claim that Christian and Muslim minorities in this Jewish state enjoy the same rights as Jews themselves? It is therefore astonishing to read the claim that 'in modern democratic politics, there is not much reason to fear a religious majority more than a secular majority' (van der Veer 2001: 20). Charles Taylor's arguments about the exclusionary tendencies in modern democratic states with religious or ethnic majorities point clearly towards the inherent possibilities in these states towards de facto singular establishment, and the wide range of exclusions and injustices that make them what they are (Taylor 1999: 138–63). To say, at this point, that religious majorities are no worse than secular majorities because different religious communities have lived in the past without coming into violent conflict is both ambiguous and misses the point. It is ambiguous because it is hard to understand what

formally established church (the Anglican Church) but few exceptions apart, only a secular state grants liberty and equality to all.

a secular majority means. If it means a group of hard-nosed secular absolutists who are deeply anti-religious, then the statement is true. But if it means a majority that wishes not to politicise religion in all kinds of unprincipled ways, then this statement is deeply wrong. The statement misses the point because peace between communities is entirely compatible with all kinds of exclusions from the domain of freedom and equality. A fearful minority is willing to buy peace at any cost – something that Indians painfully learnt again after the anti-Muslim Bombay riots in 1992–3.

What of states with multiple establishments of churches? Historically, the state of New York and the colonies of Massachusetts in the middle of the seventeenth century officially respected more than one denomination (Levy 1994: 12). These states levied a religious tax on everyone and yet gave individuals the choice to remit the tax money to their preferred church. They financially aided schools run by religious institutions but on a non-discriminatory basis. They may have punished people for disavowing or disrespecting the established religion, but did not compel them to profess the beliefs of a particular denomination.

States with substantive establishment of multiple churches are better in some ways than states with singular establishment. For example, such states are likely to be relatively peaceful. Members of different denominations are likely to tolerate one another. The state grants each denomination considerable autonomy in its own affairs. But states with establishment of multiple churches have their limitations. For a start, they may continue to persecute members of other religions, and atheists. Second, they are indifferent to the liberty of individuals within each denomination or religious group. They do little to foster a more general climate of toleration that prevents the persecution of dissenters. Closed and oppressive communities can thrive in such contexts. Third, they may not have legal provisions that allow an individual to exit from his religious community and embrace another religion, or to remain unattached to any religion whatsoever. Fourth, such states give recognition to particular religious identities but fail to recognise what may be called non-particularised identities, i.e. those that simultaneously involve several particular identities or overcoming, without cancelling, all of them. Fifth, such states are unconcerned with the *non-religious* liberties of individuals or groups. Finally, such states are entirely indifferent to citizenship rights. States that establish multiple religions face similar problems but are better than those with multiple church establishments in one important respect: there is peace and toleration and perhaps equality between all religious communities.

So are secular states better, from an ethical point of view, than theocracies and states with establishment? It would be hasty, indeed wrong, to answer this question in the affirmative. As we have seen, from a moral point of view, some secular states are deeply problematic. Amoral secular states have no commitment to any values. Anti-religious secular states have a poor record in promoting or even protecting religious freedoms. Indeed, states that fail to protect religious freedom usually trample upon other freedoms also. Overtime they also develop a hierarchy between the secular and the religious. Thus, such states are also likely to fare badly on the index of freedom and equality.

Critics who wish to rehabilitate religion in political life usually contrast states more hospitable to religions with self-aggrandising amoral or mindlessly anti-religious secular states. This is not a fair comparison. An attempt is made here to antecedently shift judgement in favour of states closely aligned with religions by deliberately pitting them against the worst forms of secular states. Little is to be gained from damning secularism, as Talal Asad does, by citing the atrocities of Hitler and Stalin or crimes committed by 'secularists' such as Saddam Hussein or Ali Hyder (Asad 2003: 10). Nonetheless, this comparison serves a point: there is not much to choose between theocracies or states with established religions on the one hand, and amoral or absolutist secular states on the other. Their deep formal structure is identical. Both fare miserably on any index of freedom or equality.

But what about the third type of secular state, one that strictly separates religion and state for the sake of religious liberty or equality of citizenship? How does the mainstream conception of secularism fare in comparison with ideal-typical theocracies and states with established religions? From a liberal and egalitarian standpoint, pretty favourably. For example, it grants the right to criticise, revise or challenge the dominant interpretations of the core beliefs of their religion to every member of all religions. In such states individuals are free not only to criticise the religion into which they are born but, at the very extreme, to reject it. Such states also grant equality of citizenship. All citizens are entitled to the same basic benefits. They have a right to vote, as also a right to participate in public deliberation and to stand for public office.

Thus, when evaluating the relative merits of religious and secular states, it is this mainstream conception that must be kept in mind for comparison and not the routinely debunked, severely anti-religious or self-aggrandising secular states. Secularism, a value-based doctrine, is as committed to denouncing these secular regimes as it is to berating religious states that violate principles of liberty and equality. The moot question is whether this mainstream conception itself has serious problems.

Critiques of mainstream, liberal-democratic secularism

The criticisms of this model are many. First, this secularism takes separation to mean exclusion of all religions on a non-preferential basis. It wishes by fiat to eliminate religion from public life and from politics more generally. For example, liberal secularism enjoins the citizen to support only those coercive laws for which there is public justification. Why so? Because if others are expected to follow a law in terms that they do not understand and for reasons they cannot endorse, then the principle of equal respect is violated (Rawls 1971: 337–8; Macedo 1990: 249; Solum 1990: 1095; Audi 1993: 701; Weithman 1997b: 6). Coercive principles must be as justifiable to others as they are to us and therefore must be based on terms that all citizens can accept on the basis of their common reason (Larmore 1996: 137). If other reasonable and conscientious citizens have good reason to reject a particular rationale in support of a coercive law then this rationale does not count as public justification. Because a religious rationale is a paradigmatic case of a reason that other citizens have good reasons to reject, it does not count as public justification; and because it does not count as public justification, a law grounded solely on a religious rationale must never be enacted. In short, purely religious convictions or commitments have no role to play in democratic and pluralist polities. This requirement that religious reasons be excluded from liberal-democratic politics is offensive to religious persons who like others wish to support their favoured political commitments on the basis of their conscience (Sandel 1993). If people believe that their politics must be consistent with their morality and that morality is derived from religion, why should they be discouraged from, or stigmatised for, so believing and seeking to act on these beliefs? Besides, it is mistaken to assume that only religious people bring passion and sectarianism into politics or, as Richard Rorty believes, that only religion is a conversation stopper (Rorty 1994: 2; Eberle 2002: 77) By asking a religious person to exercise restraint and exclude religious reasons from their justification for a coercive law, liberal secularism forces her to act against her conscience and in doing so it fails not only to respect the moral agency of that person but also violates its own principle of equal respect. Indeed, the demand that restraint be exercised is counterproductive because exclusion from the larger public sphere forces the religious to form their own narrow public where resentment and prejudice will flourish (Spinner-Halev 2000: 150–6). This would lead not only to the freezing of identities but to the building of unbreachable walls between religious and non-religious citizens. Therefore, 'engagement with religious people is typically better than shunning them' (Spinner-Halev 2000: 155).

Second, this secularism does not understand the believer's life as it is lived from the inside. It misses out on perhaps the most significant feature of most religions: that they encourage their members to choose to live a disciplined, restricted, rule-bound and desire-abnegating life. A religious life is not just a life of personal and whimsical attachment to a personal God but one in which one submits to his commands and lives obediently by them. This may be a nightmare for a standard liberal but gets the constitutive features of most religions rather better than liberal secularism does. Third, by interpreting separation as exclusion it betrays its own sectarianism; it can live comfortably with liberal, protestantised, individualised and privatised religions but has no resources to cope with religions that mandate greater public or political presence, or have a strong communal orientation. This group-insensitivity of secularism makes it virtually impossible for it to accommodate community-specific rights and therefore to protect the rights of religious minorities. In short, while this secularism copes with intra-religious domination, it does not possess resources to deal with inter-religious domination. Fourth, western secularism is a product of Protestant ethic and shaped by it. Therefore, its universal pretensions are perhaps its greatest drawback. Moreover, it presupposes a Christian civilisation that is easily forgotten because over time it has silently slid into the background. Christianity allows this self-limitation and much of the world innocently mistakes this rather cunning self-denial for its disappearance (Connolly 1999: 24). But if this is so, this 'inherently dogmatic' secularism cannot coexist innocently with other religions (Madan 1998: 298; Keane 2000: 14). Given the enormous power of the state, it must try to shape and transform them – a clear instance of illegitimate influence, if not outright violence. Thus, with all its claims of leaving religions alone, of granting religions liberty, this secularism is hostile to non-liberal, non-Protestant believers (Hamburger 2002: 193–251). Overall, it would not be wrong to say then that this secularism forces upon us a choice between active hostility or benign indifference. Fifth, liberal secularism relies excessively on a rationalist conception of reason that imposes unfair limits on the manner in which issues are to be brought into the public domain. Some issues are constitutively emotive; others become emotive because they are articulated by people who are not always trained to be rational in the way liberals mandate (Connolly 1999: 27). In short, the model of moral reasoning typical of secularism is context-insensitive, theoreticist, absolutist (non-comparative), enjoining us to think in terms of this or that, and too heavily reliant on monolithic ideas or values considered to be true or superior or wholly non-negotiable.

These are powerful critiques, with some of which I agree. But I also have a serious disagreement with the conclusion that they rebut political secularism altogether. I agree that in our imagination of social and public life, greater space must be given to non-liberal religions; such ways of life have moral integrity that liberal secularism frequently fails to realise. Yet, in our effort to accommodate such religions, we cannot ignore that these very religions also continue to be a source of severe oppression and exclusion. States that align with these religions frequently condone these morally objectionable practices. Let me offer an example each from Pakistan and India. In Pakistan, the religiously sanctioned law of evidence, *Qanoon-e-Shahadat*, holds on a par the evidence of two women or two non-Muslims with that of a single male Muslim, thereby establishing the intrinsic superiority of Muslim men over women and minorities and contravening the fundamental principle of equality (Malik 2002: 18). In Hinduism, religiously sanctioned customs related to purity and pollution continue to exclude women from the affairs of their own religion and perpetuate an institutionalised system of subordination of women. For example, at the Srimalai/Ayappa temple in Kerala, women between the ages of 15 and 55 are not allowed entry at all on the ground that their very capacity to menstruate makes their bodies impure for this entire time. This violation of the religious rights of women severely compromises the secular character of the Indian state.

What does all this show? It demonstrates three things. First, that we must be sensitive simultaneously to the moral integrity of liberal and non-liberal religious ways of living as well as to religion-based oppression and exclusions. Second, states that are strongly aligned to religions may be sensitive to the moral integrity of non-liberal religions but not always to their oppressions. Third, that a policy of non-interference (mutual exclusion) typical of liberal secularism is self-defeating. In short, a conception of secularism needs to be worked out that goes beyond liberal notions and does justice to both these dimensions referred to above. What concerns me, then, is a general failure to explore other alternative versions of secularism that are able effectively to meet the challenge of some of these critiques and imaginatively open up new possibilities of expanding our horizons. Do such versions exist? I think such a version that is not parochial, i.e. neither wholly Christian nor western, exists. This model meets the secularist objection to non-secular states and the religious objection to some forms of secular states. To my mind, when properly interpreted, Indian secularism best exemplifies this model.[9]

Alternative conceptions: Indian secularism

Seven features of Indian secularism make it distinctive, marking it out from other variants. *First*, its multi-value character. Indian secularism more explicitly registers its ties with values forgotten by western conceptions – for example, peace between communities – and interprets liberty and equality both individualistically and non-individualistically. It has a place not only for the right of individuals to profess their religious beliefs but for the right of religious communities to establish and maintain educational institutions crucial for the survival and sustenance of their religious traditions. *Second*, because it was born in a deeply multi-religious society, it is concerned as much with inter-religious domination as it is with intra-religious domination. Thus it recognises community-specific socio-religious rights. Although community-specific political rights (special representation rights for

[9] I speak of Indian secularism not out of chauvinism, but because Indian society has for centuries addressed problems that western societies are only now beginning to face. Much has been written on Indian secularism. The interested reader may consult Vanaik (1997), Bhargava (1998b), Mahajan (1998), Chandhoke (1999), Jacobsohn (2003) and Nigam (2006).

Table 4.5 *Indian secularism compared with other types of secular states*

	Levels of connection (C) or disconnection (D)			
	Amoral secular	Anti-religious secular	Mainstream value-based secular	Alternative (Indian) value-based secular
Ends: first order C/D	D	D	D	D
Institutions and personnel: second order C/D	D	D	D	D
Law and public policy: third order C/D	Opportunistic C or D	One-sided C or D	D	Principled C or D

religious minorities such as Muslims) were withheld in India for contextual reasons, the conceptual space for it is present within the model.
Third, it is committed to the idea of principled distance, poles apart
from one-sided exclusion, mutual exclusion and strict neutrality or
equidistance. Table 4.5 clarifies how this alternative, Indian conception
of secularism differs from the other types of secular states.

In addition to these features, there are others that further distinguish it from the mainstream conception. *Fourth*, it admits a distinction between depublicisation and depoliticisation, as well as
between different kinds of depoliticisation. Because it is not hostile to
the public presence of religion, it does not aim to depublicise it. It
accepts the importance of one form of depoliticisation of religion,
namely the first- and second-level disconnection of state from religion,
but the third-level depoliticisation of religion is permitted purely on
contextual grounds. *Fifth*, it is marked by a unique combination of
active hostility to some aspects of religion (a ban on untouchability
and a commitment to making religiously grounded personal laws more
gender-just) with active respect for its other dimensions (religious
groups are officially recognised, state aid is available non-preferentially
to educational institutions run by religious communities, no blanket
exclusion of religion as mandated by western liberalism). This is a
direct consequence of its commitment to multiple values and principled

distance. The Indian model accepts the view that critique is consistent with respect, and that one does not have to choose between hostility and respectful indifference. In this sense, it inherits the tradition of the great Indian religious reformers who tried to change their religion precisely because it meant so much to them. *Sixth*, it is committed to a different model of moral reasoning that is highly contextual and opens up the possibility of different societies working out their own secularisms. In short, it opens out the possibility of multiple secularisms. *Seventh*, it breaks out of the rigid interpretative grid that divides our social world into the western modern and traditional, indigenous non-western. Indian secularism is modern but departs significantly from mainstream conceptions of western secularism.

Principled distance

Let me further elucidate two of these features: its contextual character and the idea of principled distance. As seen above, for mainstream western secularism, separation means mutual exclusion. The idea of principled distance unpacks the metaphor of separation differently. It accepts a disconnection between state and religion at the level of ends and institutions but does not make a fetish of it at the third level of policy and law (this distinguishes it from all other models of secularism, moral and amoral, that disconnect state and religion at this third level). How else can it be in a society where religion frames some of its deepest interests? Recall that political secularism is an ethic whose concerns relating to religion are similar to theories that oppose unjust restrictions on freedom, morally indefensible inequalities, inter-communal domination and exploitation. Yet a secularism based on principled distance is not committed to the mainstream Enlightenment idea of religion. It accepts that humans have an interest in relating to something beyond themselves including God, and that this manifests itself as individual belief and feeling as well as social practice in the public domain. It also accepts that religion is a cumulative tradition (Smith 1991: 154–69) as well as a source of people's identities. But it insists that even if it turned out that God exists and that one religion is true and others false, then this does not give the 'true' doctrine or religion the right to force it down the throats of others who do not believe it. Neither does it give a ground for discrimination in the equal distribution of liberties and other valuable resources. Similarly, a secularism based on principled distance accepts that religion may not have special public significance antecedently written into and defining the very character of the state or the nation, but it does not follow from this that it has no public significance at all. Sometimes, on some versions of it, the wall of separation thesis assumes precisely that.

But what precisely is principled distance? The policy of principled distance entails a flexible approach on the question of inclusion/ exclusion of religion and the engagement/disengagement of the state, which at the third level of law and policy depends on the context, nature or current state of relevant religions. This engagement must be governed by principles undergirding a secular state, i.e. principles that flow from a commitment to the values mentioned above. This means that religion may intervene in the affairs of the state if such intervention promotes freedom, equality or any other value integral to secularism. For example, citizens may support a coercive law of the state grounded purely in a religious rationale if this law is compatible with freedom or equality.[10] Equally, the state may engage with religion or disengage from it, engage positively or negatively, but it does so depending entirely on whether or not these values are promoted or undermined. This is one constitutive idea of principled distance. It is different from strict neutrality, i.e. that the state may help or hinder all religions to an equal degree and in the same manner, that if it intervenes in one religion, it must also do so in others. Rather, it rests upon a distinction explicitly drawn by the American philosopher, Ronald Dworkin (1978: 125) between equal treatment and treating everyone as an equal. Treating people as equals entails that every person or group be treated with equal concern and respect. It may sometimes require equal treatment – say equal distribution of resources – but it occasionally also dictates unequal treatment. Thus treating people or groups as equals is entirely consistent with differential treatment. This idea is the second ingredient in what I have called principled distance.

---

[10] Principled distance rejects the standard liberal idea that the principle of equal respect is best realised only when people come into the public domain by leaving their religious reasons behind. Principled distance does not discourage public justification. Indeed it encourages people to pursue public justification. However, if the attempt at public justification fails, it enjoins religiously minded citizens to abandon restraint and support coercive laws that are consistent with freedom and equality based purely on religious reasons (see Eberle 2002).

I said that principled distance allows for differential treatment. What kind of treatment do I have in mind? First, religious groups have sought exemptions from practices in which states intervene by promulgating a law to be applied neutrally to the rest of society. For example, Sikhs demand exemptions from mandatory helmet laws and from police dress codes to accommodate religiously required turbans; Muslim women and girls demand that the state not interfere in their religiously required *chador*. Principled distance allows, then, that a practice that is banned or regulated in one culture may be permitted in the minority culture because of the distinctive meaning it has for its members. For the mainstream conception this is a problem because of its simple, somewhat absolutist morality, which gives overwhelming importance to one value, particularly to equal treatment, equal liberty or equality of individual citizenship. Religious groups may demand that the state refrain from interference in their practices but they may equally demand that the state give them special assistance so that they are also able to secure what other groups are able to get routinely by virtue of their dominance in the political community. For example, the state may grant authority to religious officials to perform legally binding marriages or to have their own rules of obtaining a divorce. Principled distance allows the possibility of such policies on the grounds that it may be unfair to hold people accountable to an unfair law.

However, principled distance is not just a recipe for differential treatment in the form of special exemptions. It may even require state intervention in some religions more than in others, considering the historical and social condition of all relevant religions. That is, the promotion of a particular value constitutive of secularism may actually require differential state interference in some religion. For example, suppose that the value to be advanced is social equality. This requires in part undermining caste hierarchies. If this is the aim of the state, then it may be required of the state that it interfere in caste-ridden Hinduism much more than, say, Islam or Christianity. However, if a diversity-driven religious liberty is the value to be advanced by the state, then it may have to intervene in Christianity and Islam more than in Hinduism. If this is so, the state can neither strictly exclude considerations emanating from religion nor keep strict neutrality with respect to religion. It cannot antecedently decide that it will always refrain from interfering in religions or that it will interfere in each equally. To want to do so would be plainly absurd. All it must ensure is that the relationship between the state and religions is guided by non-sectarian motives consistent with some values and principles.

Contextual secularism

A context-sensitive secularism, one based on the idea of principled distance, is what I call contextual secularism. Contextual secularism is contextual not only because it captures the idea that the precise form and content of secularism will vary from one context to another and from place to place, but also that it embodies a certain model of contextual moral reasoning. This it does because of its character as a multi-value doctrine. To accept that secularism is a multi-value doctrine is to acknowledge that its constitutive values do not always sit easily with one another. On the contrary, they are frequently in conflict. Some degree of internal discord, and therefore a fair amount of instability, is an integral part of contextual secularism. For this reason, it forever requires fresh interpretations, contextual judgements, and attempts at reconciliation and compromise. No general a-priori rule of resolving these conflicts exists: no easy lexical order, no pre-existing hierarchy among values or laws that enables us to decide that, no matter what the context, a particular value must override everything else. Almost everything then is a matter of situational thinking and contextual reasoning. Each time the matter presents itself differently and will be differently resolved. If this is true, then the practice of secularism requires a different model of moral reasoning from the one that straitjackets our moral understanding in the form of well delineated, explicitly stated rules (Taylor 1994: 16–43). This contextual secularism recognises that the conflict between individual rights and group rights, or between claims of equality and liberty, or between claims of liberty and the satisfaction of basic needs cannot always be adjudicated by recourse to some general and abstract principle. Rather, they can only be settled case by case and may require a fine balancing of competing claims. The eventual outcome may not be wholly satisfactory to either but still be reasonably satisfactory to both. Multi-value doctrines such as secularism encourage accommodation – not the giving up of one value for the sake of another but rather their reconciliation and possible harmonisation, in order to make each work without changing the basic content of apparently incompatible concepts and values.

This endeavour to make concepts, viewpoints and values work simultaneously does not amount to a morally objectionable compromise. This is so because nothing of importance is being given up for the sake of a less significant thing, one without value or even with negative value. Rather, what is pursued is a mutually agreed middle way that combines elements from two or more equally valuable entities. The roots of such attempts at reconciliation and accommodation lie in a lack of dogmatism, in a willingness to experiment, to think at different levels and in separate spheres, and in a readiness to take decisions on a provisional basis. It captures a way of thinking characterised by the following dictum: 'why look at things in terms of this or that, why not try to have both this and that' (Austin 1972: 318). In this way of thinking, it is recognised that though we may currently be unable to secure the best of both values and therefore be forced to settle for a watered-down version of each, we must continue to have an abiding commitment to search for a transcendence of this second-best condition.[11] It is frequently argued against Indian secularism that it is contradictory because it tries to bring together individual and community rights, and that articles in the Indian Constitution that have a bearing on the secular nature of the Indian state are deeply conflictual and at best ambiguous (Tambiah 1998: 445–53). This is to misrecognise a virtue as a vice. In my view, this attempt to bring together seemingly incompatible values is a great strength of Indian secularism. Indian secularism is an ethically sensitive negotiated settlement between diverse groups and divergent values. When it is not treated as such, it turns either into a dead formula or a façade for political manoeuvres.

Is secularism a Christian and western doctrine?

What then of the claim that secularism is a Christian, western doctrine, and therefore is unable to adapt itself easily to the cultural conditions of, say, India, infused as they are by religions that grew in the soil of the sub-continent? This necessary link between secularism and Christianity is exaggerated, if not entirely mistaken. It is true that

---

[11] Such contextual reasoning was not atypical of the deliberations of the Constituent Assembly, in which great value was placed on arriving at decisions by consensus. Yet, the procedure of majority vote was not given up altogether. On issues that everyone judged to be less significant, a majoritarian procedure was adopted.

the institutional separation of church and state is an internal feature of Christianity and an integral part of western secularisms. But as we have seen, this church–state disconnection is a necessary but not a sufficient condition for the development of secularism even in societies with church-based religions. It is clearly not a necessary condition for the development of all forms of secularisms. Moreover, as I have argued, the mutual exclusion of religion and the state is not the defining feature of secularism. The idea of separation can be interpreted differently. Nor are religious integrity and peace and toleration (interpreted broadly to mean 'live and let live') uniquely Christian values. Most non-Christian civilisations have given significant space to each. Therefore, none of them are exclusively Christian. It follows that, even though we find in Christian writings some of the clearest and most systematic articulation of this doctrine, even the western conception of secularism is not exclusively Christian.

All right, one might say, secularism is not just a Christian doctrine, but is it not western? The answer to this question is both yes and no. Up to a point, it is certainly a western idea. More specifically, as a clearly articulated doctrine, it has distinct western origins. Although elements that constitute secularism assume different cultural forms and are found in several civilisations, one cannot deny that the idea of the secular first achieved self-consciousness and was properly theorised in the West. One might then say that the early and middle history of secularism is almost entirely dominated by western societies. However, the same cannot be said of its later history. Nationalism and democracy arrived in the West after the settlement of religious conflicts, in societies that had been made religiously homogeneous, or had almost become so (with the exception of the Jews, of course, who continued to face persistent persecution). The absence of deep religious diversity and conflict meant that issues of citizenship could be addressed almost entirely disregarding religious context; the important issue of community-specific rights to religious groups could be wholly ignored. This had a decisive bearing on the western conception of secularism. However, for non-western societies such as India, the case is different. Both national and democratic agendas in countries such as India had to face issues raised by deep religious difference and diversity. In India, nationalism had to choose between the religious and the secular. Similarly, the distribution of active citizenship rights could not be conceived or accomplished by ignoring religion. It could be done either by actively disregarding religion (as in all political rights) or by developing a complex attitude to it, as in the case of cultural rights, where it had to balance claims of individual autonomy with those of community obligations, and claims of the necessity of keeping religion 'private' with their inescapable, often valuable presence in the public. By doing so, Indian secularism never completely annulled particular religious identities.

In addressing these complex issues, the idea of political secularism was taken further than had been evolved in the West. Mainstream theories or ideologies in modern, western societies have taken little notice of these features. Hence, they are struggling to deal with the post-colonial religious diversity of their societies. The later history of secularism is more non-western than western.[12] To discover its own rich and complex structure, western secularism can either look backward to its own past, or else look sideways at Indian secularism, which mirrors not only the past of secularism but, in a way, also its future. Doing so will certainly benefit the secularisms of many western societies. For example, French secularism needs to look beyond its own conceptions of *laïcité* in order to take into account its multicultural and multi-religious reality. It cannot continue to take refuge in claims of exceptionalism. A good hard look at Indian secularism could also change the self-understanding of other western secularisms, including a very individualist, American liberal secularism.

---

[12] And by implication, the history of secularism must include the history of other non-western societies that have sought to install and maintain secular states.

5 | *Secularism, public reason or moderately agonistic democracy?*

VEIT BADER

In recent debates on the strained relationship between liberal-democratic states and organised religions, two broad questions are at issue, both politically and theoretically: whether states and religions are, or should be, 'strictly separated'; and whether states, policies and public reasoning are, or should be, 'strictly secular'. This chapter addresses the second problem.[1] I will begin by briefly outlining my general opposition to the idea of secularism and why I prefer speaking in terms of, and attaching priority to, liberal democracy instead. My focus, however, will be on the attempt by political liberals to exclude religious reasons from public deliberation and democratic politics. I mean to challenge such attempts, using the work of John Rawls as my main example. I will conclude by considering how my critique points to the need for a sober, moderately agonistic conception of democratic institutions, virtues and practices.

Secularism or democracy?

In a critical discussion of recent sociology of religion, I have tried to develop a 'perspectivist concept' of secularisation (Bader 2007, Chapter 1). From the *perspective of religions*, it is perfectly legitimate to describe their opposite as 'secular' – a secular world based on secular communications. From the *perspective of sociology*, the concept of secularisation is inappropriate because its implied theses of an inevitable decline and an inevitable privatisation and subjectivisation of religion(s) are at odds with a great deal of empirical evidence. Moreover, the thesis of strict separation can be better reformulated as a certain minimal threshold of functional, institutional, organisational and role differentiation. From the *perspective of liberal-democratic politics and normative*

---

[1] See my earlier articles (Bader 1999; 2003b; 2003c) and my extensive treatment in 2007. My thanks to Geoff Levey for English editing.

political theory, however, the important question is not whether *societies* are 'secularised' (as they increasingly are in most European states), nor whether *cultures* might be increasingly 'secularised' (or *verweltlicht*), nor even whether *state and politics* are 'completely separated' from religions. Rather, the key question is whether these arenas are compatible with, or conducive to, minimal morality and/or minimal liberal-democratic morality. Why do I say this, and, hence, that liberal democrats and liberal-political philosophers should not be secularists?

The first and most important reason 'why I am not a secularist' is that calling the liberal-democratic state a 'secular' state is historically and structurally misleading. A *contextualist* conception acknowledges that emerging 'modern' European states had to become *indifferent* states, in the sense of respecting the relative autonomy of the state from religions and of religions from the state (i.e. what often passes under the rubric of autonomy or toleration). Compared with religions claiming supreme jurisdiction over political as well as religious affairs, such indifferent states might be called 'secular' states and may have required 'secularist' justifications. However, we need to remember that most modern states have not been 'secular' in this sense, and that not all that did eventually or have increasingly become so have remained liberal and democratic states. During the twentieth century, the minimalist morality of decent and liberal-democratic polities increasingly had to be defended against 'secular', totalitarian ideologies and states (variously fascist, 'communist' and chauvinist), which violated not only minimal liberal-democratic morality but also any minimalist decent morality. *Historical contextualisation* shows that the language of secularism, in this regard, is insufficient and myopic.

A *structural contextualisation* focuses on threats to liberal democracy that may come from religious fundamentalisms of all sorts (Christian, Jewish, Hindu, Islamist) and from secularists of all sorts; that is, not only from racist, ethno-centrist, chauvinist, fascist or 'socialist/communist' totalitarians, but also from 'scientism' as an ideology, from radical and aggressively secularist 'Enlightenment' philosophy and – perhaps least visible of all – from different kinds of 'expertocracy', including the professions, managers and bureaucrats (Bader 2007, Section 3.4.2). Thus, again, the core issue cannot be whether states and politics are 'secular' because secularism is, in fact, part of the problem.

The other reasons why I am not a secularist have to do with justifications and legitimations. If one wants to call liberal-democratic states and policies 'secular' one has to explain 'why secularism?' or 'what is secularism for?' (Bhargava 1998a: 10; 1998c: 486ff.). *Ethical secularists* argue that secularism serves substantive values such as autonomy; equality; democracy; or leading a self-chosen, fully transparent life. The trouble is that these perfectionist arguments are incompatible with reasonable pluralism concerning the Good Life. This is the second reason why I am not a secularist, one that is shared also by most 'second order' or 'political' secularists.

Second-order justifications refer to higher-order values or procedural foundations. Three such strategies predominate. The first one, an *independent political ethics* (developed by Bayle, Spinoza and Kant, and recently defended by Audi and Habermas) is based on 'secular' Reason or Rationality. It cannot resolve the paradox of second-order secularism – namely, that 'secularism presents itself as the solution after all other voices have spoken' – because it cannot consistently be decoupled from more comprehensive ethical secularism and its thick values (such as moral autonomy or demanding rationality). The second, or *common ground*, strategy (as Charles Taylor has termed it, but which historically was developed by Pufendorf, Locke and Leibniz) has been 'rather Christian in spirit', encompasses all existing religions and assumes that 'everyone shares some religious ground'. It is inherently limited because it excludes non-religious grounds; it also treats religious reasons within traditions as given and fixed, neglects internal dissent, and focuses only on some minimal common denominator instead of opening existing reasons for comparative and normative debate.

The third strategy, an *overlapping consensus*, rejects the requirement of a commonly held foundation, recognising from the outset that there cannot be a universally agreed basis, independent or religious, for the principles of political morality or justice. This 'non-foundational', 'freestanding', 'political not metaphysical' (Rawls) approach increasingly has been cleansed of secularist biases by Rawls himself. He has achieved this by softening the requirements of rational constructivism and contractualism; by accepting that his conception is one in a 'family of reasonable political conceptions' (Rawls 1999: 141); by explicitly resisting the identification of public with secular reason; and, most ambiguously, by softening but not abandoning the exclusion of religious and non-religious comprehensive reasons from public debate (all issues that I take up below). Because the 'consensus' requirements are so loosened or stripped away, this approach might more aptly be named *moderately agonistic democracy* – one that is characterised by the absence of exclusivist 'reasonability restraints', deliberations-cum-negotiations, inclusive multi- or poly-logue, and extensive free-doms of political communication.

In sum, secularist first- and second-order justifications of minimal and minimal liberal-democratic morality seem needlessly exclusive and unfair, particularly in a context in which religions increasingly have learned to bracket the 'truth question' in politics and to resolve their 'fundamentalist dilemma' (Casanova 1994: 165). The termino-logical 'confusion' of 'public' or 'liberal-democratic' with 'secular' is misleading because it seduces us into justifying the inevitable non-neutrality of liberal democracy in terms of secular-versus-religious arguments or foundations, while neglecting the existence of principled religious or theological foundations of liberal democracy, in general, and of freedom of conscience, in particular. Further, it directs our criticism of absolutism or fundamentalism in politics in a one-sided and myopic manner against religious or theological fundamentalism and tends to neglect all secular threats to liberal democracy.

The philosophical meaning of the priority for liberal democracy is thus really a radicalisation of the idea of a freestanding conception of political justice. Principles and practices of decent and liberal-democratic polities are more important than the whole variety of conflicting philosophical or religious foundations, mainly because all founda-tional theories are at least as contested as our ordinary under-standing of these principles and practices. The validity of minimal political morality fortunately does not depend upon the truth of competing moral theories. This is indicated by catchy phrases like 'priority of rights over theories of rights' (Shue 1995) and 'priority of institutions over institutional theories'. This considered commit-ment to non-foundationalism also may be described as 'philosoph-ical shallowness' (Hunter, Chapter 2 (p. 28)) or 'epistemological and moral abstemiousness' (Geuss 2002: 333). It may serve as a philo-sophical stimulus to see modern democracy as an open project, and one that helps to prevent the political form of a society being seen as the realisation of a transcendent vision (Lefort 1999: 49ff.). The public articulation of religious pluralism and the rejection of any 'symbolic', religious or philosophical *Letztbegründung* ['final foundation'] may have a constitutive function in this sense.

One core feature of *moderately agonistic democracy* is an extensive interpretation of freedoms of political communication, including: freedom of opinion, information, print/media of mass-communication, assembly, propaganda and demonstration, association or organisation, and petitions and hearings (Frankenberg and Rödel 1981: 331). These freedoms cannot guarantee idealised models of grassroots democratic deliberation, guided by 'public reason' and strictly separated from negotiations and power asymmetries. Instead, they are meant to guarantee crucial minimal preconditions for actual democratic debate (deliberation-cum-negotiation) and decision-making. They do not, and should not, discriminate between 'secular' and 'religious' opinions; on the contrary, they encourage as many voices as possible to be raised, listened to and responded to. In this regard, it is astonishing that philosophers of political liberalism have tenaciously defended issue-, content-, and reasonableness-restraints *at all*, let alone worried especially about 'religious' reasons and arguments. Freedoms of political communication, like all other human rights, are obviously not 'absolute', but the two well-known restrictions – public order/civic peace and anti-discrimination – apply or should apply equally to religious and secular speech.

Modern liberal democracy requires that all opinions and voices, ultimately expressed as votes, have to count equally when it comes to final decision-making, even if paternalistic elites think, perhaps with good reason, that they are uninformed, misinformed, false, morally wrong, disgusting and so on. This second core element, a specific, egalitarian, *anti-paternalistic mode of decision-making* requires that all defenders of 'truths', whether religious or secular (philosophical, scientistic or professional/'expertocratic'), should learn how to resolve their respective 'fundamentalist dilemma'. Since 'error has the same rights as truth', fundamentalist interpreters of religions certainly have (had) to learn to resist the temptation of 'theocracy'. Yet the same holds for philosophers and all kinds of scientific and professional experts: they have to learn to stem the philosophical 'conquest of democratic politics' (Barber 1988) and the temptation of expertocracy. In short, it is crucial not to understand or phrase the conflict between political 'absolutism' (of all sorts) and priority for democracy in terms of 'religious fundamentalism' versus 'secularism'.

Exclusion of religious reasons from public deliberation and democratic politics

Liberal-democratic constitutions guarantee freedoms of political communication and anti-paternalist decision-making. They accept deep disagreement in nearly all matters but provide mechanisms to deal with disagreement by (qualified and iterative) majority decisions that are, in principle at least, always revisable. Many political philosophers, however, do not seem to trust that these institutional and procedural modes provide enough stability and legitimacy of the liberal-democratic polity and of political decisions under conditions of deep cultural and religious diversity or 'reasonable pluralism'. They see, in various ways, a need to restrict the contents and kinds of 'reasons' in public deliberation by excluding 'religious' and other sorts of reasons that refer to comprehensive doctrines. Religious reasons, in particular, seem dangerous because they are said to be inherently conservative; to inhibit human freedoms, tolerance, or independent scrutiny and research; to fail to show due respect to citizens of other religions or non-believers; to be inherently destructive because of the intensity, heat or fervour raised by 'great ideals'; to threaten minimally required political stability and unity; and so on. The fear and distrust of religious reasons is clearly very intense, since the ways that 'exclusionary secularists' seek to control, regulate and discipline 'allowable' reasons and participants in public debate seem plainly incompatible with fairly extensive constitutional freedoms of political communication.

Many liberal philosophers (e.g. Larmore 1987; Nagel 1987; Audi 1989, 1991, 1993, 1997; Perry 1991; Foley 1992; Marshall 1993 and Macedo 1997) have identified without further consideration 'public' and 'secular' morality and reasons. Robert Audi, a sophisticated defender of 'liberalism of reasoned respect', has set out to explore appropriate liberal-democratic principles for states (institutional separation), churches (ecclesiastical and clerical political neutrality) and individuals. According to Audi (1989: 46, 52, 62), 'mature, rational religious people' should be guided by two 'principles of conscience': a principle of 'secular rationale' and secular motivation, and a second-order principle of 'theo-ethical equilibrium' between religious sources/insights and secular sources/considerations. Thus, for him, public reason is 'secular reason' by definition (Audi 1989: 178; 1997; see also the title of his reply to Weithman (1991)).

In discussing 'public-reason restraints', I nevertheless propose to focus on John Rawls, both because the changes in his position are indicative of general problems connected with the whole strategy to exclude certain reasons, and because his shift towards a more inclusive position enables us to demarcate and criticise the hard core of all exclusivist thinking. I take Rawls's to be the most considered version of public-reason-restraint arguments.[2]

The key changes in Rawls's theoretical strategy from *A Theory of Justice* (1972) to *Political Liberalism* (1993) and 'The idea of public reason revisited' in *The Law of Peoples* (1999: 129–80) are as follows. A comprehensive liberal theory (conception of person and moral autonomy) and the strategy of rational contractarianism are replaced by an explicitly political, as against metaphysical, theory (political conception of justice and autonomy), and a wide overlapping consensus. The distrust of all religion that characterises *Theory* is increasingly replaced by a fully open relationship between religion and democracy in *Political Liberalism* and even more explicitly in *Law of Peoples* (1999: 197).[3] At the same time, the identification of 'public' with 'secular reasons' is criticised, and the terminological distinction

---

[2] For a critical assessment of the positions of Audi, Foley, Marshall, Nagel, Larmore, Perry and Rawls, see Greenawalt (1995). There is an enormous range of more or less radical criticisms of exclusivist positions, including: Greenawalt (1988), Benhabib (1992; 2002), Weithman (1991; 1997), Waldron (1993; 2000), Thiemann (1996), Colemann (1997), Hollenbach (1997), Quinn (1997), Fish (1997), Neal (1997), Perry (1997; 2003), Murphy (2001), Parekh (2000: 304ff.), Eisenach (2000), Shah (2000: 132–5), Spinner-Halev (2000:142ff.), Rosenblum (2003), Connolly (1995; 1999) and Galston (2002). I refer to some of these criticisms in passing.

[3] Rawls rightly criticises not only Habermas and Benhabib, but also Gutmann and Thompson for sticking to comprehensive, secular moral theories: for the latter's 'requirement of a mundane ... completely secular justification', see Gutmann and Thompson (1996: 61, 159). The secularist suspicion even resonates in Walzer's *On Toleration* (Walzer 1997: 66–71, 81). Habermas has been rightly criticised in this regard by Shaw (1999), Koenig (2004: 98) and many others (e.g. Müller (2005)), however, believe they find an ally in Habermas's recent writing: 'In the post-secular society, the public definition of the fluid border between the secular and religious foundation of norms must be understood as a co-operative venture that requires each side to take over the viewpoint of the other' (Habermas 2001: 22; my translation). Yet in my view, Habermas has consistently refused to take the decisive step to keep the space of a final symbolic foundation open. Otherwise, he would now be really convinced by the late Rawls and drop his 'post-traditional' and epistemologically rationalist, secularist provisos (repeated in Habermas (2006)).

between 'public' and 'secular' becomes stable: 'We must distinguish public reason from what is sometimes referred to as secular reason and secular values. These are not the same as public reason' (1999: 143). Unfortunately, the importance of this distinction is still not widely recognised: Rawls's 'reasonableness-exclusivism' is clearly fairer than 'secularist' exclusivism. From *Political Liberalism* on, the exclusion of comprehensive doctrines is equally applied to religious and non-religious or 'secular' reasons and doctrines. In contrast to Audi and many other theorists of restraints, Rawls is no longer an exclusionist 'secularist', and cannot and should not be accused of secularism, though one might point out that his criticism of scientism and expertocracy has been plainly insufficient.[4] His exclusion and restraints explicitly refer to all non-reasonable doctrines and to all non-public reasons, whether 'religious' or 'secular'. Whether his 'Idea of public reason' (1993: 212–54) differs significantly from 'The idea of public reason revisited' (1999: 129–80) is less clear and more contested. In the circumstances, the best way to proceed is to examine exclusivist interpretations in relation to seven different, albeit interconnected and overlapping, aspects where public-reason-restraints might be applied.[5]

Historical and social contexts

In response to critics of his earlier 'exclusive view', such as Gutmann and Solum (see Rawls 1993: 247 n. 36), Rawls had already clarified in 1993 (251, 247ff.) that 'the appropriate limits of public reason vary depending on historical and social conditions'. In the ideal case of 'well ordered constitutional democracies', the restraints of 'public reason' are crucial, and the exclusive view is explicitly defended (Rawls 1999: 138, 139). In 'less well ordered' or in 'not well ordered societies', where a 'profound division about constitutional essentials' exists

---

[4] Mostly he refers to the 'plain truth' of religious, metaphysical, moral and political theories – including 'divine rights of monarchy', aristocracy and the 'many instances of autocracy and dictatorship' (Rawls 1999: 172ff.) – and only rarely also to unreasonable scientific doctrines and their 'plain truths', such as 'elaborate economic theories of general equilibrium, if these are in dispute' (Rawls 1993: 225). See Bader (1999: 616) and below, pp. 129–30.

[5] In a slightly modified way and a different order, I follow Greenawalt's distinctions (Greenawalt 1995).

(e.g. on slavery), Rawls (1993: 215) defends 'the more inclusive view'. Thus, Christian abolitionist views are allowed because 'the non-public reasons of certain Christian churches supported the clear conclusions of public reason' (1993: 251).[6] Clearly, this circumscribed and contextualised defence of the exclusive view depends on the possibility of a clear demarcation between 'well ordered' and 'not (so) well ordered' polities. If it is not defended from the (Hegelian or Fukuyama-like) dystopian view that we now have achieved the end-state of a perfect and ideally just polity (let alone 'society'), this line can only be drawn *retrospectively* and with great difficulty. After all, the exclusion of 'non-public reasons' in well-ordered constitutional democracies tends to immunise their present state from radical or even moderate criticism also prospectively, as is the case for the analogous demarcation of 'constitutional essentials and issues of basic justice' from other political issues dealt with below. Indeed, it is remarkable that Rawls concedes 'that it may happen that for a well-ordered society to come about in which public discussion consists mainly in the appeal to political values, prior historical conditions may require that comprehensive reasons be invoked to strengthen those values' (Rawls 1993: 215 n. 41).[7] This may have been true once upon a time, but nowadays, according to Rawls, things are different.

Range of issues

Which issues or range of subjects are covered by the public reason restraints?[8] Already in 1993 Rawls clarified that they 'do not apply to all political questions but only to those involving what we may call "constitutional essentials" and questions of basic justice' or 'fundamental questions'. In debates on 'ordinary political issues', comprehensive doctrines and 'non-public reasons' may be invoked but, again, to make this demarcation operational, one has to say who is to decide

---

[6] Also in this case, Rawls (1993: 251) applies his trick of the counterfactual form of discourse he calls 'conjecture' (Rawls 1999: 155f.).

[7] While the general argument – that conditions for the origin or emergence of polities may differ from those of their reproduction – is valid, its application, in this case, is counterproductive; it cannot really be defended against the charge of prospective immunisation. See also Connolly's (1999) criticism.

[8] See Ackerman (1989) for an attempt to *exclude* whole *issues* (such as abortion, euthanasia, biogenetics) from the public and/or constitutional agenda. See the criticism by Gutmann and Thompson (1996).

which issues are fundamental and which are normal because, clearly, these distinctions are contested in politics, with good reasons. Rawls's demarcation presupposes either some kind of broad consensus concerning it or the idea of an 'apolitical' supreme decision-making body in cases where matters are contested.[9]

Persons affected

To whom do the public reason-restraints apply? Since Audi's contributions it is common to distinguish the following categories of persons affected:[10] judges, legislators, executive officials, candidates for public office, citizens (all or some, individually or also collectively as organised in interest-groups, advocacy groups, political parties), and church-officials (see Audi 1989, 1997). In Rawls's *Political Liberalism* it seems as if – with appropriate variations – the restraints would apply only or mainly to judges and executive officials. Courts are the 'institutional exemplar' of public reason:

This means, first, that public reason is the sole reason the court exercises. It is the only branch of government that is visibly on its face the creature of that reason and of that reason alone. Citizens and legislators may properly vote their more comprehensive views when constitutional essentials and basic justice are not at stake; they need not justify by public reason why they vote as they do or make their grounds consistent and fit them into a coherent constitutional view over the whole range of their decisions. (Rawls 1993: 235, see 217f.)

Yet I agree with Greenawalt that Rawls, in *Revisited* explicitly, claims that the restraints should also extend to citizens who, in debating – or in 'citizens' reasoning' (Rawls 1999: 139) – and in voting, should behave 'ideally *as if* they were legislators' (Rawls 1999: 135, italics added), guided by public reasons alone. Rawls is fully aware that the latter are strong counterfactual claims, although it can be reasonably doubted

---

[9] The guiding paradigm of legal discourse and of Supreme Courts, in which Justices hover above the 'political turmoil', has convincingly been criticised by Unger (1983), Barber (1988), and many others.

[10] Roughly, these categories of 'persons affected' (Greenawalt 1995: 110) correspond to a simplified model of phases of the political process (Bader 1991: 232ff.). It is no surprise that the phase of 'what becomes an issue' is conspicuously absent. I return to this point below.

whether he also sees this for judges and courts.[11] In all cases, however, the basic idea is that one can achieve something like a common good, impartiality, justice and neutrality only by bracketing (*not* abstracting away) particular interests and 'non-public reasons', by insulating them in deliberations.[12]

Forums of deliberation

Do the restraints apply to 'justification rather than decision' (Greenawalt 1995: 111) or, better, to all forums of deliberation, wherever deliberation takes place? Rawls eventually spelled out, in *Political Liberalism*, that there is no such thing as 'private reasons' (1993: 220). Hence, the different societal forums or arenas cannot be distinguished in the traditional terms of private versus public spheres. The difficulty in understanding Rawls's claim that public reason restraints apply only in the 'public political forum' but not in the 'non-public political culture' of 'civil society' has to do with his very peculiar definition of 'public', which is at odds both with its common understanding and with its predominant use in social sciences and political philosophy. Let me clarify what Rawls means by 'public', before offering my criticism of his 'public reason restraints' approach.[13]

For Rawls, the arenas of deliberation and the appropriate reasons are neatly divided into three. First, there is the *'domestic' sphere*, in which domestic reason or 'the reason of families' is apt. Second, there is the *'non-public political' forum* that is linked to the 'background culture' of 'civil society' or the 'non-public political culture' (Rawls 1999: 134, 152, 153, 171f.), and where 'non-public political reasons' (p. 134) or 'social reason' (p. 142) are appropriate. As he puts it,

---

[11] Assuming that he recognises this, he is still seduced into reproducing the 'necessary illusions' of judges (Unger 1983) that there is 'one reasonable solution only', even in all hard cases (the common core of the positions of Dworkin, Habermas and Rawls). His 'idea' of public reason serves as an 'ideal' that is realised when and to the degree that people 'act from and follow the idea' (Rawls 1999: 135). Only then do they fulfil their moral duty of civility.

[12] The 'as if' is as telling as are the references to the Rousseauian and Kantian origins of this pattern of thinking.

[13] Benhabib 'means by the public sphere what Habermas does, namely what *Political Liberalism* calls the background culture of civil society in which the ideal of public reason does not apply. Hence political liberalism is not limiting in the way she thinks' (Rawls 1993: 142 n. 28).

Among the non-public reasons are those of associations of all kinds: churches and universities, scientific societies and professional groups ... This way of reasoning is public with respect to their members, but non-public with respect to political society and citizens generally. Non-public reasons comprise the many reasons of civil society and belong to what I have called the 'background culture'. (Rawls 1993: 220)

In this sphere, the 'liberties of thought and speech, and the right of association' are ensured (Rawls 1999: 134). Third, in *'the public political forum'* (p. 133) only 'public reason' (singular) is appropriate.[14]

Now Rawls clearly and consistently limits the restraints of public reason already in *Political Liberalism* to the public-political forum: 'its limits do not apply to our personal deliberations and reflections about political questions, or to the reasoning about them by members of associations. Plainly, religious, philosophical, and moral considerations of many kinds may here properly play a role' (Rawls 1993: 215). Less clear is where he means to draw the line that separates the public from the non-public political forum. The role of interest-groups, political advocacy groups and political parties, in particular, is not clarified in this regard. Still, I take it to be Rawls's considered view that 'ideally' they should operate exactly as citizens should on entering the public forum. Thus, whenever they engage in public debate and political decision-making, only public reason is allowed and will be decisive. The limits of public reason do 'hold for citizens when they engage in political advocacy in the public forum, and thus for members of political parties and for candidates in their campaigns', and for citizens as voters in elections when constitutional essentials and matters of basic justice are at stake (1993: 215f.).

Three points of criticism are important for my purposes. First, as Greenawalt (1995: 113) rightly observes, it is doubtful that personal deliberation, associational deliberations and deliberations in civil society are free from the restraints of public reason since this requirement 'would infect thought and discussion of relevant issues in all settings'. The public reason condition is simply more significant and less innocent than one might initially suppose.

Second, and more important, is the spill-over that occurs from non-public reasons in the non-public political forums (plural) of civil

---

[14] 'There are many non-public reasons and but one public reason' (Rawls 1993: 220).

society into the public forum (singular!). That everyday politics typically treats discussions in civil society as 'public debate', and that
political parties are situated somewhat uneasily between private and
public law in most constitutions and legal systems, already suggests
that such spill-over not only happens regularly (Rawls could defend
his position by saying that murky reality obviously deviates from the
ideal), but is also seen as lawful. While Rawls seems to restrict the freedoms of political communication to civil society, liberal-democratic
constitutions and legal systems also tend to protect them in the 'public
political forum', such as the parliament. Even if one says that the duties
of self-restraint are moral rather than legal duties,[15] they do not easily
fit into the legal framework of democracy, which, indeed, seems to
welcome a (moderately) agonistic form of deliberation in parliament as
well as in civil society.

More important still are normative arguments, which insist that the
different arenas of deliberation – or, in common language, of public
debate – should be open to 'all comers' and not simply be the preserve
of elites, and that an inclusive debate in civil society should have an
important impact on 'formal' or 'official' forums of deliberation.[16]
Then there are the arguments that directly refute the restrictive legalistic
and jurisdictional model of 'deliberation' and 'public reason' or discourse that inspires Rawls's theory.[17] Both these critical strands challenge the neat separation of forums, discourses and reasons, as well as
the idea of insulating a certain public reason that is the exclusive province of constitutions and hero judges. Both strands also insist that
changes to constitutional provisions or in their juridical interpretation
depend crucially on blurring these boundaries and breaking through
these exclusions.

---

[15] Rawls (1993: 217; 1999: 136).
[16] All post-Rawlsian deliberative democrats share this criticism. In this regard,
Rawls's *terminological* defence against Benhabib's charge simply misses the
point. The criticism is, however, made most effectively by so-called
empowered democrats, strong democrats and agonistic democrats (see already
Dewey (1927)).
[17] Rawls hopes for a 'trickle down' effect from the idealised discourse of the
exemplary Supreme Court Justices to executive officials, legislators and,
eventually, citizens and political parties. Normative counter-models hope for a
lively politicisation of debates not only in parliament, but also in Supreme
Courts, guided by second-order principles like relational neutrality (see van
Dommelen (2003)).

Finally, the 'public reason restraints' strategy ultimately turns on a cardinal misunderstanding of the idea that 'the whole truth in politics' is 'incompatible with democratic citizenship and the idea of legitimate law' (Rawls 1999: 138). The core of priority for democracy, as I have interpreted it above, is indeed a specific version of an incompatibility-thesis. 'The zeal to embody the whole truth in politics is incompatible' (Rawls 1999: 133) if it refers to democratic *decision-making*: 'those who believe that fundamental political questions should be *decided* by what they regard as the best reasons according to their own idea of the whole truth – including their religious or secular comprehensive doctrine' (p. 138, italics added). Yet this stricture does not require the exclusion of the competing 'whole truths' from *public debate in the 'public political forum'*. What it does require is that legitimate law will be 'politically (morally) binding' even if it 'be thought not to be the most reasonable, or the most appropriate by each [party]' (p. 137), since no unanimity or 'general agreement' can be expected. Thus, majority decisions enjoy a status not so much of being 'true' or 'correct' as simply 'reasonable and legitimate law' (pp. 168–70). 'Reasonable' public debate and the acceptance of majority decisions, for the time being, certainly require that people's 'zeal' be tempered by virtues of moderation (see below), but this is very different from the much more demanding moral duty to exclude 'the whole truth as we see it' (p. 218) from public discussion.

Kinds of reasons and content of public reason

From *Political Liberalism* on, Rawls consistently excludes all 'non-accessible' reasons or grounds, whether religious or secular, from deliberation on constitutional essentials and matters of basic justice in the public political forum. I will try to spell out the possible changes in his account concerning the ever more complex relation between comprehensive doctrines and the purely political (moral) conception of public reason, the content of public reason and the specification of the standards of exclusion. But first it is worth noting the central tension in the whole endeavour between, on the one hand, his conception of a wide overlapping consensus that allows for all possible reasons if they result in endorsing or backing the principles and core institutions of constitutional democracies, and, on the other hand, his ceaseless effort to exclude these reasons from public discourse in these

same polities. And this despite the fact that Rawls increasingly recognises that we are confronted with 'many liberalisms' and 'many
forms of public reason', so that we cannot and should not try to 'fix
public reason once and for all' (1999: 141) and thereby exclude new
variations. In addition, he clearly acknowledges that we are confronted with problems of moral pluralism ('public reason often allows
more than one reasonable answer to any particular question' (1993:
240)), of indeterminacy or, better, under-determinacy, of principles,
and of contested interpretations and applications. What, then, of the
changes in his account?

For a start, Rawls's 'wide view of public political culture' (1999:
152ff.) introduces more complexity in the relation between comprehensive doctrines and purely public reason. Reasonable comprehensive doctrines 'may be introduced in public political discussion at any
time, provided that in due course proper political reasons ... are
presented that are sufficient' as support (more on this flexible proviso
below). This does not imply

> restrictions on how religious or secular doctrines themselves [are] to be
> expressed; these doctrines need not, for example, be by some standards
> logically correct, or open to rational appraisal, or evidentially supportable.
> Whether they are or not is a matter to be decided by those presenting them,
> and how they want what they say to be taken'. (Rawls 1993: 153)

His wide view also allows for more 'positive reasons for introducing
comprehensive doctrine into public political discussion' (1999: 152): they
provide important 'roots of democratic citizens' allegiance', a 'vital social
basis, giving them enduring strength and vigour' (p. 153).[18] In addition,
Rawls believes that 'a true judgment in a reasonable comprehensive
doctrine never conflicts with a reasonable judgment in its related political
conception' (1999: 173), because even if the latter may be ranked lower,
it cannot be overridden by higher 'great values' (1993: 218).

There are also changes regarding the *content* of public reason. This
relates both to the principles of political justice and to 'guidelines of

---

[18] See Rawls (1993: 241ff.; 1999: 172ff.) for 'underwrite' and 'affirm' (see also
Müller (2005)). Critics who argue that Rawls's idea requires that all kinds of
'believers' would have to 'abstract' from their doctrines or 'privatise' them
(e.g. Loobuyck (2006)), or 'to pluck out their religious convictions' and to
think as if 'they [had] started from scratch' (Greenawalt 1988: 155), are clearly
mistaken (see Rawls's comment, 1993: 244).

inquiry' (1993: 223) or standards. Regarding the *principles* of public reason, Rawls has eventually conceded that they are spelled out by a 'family of [competing] political conceptions of justice, not by a single one' (p. 141), and that the content of public reason cannot be fixed once and for all ('content and idea may vary' [p. 226]). His own theory of principles of political justice changes from a wider version, in which 'constitutional essentials and basic justice' clearly include 'equal opportunity' and the 'difference principle' (in *Theory*), to a narrow version in which these 'more demanding' principles, which are 'nearly always open to wide differences of reasonable opinion' (1993: 228f.), are excluded in favour of the hard core of 'basic rights and needs' (see Greenawalt 1995: 201f., 227–9; see Bader 2007, Chapter 2 for a more elaborate defence of moral minimalism). Even then, Rawls has to concede that this hard core also may be open to wide differences of reasonable opinion as a consequence of three facts: moral pluralism, under-determinacy of principles, and contested interpretations and applications.

Consider first *moral pluralism*. According to Rawls (1993: 240),

> Public reason often allows more than one reasonable answer ... because there are many political values and many ways they can be characterized. Suppose then that different combinations of values, or the same values weighed differently, tend to predominate in a particular fundamental case. Everyone appeals to political values but agreement is lacking and more than marginal differences persist.

Now, adding that the 'many political values' often are in tension with or even contradict each other, gives us the full problem of moral pluralism. Rawls's response to Greenawalt is highly instructive and symptomatic in this regard: 'Should this happen, as it often does, some may say that public reason fails to resolve the question, in which case citizens may legitimately invoke principles appealing to non-political values to resolve it in a way they find satisfactory' (1993: 240, also n. 30). Some, including myself, would maintain that this kind of appeal to comprehensive doctrines and to preferred but contested institutions in which these principles are 'realized' (1999: 144) is *always* happening; indeed, it is unavoidable when conflicting principles are combined, weighed and put into (contextual or context-independent) lexical orderings.

Rawls anticipates this challenge by saying that the 'ideal of public reason urges us not to do this [i.e. to appeal to comprehensive doctrines, etc.] in cases of constitutional essentials and matters of basic justice. Close agreement is rarely ever achieved and abandoning public reason whenever disagreement occurs in balancing values is in effect abandoning it altogether' (1993: 241). I rather think that abandoning legal theorists' 'necessary illusion' of there being just one right answer in all these hard cases is not a bad idea, as a first step. More importantly, I would argue that while the inclusion of reasons from comprehensive doctrines may not require us to abandon the idea of public reasoning altogether, it does suggest the need to reconceptualise it more in terms of 'embedded impartiality' and 'relational neutrality', as proposed by my version of moral minimalism. We thus arrive at *inclusive*, rather than exclusive, public reasons. Only in this way, I suggest, can we effectively challenge predominant particularist interpretations hiding behind the 'universal' version of a fixed, predominant idea of public reason.

The same arguments above apply to the problems of *under-determinacy of principles* and of *contested interpretations and applications*. These problems are more commonly recognised and debated in moral and political philosophy and more clearly acknowledged by Rawls. As Greenawalt (1995: 113–14) shows, if everything is 'up for argument' and important disagreements inevitably arise 'about a range of debated applications', then agreement will be difficult to achieve, if at all, and will probably be 'limited to general abstractions'. Greenawalt (1995: 117) also clearly shows how comprehensive views 'influence someone's sense of the application of fundamental values' and that 'it is highly doubtful that people should feel so constrained, attempting to reach interpretations of essentials that correspond with a balance of public reasons alone, even when their comprehensive views lead them to other plausible interpretations'.[19] Accordingly, he 'calls into question the desirability of a standard of public reason that asks citizens to aim for justifications on particular issues that do not rely on comprehensive views' (1995: 117).[20]

Rawls himself admits that the use of 'public reason' results in major disagreements, though he is more reluctant to concede that it may be

---

[19] Clearly, this also holds for Justices of Supreme Courts.

[20] In his response to Greenawalt's criticism, Rawls (1993: 244 n. 33) himself blurs his concept of an overlapping consensus with his exclusivist public reason restraints, which is symptomatic of the tension indicated above.

impossible to reach a decision even on the basis of purely public political values alone.[21] The force of public reasons, then, relies on three supplements: (a) the 'proviso' as a kind of escape clause, (b) an idealised completeness requirement and (c) an idealised sincerity requirement. Let us take each in turn.

The proviso: as we have seen, comprehensive doctrines may be introduced into the public political forum 'at any time', 'provided that, in due course' we give 'properly public reasons' that are 'sufficient' (Rawls 1999: 143f. as quoted, repeated 152ff.). Though Rawls does not answer the two questions 'when?' (same day or later?) and 'to whom does this obligation apply?',[22] he insists that, eventually and for somebody, only purely public reasons are allowed so that the proviso 'does not challenge the nature and content of justification in public reason itself' (Rawls 1999: 153). In order to prevent a dynamic, as the Dutch say, of *van uitstel komt afstel* ('to postpone is to abandon/relinquish'), however, Rawls adds a 'good faith' (or sincerity) requirement.

The *completeness requirement* asks that political conceptions of public reason 'should be complete' (Rawls 1999: 144). 'This means', Rawls explains, 'that the values specified by that conception can be suitably balanced or combined, or otherwise united, as the case may be, so that those values alone give a reasonable answer to all, or to *nearly all*, questions involving constitutional essentials and basic questions of justice' (1993: 225, italics added; see also pp. 241, 244) or 'matters of basic structure' (1999: 145). If a political conception is not complete, 'it is not an adequate framework of thought in the light of which the discussion of fundamental political questions can be carried out' (1999: 145).[23] When one takes into account that even Rawls's own political conception is not complete in the sense that it consistently combines, balances and prioritises all relevant political

---

[21] See also Quinn (1997: 150 ('too weak to single out')); Valadez (2001: 58ff.) and Bohman (2003b).

[22] Details 'must be worked out in practice and cannot feasibly be governed by a clear family of rules given in advance' (Rawls 1999: 153).

[23] In n. 35, Rawls again stresses that 'different political conceptions of justice will represent different interpretations of the constitutional essentials', and also that 'there are different interpretations of the same conceptions ... There is not, then, a sharp line between where a political conception ends and its interpretation begins, nor need there be. All the same, a conception greatly limits its possible interpretations' (Rawls 1999: 145).

values, the idealisation of the completeness requirement becomes obvious. In fact, it has to compete with different conceptions and different interpretations. Thus, one is left in total disarray when it comes to answering questions concerning which content of which conception of political justice should serve as a guide for this requirement of exclusion that is still stubbornly defended. The ventured (and escape) stipulation of 'all, or nearly all' matters concerning the basic structure and basic justice actually dissolves into 'nearly none'.

Finally, the *sincerity requirement* means 'that a person must sincerely think his view is based on political values others can reasonably be expected to endorse' (1993: 241) instead of having a purely 'manipulative' or 'strategic' use (pp. 137, 140, 156).[24] As in Audi's and Habermas's theories, it adds an idealised motivational condition to the strict analytical split between 'reason' and 'negotiation' or 'compromise'.[25] If principles and public reason cannot fill the under-determinacy and decision gaps, sincere individuals have to try as hard as they can.

So much for the normative content of public reason: it turns out that the meaning of the restraints becomes increasingly hollow under the force of contested political conceptions, contested ideas of public reason, huge disagreements due to moral pluralism, the under-determinacy of interpretation, and principles that cannot be filled with decisive content by completeness and sincerity requirements. The situation becomes even more hopeless when we examine the guidelines or standards for inquiry, the second aspect of content restraints.

Burdens of judgement

Standards or 'guidelines of inquiry specify ways of reasoning and criteria' without which 'substantive principles cannot be applied' and

---

[24] It requires more than 'practical reasons for wanting to make their views acceptable to a broader audience' (Rawls 1999: 153). See also Greenawalt (1995: 112) for resolving the remaining uncertainty in interpreting Rawls's intentions. Like Habermas, Rawls sincerely distrusts the cunning of institutional reason and the disciplining force of reasoning in public. Both have to rule out the mix of strategic and moral reasoning that is characteristic of actual public deliberation.

[25] Audi's principle of secular motivation requires secular reasons to be 'motivationally sufficient'. It leads him into a very 'subtle' treatment of the relationship between motives, reasons and actions (see Audi (1989: 281ff.) vs. rationalisations).

any political conception would remain incomplete and fragmentary. These 'principles of reasoning and rules of evidence ... have the same basis as the substantive principles of justice' (Rawls 1993: 224–5). They are specified in detail as 'the burdens of judgment' (1999: 177, also n. 95) in *Political Liberalism*, Lecture II.2 (1993: 54ff.). They 'always exist and limit the extent of possible agreement', so we have to be willing to recognise them and 'to accept their consequences for the use of public reason'. Cognitive, empirical and normative aspects are intertwined. I will highlight the cognitive and empirical factors and only indicate the normative ones here, as I have discussed these previously.

We 'share a common human reason, similar powers of thought and judgment', we 'can draw inferences, weigh evidence, and balance competing considerations'. Reasonable disagreement comes about because, first, we have to balance our various ends (difficult judgements of rationality); second, we have difficulties in making sound reasonable judgements (assessing the strength of people's claims against one another, or about our common practices and institutions); and third, we have difficulties in appraising our use of our theoretical powers (beliefs and schemes of thought). In elaborating this last point, Rawls emphasises several factors: (a) the evidence (empirical and scientific) is conflicting and complex, hard to assess and evaluate; (b) we disagree about their weight and so arrive at different judgements; (c) all our concepts are vague and subject to hard cases (under-determinacy); (d) the way we assess evidence and weigh moral and political values is shaped by our total experience (given broad structural and cultural diversity in modern society: citizens' total experiences are disparate enough for their judgements to diverge);[26] (e) we appeal to different kinds of normative considerations of different force; and (f) we are confronted with hard decisions that seem to allow no clear answers because of the limited values of any system of social institutions.[27] For all these reasons, 'it is unrealistic – or worse it arouses mutual suspicion and hostility – to suppose that all our differences are rooted solely in

---

[26] Here, it seems, Rawls concedes what he rejects in his response to Greenawalt's objections.

[27] Here, it seems, Rawls thoroughly acknowledges the problem of moral pluralism and in a way that contradicts his 'completeness' requirement.

ignorance and perversity, or else in the rivalries for power, status, or economic gain' (Rawls 1993: 58).

So, with regard to the second, cognitive and empirical side of the content of public reason, 'we are to appeal only to presently accepted general beliefs and forms of reasoning found in common sense, and the methods and conclusions of science when these are not controversial'. We are not to appeal to comprehensive religious and philosophical doctrines, nor to 'elaborate economic theories of general equilibrium, say, if these are in dispute. As far as possible, the knowledge and ways of reasoning ... are to rest on the plain truths now widely accepted, or available, to citizens generally' (Rawls 1993: 225). If we were to take this recommendation seriously – much more seriously than Rawls himself – then it would not leave much to talk about in the public political forum, because most 'truths' – theories and evidence in the sciences and, especially, in the social sciences – are contested in these fields themselves. Quite often, this only becomes evident if scientists go 'public' under democratic conditions and are confronted, for example, in science hearings, with competing theories and counter-evidence by other scientists and scientists from other disciplines. Then they are forced to see a lot of hidden 'truth-power' and illegitimate 'scientism' that is otherwise obscured by the irenic and idealised democratic model of the scientific field, driven, as it is, by assumptions of cognitive truth and supposedly rigorous standards of 'falsification'.[28] The amount of cognitive and evidential disagreement actually seems limitless, and the attempted exclusions become ever more counterproductive.

---

[28] There is a clear *analogy* between public reason content restraints and the exclusion of normative arguments and interests from the irenic model of sciences. Habermas, for example, really believes that actual debate in the sciences fully approximates to the conditions of ideal *herrschaftsfreie Diskurse* (see my criticism: Bader (1988)). There may be a selective affinity between democracy and truth but the actual democratisation of scientific communities took a long time, and required strong pressure against entrenched bulwarks of dominant schools, both from within and from general democratic publics. In the case of sciences also, the 'inclusive' model and its institutional elaboration in forms of associative democracy (see Novotny, Scott and Gibbons (2001) and Bader (2003a)) is much more apt, in my view, to realise relational objectivity compared with the exclusionary model and with the abandonment of objectivity principles by adherents of the strong programme and by postmodernist deconstructivists in philosophy of sciences.

Reasonability

Partly as a consequence of criticism like the above, the attempts to regulate the content of public reason via standards of 'reasonability' and 'rationality' such as logical and conceptual consistency, inference, cognitive adequacy (theoretical truth and objective empirical validity), and also normative and practical validity, are becoming more muted and less rigidly applied by their protagonists. Audi, for example, tries to dilute the criteria for his required 'adequate secular reasons'. They should be 'well-grounded' rather than 'ill-grounded', where this means that they need not be 'objectively correct' or 'true propositions'. Even 'false propositions' are admissible if they are 'sufficiently well-justified' (Audi 1997: 55 n. 25). Yet, if 'truth' is relaxed in favour of 'justificatory sufficiency' (whatever that may be) as the standard, then how can he nevertheless invoke 'error' ('false premise or invalid inference', p. 56) as a criterion of exclusion? Gutmann and Thompson (1996: 56) moderate the standards of exclusion even further by insisting that they should not be 'impervious to the standards of logical consistency or to reliable methods of inquiry'. In the empirical dimension, admissible reasons should be 'consistent with relatively reliable methods of inquiry' or at least 'not be implausible', and 'claims need not be completely verifiable,[32] but they should not conflict with claims that have been confirmed by the most reliable methods' (Gutmann and Thompson 1996: 56). Still, Gutmann and Thompson think that these softer restraints would help to filter out 'inadmissible' from 'admissible' reasons.[29]

---

[29] Gutmann and Thompson's attempt to 'regulate public reason' (Gutmann and Thompson 1996: 55) is more inclusive than Audi's, stresses more the limits of cognitive and normative consensus (p. 370), focuses on actual debate (p. 373; see also Habermas's criticism (1990; 1995)), and invites us more openly and directly to learn to live with moral deliberative disagreement. Their principle of reciprocity still refers to the 'kinds of reasons'. The *moral* requirement to offer each other mutually acceptable normative reasons is more moderate because, fully in line with Rawls, it points out the 'aim to find fair terms for social cooperation' and the obligation 'to seek agreement on substantive moral principles', but it clearly recognises that we often do not reach agreement and thus have to live with moral disagreement and find ways of 'accommodation based on mutual respect'. The *empirical* requirement that our reasons should not be 'implausible' may go together with much disagreement among scientists about concepts, theories, methods, empirical evidence etc. As a consequence, in my view, their criteria of exclusion resolve

In my view, even the weakest versions of content restraints are plagued with three vexing problems. First, there is the problem of determining which standards or which interpretation of the same standards ('which rationality?' or 'which public reason?') should prevail. Second, there is the question of who exactly is supposed to apply the restrictions ('whose rationality?'). If the answer is, as it should be, that it has to be 'self-restraint' resulting from the *moral* duty of civility (Rawls 1993: 217), then the problem remains because each person would use his or her (contested, competing) standards or interpretations of the same standard. Were the answer, instead, that *others* should do the restraining, threatening sanctions to uphold the *legal* duty of self-restraint, this plainly would be incompatible with freedoms of political communication. Third, there is the difficulty that 'whose rationality' almost always turns out to be the rationality, reason or standards of *elites*. The whole idea of content restraints is vulnerable to charges of elitism. Audi's principles of 'secular rationale' and 'theo-ethical equilibrium', for example, require that reasons be transparent, propositionally articulated and cognitively balanced to achieve 'reflective equilibrium' (Audi 1989). He still privileges a very specific understanding of 'mature, rational people' and a very specific understanding of knowledge, neglecting or discounting practical knowledge and, of course, passions.

During the post-Rawlsian shift towards 'reasonable' public deliberation and deliberative democracy, the concept of reason itself has been thoroughly criticised, partly also in order to get rid of this elitist bias. Bhikhu Parekh (2000: 304–13) has drawn seven important lessons from a detailed discussion of the 'logic of political discourse', producing a concise and sharp criticism of both Rawls's and Habermas's versions of public reason:

Political deliberation is contextual and culturally embedded, is never wholly cerebral or based on arguments alone, and no single model of it fits all

in *attitudes*, *virtues* and *good practices*. Compared with Rawls's view in 1999, however, I see no decisive changes. James Bohman (2003a) replaces Rawls's 'inclusive view' by an 'open view with no constraints'. This 'decidedly non-Rawlsian' rethinking and transformation of 'the current reflexive equilibrium' shifts the emphasis from 'beliefs to the structure of communication' and from 'reasons to perspectives', but is still based on Habermasian emphatic concepts of integrity, reflexivity, mutuality and discursive openness in a 'deliberative community'.

societies. Rawls' theory of public reason does not seem to appreciate these basic features of it. It has a rationalist bias, homogenizes and takes a one-dimensional view of public reason, assimilates the political to judicial reason, and, unwittingly, universalizes the American practice, and that too in its highly idealized version. In spite of all its strengths, even Habermas' discourse ethic is vulnerable on all three counts. He sets up a single model of political discourse and fails to appreciate the depths of national diversity. Like Rawls, he too takes a narrowly rationalist view of it, stresses arguments and largely ignores other forms of reasons, takes a homogenous view of political arguments, postulates a culturally unmediated or 'pure inter-subjectivity' and a language 'purified' of history, concentrates on 'what' is said and ignores 'who' said it, and often comes close to assimilating political discourse to an idealized model of philosophical discourse (Parekh 2000: 312–13).[30]

In opposition to the remnants of inherently elitist 'cognitivist rationalism', it is increasingly seen that 'reasons' should not be reduced to (clearly and propositionally articulated) 'arguments', that they should be fully open not only to theoretical but also to practical knowledge, that they should not exclude emotions and passions,[31] that homogeneous views of public reason (singular) have to be rejected and that the plurality or multiplicity of perspectives has to be explicitly recognised. 'Public reason' does not guarantee, and public reasoning does not result in, consensus. Even 'reasonable reasons' are not reasons 'that might be *shared* by all citizens as free and equal' (Rawls 1999: 138, italics added) or reasons with which we all can 'agree'. They should be 'understandable', 'comprehensible', 'intelligible' or 'accessible', but it is crucial to resist the often unrecognised slide from the requirement of a moderate threshold of 'understanding' to the demanding requirement of

---

[30] See, for similar criticisms: Tully (1999), Valadez (1999), Williams (2000), Archard (2001), v. d. Brink (2002), Ferrara (2002), Deveaux (2005). Waldron's (1993: 848) insistence on 'reasons' is somewhat ambiguous: to the extent that he criticises elitist, rationalist and cognitivist approaches, his appeal to reasons does not exclude much. If so, why not directly focus on 'an open, challenging, and indeterminate form of public deliberation in which nothing is taken for granted'? (See also Waldron 2000).

[31] See Walzer (2005), Williams (2000) and other feminist criticism. Connolly (2004: 71, 76, 80, with Assad) also points out that the 'rationalism' of secularism and the Enlightenment is 'too unalert' to enactment, discipline, ritual, embodiment in repetitive practices, but his style of criticism shows the remnants of post-modernist radicalism (see Connolly (1995: xii), assimilating 'reason' with 'race').

'agreement'. Such a slide is systematically exploited, for example, in Habermas's formal pragmatics, and trades on the ambiguity of the German term *Verständigung*.[32]

So liberal attempts to restrain public reason, in the end, do not seem to exclude much. Reasonable conceptual, moral, theoretical and empirical disagreement continues unabated. And the criteria of exclusion ultimately seem to boil down to attitudes, virtues and good practices of liberal democracy.

Conclusion: towards moderately agonistic democracy

Recently, we have witnessed a remarkable theoretical shift in emphasis from principles to institutions, virtues and good practices. Contrary to liberal fears, the breakdown of public reason restraints and their replacement by an explicitly wide and inclusive view of public reasoning do not lead to chaotic talk or the breakdown of democratic decision-making and legitimate law if citizens behave in a civilised way. The Rawlsian 'political virtues as reasonableness and a readiness to honour the (moral) duty of civility' presuppose such an attitudinal basis (Rawls 1993: 224). Similarly, in my view, Gutmann and Thompson's (1996: 77) 'principle of reciprocity' ends up being less a principle than a virtue: 'uncertainty about the truth of their own position', as opposed to rigidity, dogmatism and arrogance.[33]

We also may hope that some sort of *cunning of institutional reason* is at work: participating in public debate, under the dual conditions of guaranteed and sanctioned freedoms of political communication and an effective ban on violence, eventually inculcates some minimally required and attitudinally based virtues of moderation and toleration. In addition, the line between the 'disciplining' of passions by interests (Hirschman 1981) and by morality is as blurred as are strategic and

---

[32] See my criticism in Bader (1984). Forst's (2006) criterion 'sharable among all persons affected' is weaker than Habermas's because it stresses that criteria of reciprocity and generality do not lead to consensus.

[33] The duty to say whatever one wants to say, even the 'whole truth' in an 'understandable' way (or in a short phrase: the understandability requirement stated above), can also be seen as a virtue with an attitudinal basis. The 'discipline' of public reason without content restraints directly indicates attitudinal disciplining.

moral motives, negotiations and deliberations. Defenders of deliberative democracy such as Bohman (2003b) and Deveaux (2005) increasingly recognise this, though they have failed to spell out the institutional requirements of public debate and democratic decision-making under 'non-ideal' conditions of structural inequalities. Moderately agonistic theories of democracy have to combine plausible accounts of civic and democratic virtues with institutional designs that enable lively and inclusive public debate.

There is much theoretical work, then, that still needs to be done. Here is my shortlist of tasks. First, the strategy of replacing principles with virtues or attitudes, now so prominent among post-modernist theorists, needs to be challenged by showing how a productive complementarity of principles and virtues is more helpful, and what it might look like. Second, we need finer-grained and more detailed analyses of the long and complex list of civic and democratic virtues, ranging from civic minimalism to democratic maximalism. Third, more attention needs to be paid to explaining where and how these virtues are learned. Finally, and most importantly, we need research that combines theory with practical democratic experience that spells out which institutional arrangements are minimally conducive to the learning of civic and democratic virtues. All this, however, lies ahead.[34]

---

[34] For first attempts in the tradition of associative democracy, see Bader (2007), Section 6.1, Chapters 9 and 10.

PART II

Secularism and multicultural citizenship

6 | Immigration and the new religious pluralism: a European Union–United States comparison

JOSÉ CASANOVA

In the last four decades the United States and western European societies have become the main destinations of new global migration flows. In the case of the United States, the 1965 new immigration law overturned the draconian anti-immigration laws of the 1920s and brought a resumption of a long tradition of immigration. Unlike the nineteenth-century immigrants, however, who came mainly from Europe, the new immigrants originate primarily from the Americas and Asia and increasingly from all regions of the world. In the case of western Europe, the new immigration has meant a radical reversal of a long history of European emigration to the rest of the world (Cohen 1995; Hirschman, Kasinitz and de Wind 1999; Moch 2003).

Throughout the modern era, western European societies had been the primary source of immigration in the world. During the colonial phase, European colonists and colonisers, indentured servants and penal labourers, missionaries and entrepreneurs settled in all the corners of the globe. During the age of industrialisation, from the 1800s to the 1920s, it is estimated that around 85 million Europeans emigrated to the New World and to the southern hemisphere, 60 per cent of them to the United States alone. In the last decades, however, the migration flows have reversed and western European societies have become instead centres of global immigration.

It began in the 1950s with guest worker programmes attracting migrant labour from the less developed southern European countries (Italy, Spain, Portugal, Yugoslavia, Greece and Turkey). Decolonisation brought former colonial subjects from north and west Africa, south and southeast Asia, and the Caribbean to the colonial metropolises (France, Great Britain and the Netherlands). Economic disruptions, famines, political violence, wars and global smuggling rings added refugees, asylum seekers and illegal migrants from less privileged regions, long after the post-World War II economic boom had come to an end in the 1970s, bringing a stop to regulated labour migration programmes also. The fall of communism in 1989 opened the gates to new immigrants from eastern Europe and the former Soviet Union. Most of the initial guest workers from poorer neighbouring European countries either returned home or have been successfully integrated into the host countries. But policies of voluntary repatriation of non-European immigrants have proved less successful, as the guest workers not only overstayed their welcome but have settled permanently with their reunited families. In 2004, Spain and Italy, which only three decades earlier had been immigrant-sending countries, received the largest number of legal immigrants in Europe, around 500,000 and 400,000 respectively, while traditional immigrant-receiving countries such as Germany, France and Great Britain were able to reduce drastically their legal immigration to 100,000 entries or less.

Although the proportion of foreign immigrants in many European countries (United Kingdom, France, the Netherlands, West Germany before reunification), at approximately 10 per cent, is similar to the proportion of foreign-born in the United States today, most European countries still have difficulty viewing themselves as permanent immigrant societies, or viewing the foreign-born, and even the native second and third generation, as nationals, irrespective of their legal status. The United States, by contrast, tends to view itself as the paradigmatic immigrant society, and the distinction between native citizen, naturalised immigrant, immigrant alien and undocumented alien, while legally clear, is not immediately evident in ordinary social encounters or relevant in most social contexts (Bauböck 1994; Bauböck, Heller and Zolberg 1996; Bauböck and Rundell 1998).

The challenge of the new religious diversity in secular Europe

One of the most significant consequences of the new immigration has been a dramatic growth in religious diversity on both sides of the Atlantic. But while in the United States the new immigrant religions have mainly contributed to the further expansion of an already vibrant American religious pluralism, in the case of Europe, immigrant religions present a greater challenge to local patterns of limited religious pluralism and, even more importantly, to recent European trends of drastic secularisation. It is true that European societies distinguish themselves not only from the United States but also from one another, in the different ways in which they try to accommodate and regulate immigrant religions, particularly Islam. European societies have markedly different institutional and legal structures regarding religious associations, and very diverse policies of state recognition, state regulation and state aid to religious groups, as well as diverse norms concerning when and where one may publicly express religious beliefs and practices (Ferrari and Bradney 2000).

In their dealing with immigrant religions, European countries, like the United States, tend to replicate their particular model of separation of church and state and the patterns of regulation of their own religious minorities (Jelen and Wilcox 2002; Madeley and Enyedi 2003). France's etatist secularist model and the political culture of *laïcité* require the strict privatisation of religion, eliminating religion from any public forum, while at the same time pressuring religious groups to organise themselves into a single, centralised churchlike institutional structure that can be regulated by and can serve as interlocutor to the state, following the traditional model of the concordat with the Catholic Church. Great Britain, by contrast, while maintaining the established Church of England, has historically accommodated a much greater religious pluralism and today allows greater freedom of religious associations, which deal directly with local authorities and school boards to press for changes in religious education, diet and so on, with little direct appeal to the central government. Germany, following the multi-establishment model, has tried to organise a quasi-official Islamic institution, at times in conjunction with parallel strivings on the part of the Turkish state to regulate its diaspora. But the internal divisions among immigrants from Turkey and the public expression and mobilisation of competing identities (secular and Muslim, Alevi and Kurd) in the German democratic context have undermined any project of institutionalisation from above. The Netherlands, following its traditional pattern of pillarisation, seemed, until very recently at least, bent on establishing a state-regulated but self-organised separate Muslim pillar. Lately, however, even the liberal, tolerant Netherlands is expressing second thoughts and seems ready to pass more restrictive legislation, setting clear limits to the kinds of un-European, unmodern norms and habits it is ready to tolerate.

Looking at western Europe as a whole, however, there are two fundamental differences with the situation in the United States. In the first place, in continental Europe at least, immigration and Islam are almost synonymous. Except for the United Kingdom, where one finds a much greater diversity of immigrants from former colonies of the British Empire, until very recently a majority of immigrants in most European countries have been Muslims. Moreover, despite the symbolic presence of small groups of European converts to Islam, the overwhelming majority of western European Muslims are immigrants. This identification of immigration and Islam appears even more pronounced in those cases where the majority of Muslim immigrants tend to come predominantly from a single region of origin (for example Turkey in the case of Germany, the Maghreb in the case of France). This entails a superimposition of different dimensions of otherness that exacerbate issues of boundaries, accommodation and incorporation. The immigrant, the religious, the racial and the socioeconomically disprivileged Other all tend to coincide (Vertovec and Peach 1997; Maréchal *et al.* 2003; Cesari 2004).

In the United States, by contrast, Muslims constitute at most 10 per cent of all new immigrants, a figure that is likely to decrease, if the strict restrictions on Arab and Muslim immigration imposed after 11 September 2001 continue. Since the US Census Bureau, the Immigration and Naturalization Service and other government agencies are not allowed to gather information on religion, there are no reliable estimates on the number of Muslims in the United States. Available but self-interested estimates range widely between 2.8 million and 8 million. It is safe to assume that the actual number lies somewhere in the middle – between 4 and 6 million. More reliable is the estimate that between 30 and 42 per cent of all Muslims in the United States are African American converts to Islam, making more difficult the characterisation of Islam as a foreign, un-American religion. Furthermore, the Muslim immigrant communities in the United States are extremely diverse, in terms of geographic region of origin from all over the Muslim world, in terms of discursive Islamic traditions and in terms of socioeconomic characteristics. As a result, the dynamics of interaction with other Muslim immigrants, with African American Muslims, with non-Muslim immigrants from the same regions of origin and with their immediate American hosts, depending upon socioeconomic characteristics and residential patterns, are much more complex and diverse than anything one finds in Europe (Haddad 2002; Leonard 2003).

The second main difference between western Europe and the United States has to do with the role of religion and religious group identities, in public life and in the organisation of civil society. Internal differences notwithstanding, western European societies are deeply secular societies, shaped by the hegemonic knowledge regime of secularism.[1] The progressive, though highly uneven, secularisation of Europe is an undeniable social fact (Martin 1978; Greeley 2003). It is true that the rates of religiosity vary significantly across Europe. East Germany is by far the least religious country of Europe by any measure, followed at a long distance by the Czech Republic and the Scandinavian countries. At the other extreme, Ireland and Poland are by far the most religious countries of Europe, with rates comparable to those of the United States. In general, with the significant exception of France and the Czech Republic, Catholic countries tend to be more religious than Protestant or mixed countries (West Germany, the Netherlands), although Switzerland (a mixed and traditionally pillarised country comparable to the Netherlands) stands at the high end of the European religious scale, with rates similar to those of Catholic Austria and Spain, both of which, however, have been undergoing drastic rates of decline.

In any case, across Europe since the 1960s an increasing majority of the population has ceased participating in traditional religious practices, at least on a regular basis, while still maintaining relatively high levels of private individual religious belief. In this respect, one should perhaps talk of the unchurching of the European population and of religious individualisation, rather than of secularisation. Grace Davie (1994; 2000) characterises this general European situation as 'believing without belonging'. At the same time, however, large numbers of Europeans, even in the most secular countries, still identify themselves as Christian, pointing to an implicit, diffused and submerged Christian cultural identity. In this sense, Danièle Hervieu-Léger (2004) is also correct, when she offers the reverse characterisation of the European situation as 'belonging without believing'. From France to Sweden and from England to Scotland, the historical churches (Catholic, Lutheran, Anglican or Calvinist), although emptied of active membership, still

---

[1] The following section draws upon an argument developed more extensively in Casanova (2006).

function, vicariously as it were, as public carriers of the national religion. In this respect, 'secular' and 'Christian' cultural identities are intertwined in complex and rarely verbalised modes among most Europeans.

Indeed, the most interesting issue sociologically is not the fact of progressive religious decline among the European population since the 1950s, but the fact that this decline is interpreted through the lenses of the secularisation paradigm and is therefore accompanied by a secularist self-understanding that interprets the decline as normal and progressive, that is, as a quasi-normative consequence of being a modern and enlightened European. We need to entertain seriously the proposition that secularisation became a self-fulfilling prophecy in Europe once large sectors of the population of western European societies, including the Christian churches, accepted the basic premises of the theory of secularisation: that secularisation is a teleological process of modern social change; that the more modern a society, the more secular it becomes; and that secularity is 'a sign of the times'. If such a proposition is correct, then the secularisation of western European societies can be explained better in terms of the triumph of the knowledge regime of secularism than in terms of structural processes of socioeconomic development, such as urbanisation, education, rationalisation and so on. The internal variations within Europe, moreover, can be explained better in terms of historical patterns of church–state and church–nation relations – as well as in terms of different paths of secularisation among the different branches of Christianity – than in terms of levels of modernisation.

It is the secular identity shared by European elites and ordinary people alike that paradoxically turns religion and the barely submerged Christian European identity into a thorny and perplexing issue, when it comes to delimiting the external geographic boundaries and to defining the internal cultural identity of a European Union in the process of being constituted. The contentious debates over the potential integration of Muslim Turkey into the European Union are superimposed on the debates over the failure to integrate second- and third-generation Muslim immigrants into Europe – all contributing to the spectre of Islam as the Other of the modern, liberal, secular West. Moreover, the debates over textual references to God or to the Christian heritage in the preamble to the new European constitution have shown that Europe, rather than Turkey, is actually the 'torn country', deeply divided over its cultural identity, unable to answer the question whether European unity, and therefore its external and internal boundaries, should be defined by the common heritage of Christianity and western civilisation or by its modern, secular values of liberalism, universal human rights, political democracy, and tolerant and inclusive multiculturalism. Publicly, of course, European liberal, secular elites could not share the Pope's definition of European civilisation as essentially Christian. But they also could not verbalise the unspoken cultural requirements that make the integration of Turkey into Europe such a difficult issue. The spectre of millions of Turkish citizens already in Europe but not of Europe, many of them second-generation immigrants, caught between an old country they have left behind and their European host societies, unable or unwilling to fully assimilate them, makes the problem only more visible. Guest workers can be successfully incorporated economically. They may even gain voting rights, at least on the local level, and prove to be model or at least ordinary citizens. But can they pass the unwritten rules of cultural European membership or are they to remain 'strangers'? Can the European Union open new conditions for the kind of multiculturalism that its constituent national societies find so difficult to accept? Contemporary debates across Europe illustrate a fundamental tension between cosmopolitan secularism and the kind of multiculturalism that could bring public recognition of the mores, customs, and life-worlds of Muslim and other immigrant religious communities (Modood 2005).

As liberal, democratic polities, all European societies respect and protect constitutionally the private exercise of religion, including Islam, as an individual human right. It is the public and collective free exercise of Islam as an immigrant religion that most European societies find difficult to tolerate, precisely on the grounds that Islam is perceived as an essentially un-European religion. The stated rationales for considering Islam un-European vary significantly across Europe and among social and political groups. For the anti-immigrant, xenophobic, nationalist right, represented by Jean-Marie Le Pen's discourse in France and by Jörg Haider in Austria, the message is straightforward. Islam is unwelcome and unassimilable simply because it is a 'foreign' immigrant religion. Such a nativist and usually racist attitude can be differentiated clearly from the conservative Catholic position, paradigmatically expressed by the Cardinal of Bologna, when he declared that Italy should welcome immigrants of all races and regions of the world, but should particularly select Catholic immigrants in order to preserve the Catholic identity of the country. Christian democratic parties have in fact become the cultural defenders of a narrow, nativist and territorial definition of European Christianity, at a time when the millennial identification of Christianity and European civilisation has come to an end, owing to a dual process of advanced secularisation in post-Christian Europe and increasing globalisation of a de-territorialised and decentred non-European Christianity.

Liberal, secular Europeans tend to look askance at such blatant expressions of racist bigotry and religious intolerance coming from nationalists and religious conservatives. But when it comes to Islam, secular Europeans also tend to reveal the limits and prejudices of modern, secularist toleration. One is not likely to hear among liberal politicians and secular intellectuals explicitly xenophobic or anti-religious statements. The politically correct formulation tends to run along such lines as 'we welcome each and every immigrant irrespective of race or religion as long as they are willing to respect and accept our modern, liberal, secular European norms'. The explicit articulation of those norms may vary from country to country. The controversies over the Muslim veil in so many European societies and the overwhelming support among the French citizenry, including apparently among a majority of French Muslims, for restrictive legislation prohibiting the wearing of Muslim veils and other ostensibly religious symbols in public schools as 'a threat to national cohesion', may be an extreme example of illiberal secularism (Bowen 2004; Asad 2006). But in fact one sees similar trends of restrictive legislation directed at immigrant Muslims in the liberal Netherlands, precisely in the name of protecting its liberal, tolerant traditions from the threat of illiberal, fundamentalist, patriarchal customs, reproduced and transmitted to the younger generation by Muslim immigrants.

Revealingly enough, French Prime Minister Jean-Pierre Raffarin, in his address to the French legislature defending the banning of ostensibly religious symbols in public schools, made reference in the same breath to France as 'the old land of Christianity' and to the inviolable principle of *laïcité*, exhorting Islam to adapt itself to the principle of secularism as all other religions of France have done before: 'For the most recently arrived ... I'm speaking here of Islam ... secularism is a chance, the chance to be a religion of France' (Sciolino 2004). The Islamic veil and other religious signs are justifiably banned from public schools, he added, because 'they are taking on a political meaning', while according to the secularist principle of privatisation of religion, 'religion cannot be a political project'. Time will tell whether restrictive legislation will have the intended effect of stopping the spread of 'radical Islam', or whether it is likely to bring about the opposite result of radicalising further an already alienated and maladjusted immigrant community.

The positive rationale one hears among liberals, in support of such illiberal restriction of the free exercise of religion, is usually put in terms of the desirable enforced emancipation of young girls, if necessary against their expressed will, from gender discrimination and from patriarchal control. This was the discourse on which the assassinated Dutch politician Pim Fortuyn built his electorally successful anti-immigrant platform in the liberal Netherlands, a campaign that is now bearing fruit in new restrictive legislation and in further violence. While conservative religious people are expected to tolerate behaviour they may consider morally abhorrent – such as homosexuality – liberal, secular Europeans are openly stating that European societies ought not to tolerate religious behaviour or cultural customs that are morally abhorrent, insofar as they are contrary to modern, liberal, secular European norms. What makes the intolerant tyranny of the secular, liberal majority justifiable in principle is not just the democratic principle of majority rule, but rather the secularist teleological assumption built into theories of modernisation that one set of norms is reactionary, fundamentalist and anti-modern, while the other set is progressive, liberal and modern.

Anti-immigrant xenophobic nativism, secularist anti-religious prejudices, liberal-feminist critiques of Muslim patriarchal fundamentalism and the fear of Islamist terrorist networks are being fused indiscriminately throughout Europe into a uniform anti-Muslim discourse, which practically precludes the kind of mutual accommodation between immigrant groups and host societies that is necessary for successful immigrant incorporation.[2] The parallels with Protestant-Republican anti-Catholic nativism in mid-nineteenth-century America are indeed striking. Today's totalising discourse on Islam as an essentially anti-modern, fundamentalist, illiberal and undemocratic religion and culture echoes the nineteenth-century discourse on Catholicism (Casanova 2001).

[2] For a notorious expression of Islamophobia, see Fallaci (2002). On the issue, see Runnymede Trust (1997), and Sayyid (2003 [1997]).

European societies tend to tolerate and respect individual religious freedom. But owing to the pressure towards the privatisation of religion, which among European societies has become a taken-for-granted characteristic of the self-definition of a modern, secular society, those societies have a much greater difficulty in recognising some legitimate role for religion in public life and in the organisation and mobilisation of collective group identities. Muslim-organised collective identities and their public representations become a source of anxiety, not only because of their religious otherness as a non-Christian and non-European religion, but more importantly because of their religiousness itself as the Other of European secularity. In this context, the temptation to identify Islam and fundamentalism becomes the more pronounced. Islam, by definition, becomes the Other of western secular modernity, an identification that becomes superimposed upon the older image of Islam as the Other of European Christianity. Therefore, the problems posed by the incorporation of Muslim immigrants become consciously or unconsciously associated with seemingly related and vexatious issues concerning the role of religion in the public sphere, which European societies assumed they had already solved according to the liberal, secular norm of privatisation of religion (Casanova 1994).

Immigrant religions and the expansion of American denominationalism

The structural conditions that immigrants encounter in the United States are substantially different.[3] It is not only that Americans are demonstrably more religious than the Europeans and therefore that there is a certain pressure for immigrants to conform to American religious norms. Even more significantly, today, as in the past, religion and public religious denominational identities play an important role in the process of incorporation of the new immigrants: thus the paradox observed again and again by students of immigrant communities

---

[3] The following section draws substantially upon the still unpublished findings of the Religion and Immigrant Incorporation in New York (RIINY) research project, led by José Casanova and Aristide Zolberg at the International Center for Migration, Ethnicity, and Citizenship at the New School for Social Research in New York. RIINY (1999–2002) was one of seven 'Gateway Cities' projects financed by the Pew Charitable Trusts.

that, in the words of Raymond Williams (1988: 29), 'immigrants are religious – by all counts more religious than they were before they left home'.[4]

It is important to realise, therefore, that immigrant religiosity is not simply a traditional residue, an Old World survivor likely to disappear with adaptation to the new context, but rather an adaptive response to the New World. I find unconvincing, however, Timothy Smith's (1978) explanation that it is the immigration experience per se that calls forth such a religious response because immigration itself is a 'theologising' experience, because the uprootedness it entails from traditional ways, the uncertainty of the journey and the anomic experience of being strangers in a new land calls forth a religious response.

It is often the case that phenomenologically many immigrant groups, in trying to express and verbalise the experience of the immigrant journey, resort to religious language and draw upon available discursive archetypes from various religious traditions, framing it in terms of a pilgrimage (Christians and Hindus), an exodus to a promised land (Puritans, Jews and African Americans) or a new hegira (Muslims). The problem begins when this particular phenomenological observation is turned into a neo-Durkheimian general explanation, in terms of reactive responses to the cultural strains and anomic disintegration associated with the uprooting experience of immigration. Such a general explanation is not convincing, because one actually finds an enormous range in the religious responses of contemporary immigrant groups in America: from Korean Americans, who are arguably more religious than any other ethnic group in America, immigrant or native; to Soviet Jews, who are as little religious as they were in the old country. But, more importantly, it is not plausible as a general explanation, because it is not confirmed by the comparative evidence from other immigrant societies, today or in the past.[5]

---

[4] The claim that immigrants become more religious as they become more American was central to Will Herberg's (1960) thesis in his classic study *Protestant–Catholic–Jew*. The same claim has been restated by most contemporary studies of immigrant religions in America. See, for example, Warner and Wittner (1998), and Ebaugh and Chafetz (2000).

[5] Rural Italian immigrants from the south at the turn of the twentieth century, for instance, tended to adopt anti-clerical socialist and anarchist identities when they migrated to urban industrial centres in northern Italy or to Catholic Argentina, while they tended to become 'better' practising Catholics when they migrated to urban industrial centres in the United States. One could make

It is not the general context of immigration, but the particular context of immigration to America, and the structural and institutional context of American society that provoke this particular religious response. The thesis of Will Herberg concerning the old European immigrant, that 'not only was he expected to retain his old religion, as he was not expected to retain his old language or nationality, but such was the shape of America that it was largely in and through religion that he, or rather his children and grandchildren, found an identifiable place in American life', is still operative with the new immigrants (Herberg 1960: 27–28). The thesis implies not only that immigrants tend to be religious because of a certain social pressure to conform to American religious norms; more importantly, it implies that collective religious identities have been one of the primary ways of structuring internal societal pluralism in American history.

Since Americans in general tend to be religious, more religious probably than most people in other modern societies, immigrants in America will tend to conform to the American norm: 'When in Rome do as the Romans.' About the pressure to conform to American standards of religiosity, there can be little doubt: ask any political candidate whether they can afford to confess that they have 'no religion'. What is relevant is the 'definition of the situation'. Since Americans define themselves as a religious people, they think and act accordingly. Even more striking is the fact that they tend to lie to the pollsters and to inflate their rates of church attendance and to exaggerate the depth and seriousness of their religious beliefs (Hadaway, Marler and Chaves 1993). Indeed, the very tendency of the Americans to exaggerate their religiousness, in contrast to the opposite tendency of the Europeans to discount and under-count their own persistent religiosity – tendencies that are evident among ordinary people, as well as among scholars, on both sides of the Atlantic – are themselves part of the very different and consequential definitions of the situation in both places. Obviously, Americans think that they are supposed to be religious, while Europeans think that they are supposed to be irreligious. This would explain, at least in part, the reason why the same groups of immigrants tend to be more religious and to carry their religious

similar comparisons in the present day between Hindu immigrants in London and New York or between francophone west African Muslims in Paris and New York.

identity more openly in public in the United States than in most European countries.

But more important than the diffuse social pressure to conform to American religious norms are, in my view, the structural conditions shaping American religious pluralism. The fact that religion, religious institutions and religious identities played a central role in the process of incorporation of the old European immigrants has been amply documented. Rather than decreasing, as one would expect from conventional theories of modernisation and secularisation, religious identities tended to gain salience in the particular context of immigration to America. Herberg's (1960: 27) thesis implied that collective religious identities have been one of the primary ways of structuring internal societal pluralism in American history, the reason being that 'almost from the beginning, the structure of American society presupposed diversity and substantial equality of religious associations'.

The particular pattern of separation of church and state codified in the dual clause of the First Amendment, 'free exercise of religion' and 'no establishment', served to structure this diversity and substantial equality. After independence, the establishment of any particular church at the federal/national level was probably precluded by the territorial distribution and the relative equal strength of the three colonial churches: Congregational, Presbyterian and Anglican. However, either multiple establishment or the establishment of a generalised Christian (i.e. Protestant) religion could have been likely outcomes, had it not been for the active coalition of Jefferson, Madison and dissenting Baptists in Virginia.

The American constitutional formula challenged the notion, taken for granted and shared at the time by religionists and secularists (deists) alike, that the state or the political community of citizens needed a religion, ecclesiastical or civil, as the base of its normative integration and that, moreover, it was the business of the sovereign to regulate the religious sphere. The First Amendment raised not only a 'wall of separation' protecting the state from religion (no establishment) and religion from the state (free exercise), but actually established a principle of differentiation between the political community of citizens and any and all religious communities. Eventually, all religions in America, churches as well as sects, irrespective of their origins, doctrinal claims and ecclesiastical identities, would turn into 'denominations', formally equal under the Constitution and competing in a relatively free, pluralistic and voluntaristic religious market. As the organisational form and principle of such a religious system, denominationalism constitutes the great American religious invention (Greeley 1972; Mead 1976).[6]

At first, this diversity and substantial equality was institutionalised only as internal denominational religious pluralism within American Protestantism. America was defined as a 'Christian' nation and Christian meant solely 'Protestant'. But eventually, after prolonged outbursts of Protestant nativism, directed primarily at Catholic immigrants, the pattern allowed for the incorporation of the religious others, Catholics and Jews, into the system of American religious pluralism (Billington 1938; Davis 1960; Higham 1988, 1999). A process of dual accommodation took place, whereby Catholicism and Judaism became American religions, while American religion and the nation were equally transformed in the process. America became a 'Judeo-Christian' nation, and Protestant, Catholic and Jew became the three denominations of the American civil religion. It is this final outcome – the assimilation of immigrant European Catholics and Jews into the American mainstream – that Herberg's book celebrates.[7] And it is worth remembering that it is this same self-congratulatory context and the inaugural speech of the first Catholic president – John F. Kennedy – that serves as the background for Robert Bellah's (1967) thesis of civil religion in America a decade later.

Herberg's thesis of American ethno-religious pluralism has serious shortcomings. The most blatant is the fact that Herberg is absolutely blind to issues of race, and thus *Protestant–Catholic–Jew* examines only the process of incorporation of European immigrants, while being absolutely silent about non-European immigrants. The crucial problem is not that Herberg ignores other non-European immigrant minorities and their non-Judeo-Christian religions, such as Japanese

---

[6] In western Europe, by contrast, the model has remained that of one single church that claims to be coextensive with the nation, or that of two (Catholic and Protestant) competing but territorially based national churches along with an indefinite number of religious minorities, which tend to assume the structural position of sects vis-à-vis the national church or churches. Post-independence Ukraine may be the only European society that resembles the denominational model. See Casanova (1998).

[7] Actually, on theological monotheistic grounds, Herberg himself was personally highly critical of the idolatrous immanent character of the American or any national civil religion.

Buddhists or Chinese Daoists or Arab Muslims – groups that were already part of the old immigration. Though a serious oversight, one could still argue defensively that those were at the time relatively small minorities. The real problem is that Herberg ignores the truly relevant racial minorities among the religious groups he is studying, the Christian others: black Protestants and Hispanic Catholics. After all, Herberg wrote his study in the 1950s, at the high point of the great internal migration of African Americans from the rural south to the northern urban industrial centres, and of the Puerto Rican migration to New York, leaving aside for the moment the other relevant Hispanic Catholics: the 'Chicanos' from the southwest, who were themselves mostly, with the exception of the braceros, not migrants (Glazer and Moynihan 1963; Dolan and Vidal 1994; Lemann 1996). As in the case of Puerto Rico, it was the US borders that had migrated to their ancestral territories. Strictly speaking, of course, African Americans and Hispanics were not immigrant aliens. But it is the fact that Herberg constructs Protestant, Catholic and Jew as the three imagined religious communities making up the imagined community of the American nation that makes the omission of African Americans and Hispanics the more problematic and revealing. What the omission of black Protestants and Hispanic Catholics reveals is that in the 1950s those groups remained the invisible racial alien at a time when European immigrants, Catholics and Jews, had been incorporated into the imagined community of the American nation.

Rightly, the new literature on immigration studies has placed issues of race, racialisation and racial identities at the very centre of the analysis of processes of immigrant incorporation. Blacks and Hispanics have become, indeed, the truly relevant *tertium comparationis* in all comparative studies of the old and the new immigration. At least implicitly, the three terms of comparison in all contemporary debates are (a) European white ethnics (the old immigrants), (b) American racial minorities (African American and Hispanic) and (c) the new immigrants from all over the world (Asian, Caribbean, Latin American, African etc.). Once the comparative framework is constructed in such a way, it becomes immediately obvious that race matters, and that matters of race are crucial in the process of immigrant incorporation. But what Herberg's study shows is that religion matters also and that matters of religion may be equally relevant in processes of immigrant incorporation in America. Not religion alone, as Herberg's study would seem to imply, and not race alone, as contemporary immigration studies would seem to imply, but religion and race and their complex entanglements, have served to structure the American experience of immigrant incorporation and indeed are the keys to 'American exceptionalism' (Lincoln 1984; Wood 1990).[8]

Simplifying a complex story, one could say that assimilation into the American mainstream meant at first becoming WASP or WASP-like. Of the four markers of American identity – white, Anglo-Saxon, Protestant – the truly relevant ones, however, were the first and the last: race and religion.[9] One could be as white as it gets, but if one was not Protestant, it was hard to pass as an American. Irish Protestants (and do not forget that the majority of Americans of Irish descent are of Protestant origin, descendants of the Scottish-Irish) never had a problem passing as white. It was the Irish Catholics and other Catholics (Italians, Slavs etc.) who were racialised as the Other. Becoming as devoutly Protestant as most African Americans did was also not enough. If one was not white, one could not be fully American (King 2000). Today, religion and race are becoming, once again, the two critical markers identifying the new immigrants either as assimilable or as suspiciously alien. In this respect, religious and racial self-identifications and ascriptions represent parallel, and at times alternative, ways of organising American multiculturalism (Lawrence 2002).

Immigration as a context for United States religious pluralism

The United States has become an immigrant society again. During the past decade alone, approximately one million immigrants annually entered the United States, the largest wave in the nation's history, even outnumbering the nine million immigrants who came during the first decade of the twentieth century. Moreover, the trend may have slowed down slightly after 9/11, but there are no clear indications that it is likely to be reversed in the near future. More important than the increase in numbers, however, are the changes in the regions of origin

[8] Until recently the new field of immigration studies had paid little attention to religion, but this situation has been radically altered in the last decade.

[9] For a prominent voice of Anglo-Protestant nativism directed at the threat of Hispanic Catholics, see Huntington (2004).

and in the characteristics of the new immigrants. In comparison with the old immigrants, two characteristics of the new immigrants are most relevant: (a) they are primarily non-European, increasingly from all regions of the world, but predominantly from Asia and the Americas, and (b) in addition to the tremendous range in all forms of human diversity (racial, ethnic, religious, cultural, linguistic) that they bring, the new immigrants are also extremely diverse, almost bifurcated, in the levels of human and social capital, skills, and resources that they bring (Portes and Rumbaut 1996).

From the particular perspective of this essay, the most important characteristic is the extraordinary religious pluralism and diversity that they bring to a country that was already the most religiously diverse and pluralistic in the world (Eck 2002). Since US government agencies cannot gather information on the religious makeup of the population, we must rely on other sources for reliable data on the denominational affiliation of the new immigrants.[10] Attempts to extrapolate from the religious composition of the country of origin have to be sensitive to the fact that today, as always, religious minorities tend to immigrate to America in disproportionate numbers. Arab Christians and Russian Jews in the past, Korean Christians and Latino Protestants today, would be obvious examples. Moreover, one has to be aware of the intrinsic difficulties in applying western categories of religious affiliation to non-western religions. Nominal affiliation is in any case problematic as a measure of individual religiosity, since it does not tell how truly religious the nominally affiliated are: that is, whether, how and how often they practise their religion. Much less, of course, can denominational affiliation categories, or 'religious preference', measure the religion of the unaffiliated, namely those religious practices and forms of religion that are not defined by membership or affiliation in an organised religious institution, congregation or community.

In any case, it is safe to assume that the immense majority of all new immigrants are Christian, Protestant and Catholic in various proportions, with small numbers of Eastern Orthodox, depending upon the port of entry. In the case of New York, our own very rough estimate from the Religion and Immigrant Incorporation in New York (RIINY)

---

[10] The New Immigrant Survey (NIS) fortunately provides such a source of data. See http://nis.princeton.edu and note 11 below.

project is that close to 50 per cent of all new immigrants are nominally Catholic, while approximately 25 per cent of the new immigrants are nominally Protestant. Protestants and Catholics together, therefore, constitute around 75 per cent of all new immigrants to New York. For the United States as a whole the proportion of Christians among the new immigrants is likely to be slightly lower, somewhere between two-thirds and three-quarters.[11] In this respect, the most significant religious impact of the new immigrants is likely to be the replenishing and renovation of American Christianity. But since they bring non-European versions of Christianity, the new immigrants are also going to contribute to the de-Europeanisation of American Protestantism and American Catholicism. The Hispanisation or Latin-Americanisation of American Catholicism is one of the most obvious and relevant trends. But it is accompanied by the no less significant trend of Protestanti-fication of Latin America and of Latino-Americans.[12]

But the most striking new development with extraordinary potential repercussions, both national and global, is the arrival of increasing numbers of Muslims, Hindus, Buddhists, indeed of representatives of all world religions. The numbers may not yet be as large as the exaggerated estimates of 6 to 7 million Muslims, 2.8 to 4 million Buddhists, and 1.2 to 2 million Hindus that one sees floating around. But the battle over numbers and the attempts by the National Opinion Research Center and the American Jewish Committee to deflate those exaggerated esti-mates in order to prove that, as a *Chicago Tribune* (2002) headline put it, 'Christians, Jews still predominate' misses the point (see Smith 2001).

In terms of numbers, American Jews never presented a real chal-lenge to Christian predominance, but the incorporation of Judaism as

---

[11] According to the New Immigrant Survey Pilot (NIS-P 1996) and the NIS-2003, almost two thirds of new immigrants are nominally Christian (Catholic 41.9%; Protestant 18.6%; Orthodox 4.2%), 2.6% denominated themselves Jewish, while close to 17% chose non-Judeo-Christian religions as their denomination (Muslim 8%; Buddhist 4%; Hindu 3.4%; other 1.4%) and 15% chose 'no religion' as their 'religious preference'. While the NIS-Pilot drew on a small sample (976) of respondents, its findings on the religious preference or nominal affiliation of the new immigrants were largely confirmed by the much larger adult sample of the NIS-2003. See http://nis.princeton.edu/key-findings.html, and Jasso *et al.* (2003).

[12] On the Hispanisation of American Catholicism and Protestantism and the parallel Protestantification of Latin America, see Dolan and Deck (1994), and Diaz-Stevens and Stevens-Arroyo (1998).

an American religion radically transformed the American religious landscape and the self-definition of the American nation. It is true that unlike the deeply seated Protestant anti-Catholic nativism, Judaism in America did not encounter similar religiously based anti-Semitism, and in general American Protestantism has tended to maintain a philo-Hebraic attitude. But the addition of Catholicism and Judaism as American denominations altered the very system of American denominationalism. The perceived threat posed by immigrant Catholicism was not primarily due to its size, but rather to the fact that it was viewed as an un-American religion, insofar as Republicanism and Romanism were defined as being incompatible.

American religious pluralism is expanding and incorporating all the world religions in the same way as it previously incorporated the religions of the old immigrants (Pluralism Project CD-ROM 1997). A complex process of mutual accommodation is taking place. Like Catholicism and Judaism before, other world religions (Islam, Hinduism, Buddhism) are being Americanised, and in the process they are transforming American religion, while the religious diasporas in America are simultaneously serving as catalysts for the transformation of the old religions in their civilisational homes, in the same way as American Catholicism had an impact upon the transformation of world Catholicism and as American Judaism had transformed world Judaism (Dolan 1985; Moore 1986; Hertzberg 1989).

A similar story and similar patterns of conflictive incorporation and mutual accommodation are being repeated today. It is true that the models of immigrant incorporation have been radically altered by the expanding multiculturalism at home and by the proliferation of global transnational networks. The increasing global migration in turn leads to a spiralling acceleration of multiculturalism and religious pluralism, now encompassing all world religions. We have entered a new phase in the American experiment. The United States is called to become not just 'the first new nation', made up primarily of all the European nations. The traditional model of assimilation, turning European nationals into American 'ethnics', can no longer serve as a model of incorporation now that immigration is literally worldwide. America is bound to become 'the first new global society', made up of all world religions and civilisations, at a time when religious civilisational identities are regaining prominence on the global stage (Protero 2005).

It is due to the corrosive logic of racialisation, so prominent and pervasive in American society, that the dynamics of religious identity formation assume a double positive form in the process of immigrant incorporation. Owing to the institutionalised acceptance of religious pluralism and religious identities for the structural reasons mentioned above, it is not surprising that the affirmation of religious identities is enhanced among the new immigrants. This positive affirmation of religious identities is reinforced further by what appears to be a common defensive reaction by most immigrant groups against ascribed racialisation, particularly against the stigma of racial darkness. If anything, the new patterns of global migration are making our absurd binary racial categories ever more confusing and untenable. In this context, the positive affirmation of religious identities by Hindus from India and the Caribbean, by Muslims from west Africa or by Creole Catholics from Haiti is adding a dimension of resistance to the dynamics of racialisation. In this respect, religious and racial self-identifications and ascriptions represent alternative ways of organising American (and global) multiculturalism.[13] One of the obvious advantages of religious pluralism over racial pluralism is that under proper constitutional institutionalisation it is more reconcilable with principled equality and non-hierarchic diversity and therefore with genuine multiculturalism.

American denominationalism functions at three different levels, each affecting diversely the transformation of immigrant religions in America. The first is the basic 'congregational' level of the local religious community. This is the most important level in which the fundamental process of Americanisation takes place. As Stephen Warner (2005) rightly points out, all immigrant religions in America, irrespective of their institutional form in their traditional civilisational settings, tend to adopt a typically Protestant congregational form. It happened to the old immigrants, Catholics and Jews, and it is happening to the new immigrants, irrespective of whether they already had a quasi-congregational form, like the Muslims, or have no congregational tradition, like Buddhists or Hindus. All religious communities in America tend to assume a voluntary associational form and become incorporated as a non-profit organisation, led by the laity. Churches,

---

[13] For a poignant illustration, see Kurien (2005).

synagogues, temples, masjids, and so on, tend to become more than houses of worship or prayer, being authentic community centres, with different kinds of educational and social services, fellowship and rec-reational activities, and task-specific associational networks. Indeed, they become, as Tocqueville has already pointed out, schools of demo-cracy and the centres of associational life of the immigrant communities (Tocqueville 1945).

This is the fundamental difference between the American deno-minations and the European churches, which never made the full transition to congregational voluntary associations and remained anchored in the territorially based national church and local parish. Structurally significant is the fact that at least for some groups the American experience of immigration seems to call forth the reflexive affirmation of religious identities; that is to say, the practice of naming oneself and of being named by others according to some religious denomination. This active, achieved and reflexive denomination, more-over, is very different from the passive, ascribed and nominal affi-liation to a religion into which one is born. This was, of course, the experience of immigrant Catholics and Jews in America. They could not simply maintain the nominal affiliation, at least not if they wanted to pass on the same affiliation to their children. They had to become voluntary members of an association and actively maintain and pass on their family traditions.

The second level is the denominational proper, in the sense in which it originally emerged as doctrinally, organisationally or ethno-racially differentiated plural denominations within American Protestantism. While the hierarchically organised Roman Catholic Church was able to incorporate all Catholic immigrants (with the exception of the Polish National Church) into a single American Catholic Church through the ethnic parish system, American Judaism also became differentiated into three main denominations (Reform, Conservative and Ortho-dox). It is still unclear whether various branches or traditions of the other world religions (Islam, Hinduism and Buddhism) will become institutionalised as separate denominations in America, or whether other denominational divisions will emerge.

Finally, there is the national level of 'imagined community' in the sense in which Herberg talks of Protestant, Catholic and Jew as the three denominational forms of the American civil religion. This is also the level at which the immigrant religions gain symbolic recognition and are thus incorporated into the nation as 'American', irrespective of whether they also develop unified national organisations.

The particular challenge of American Islam

Of all the new immigrant religions, Islam represents the most interesting testing ground and challenge to the pattern of immigrant incorporation. Because of geopolitical rationales and the common portrayal of Islam as fundamentalist, Islam today, as Catholicism before, is often represented as the Other and therefore as un-American. Tragically, these debates have only been exacerbated in the wake of the 9/11 terrorist attacks by Muslim militants and the US military response. Paradoxically, however, these developments are forcing not only a debate about the alleged civilisational clash between Islam and the West, but also a recognition that Islam has taken roots in America and is becoming a major American religion (Esposito 2007).

Certainly, one can observe striking similarities between today's discourse on Islam as a fundamentalist, anti-modern religion incompatible with democracy, and yesterday's discourse on Catholicism. From the 1830s to the 1950s anti-Catholic Protestant nativism in America was based on the alleged incompatibility between Republicanism and Romanism. In his portrayal of Catholics in America, Tocqueville had already tried to refute this thesis, as well as the widely held perception on both sides of the French Republican-laicist–monarchist-Catholic divide that Catholicism was incompatible with modern democracy and with individual freedoms (Tocqueville 1945).

As in the case of Catholicism before, the internal and external debates over the compatibility between Islam and democracy and modern individual freedoms is taking place at three separate yet interrelated levels: debates over the proper articulation of a Muslim *umma* in diasporic contexts outside Dar al-Islam; debates over the democratic legitimacy of Muslim political parties in Turkey and elsewhere, which like their – at first equally suspect – Catholic counterparts, may establish new forms of Muslim democracy, akin to Christian democracy; and debates over the alleged clash of civilisations between Islam and the West at the geopolitical level, with clear parallels to earlier debates on the clash between Republicanism and Romanism. Under conditions of globalisation, all three issues become ever more entangled (Roy 2004).

One can also witness, however, an ambiguous and tortuous process of public symbolic recognition of Islam as an American religion that resembles the processes of incorporation of Catholicism and Judaism. The self-defining discourse of America that had changed from that of a 'Christian' to a 'Judeo-Christian' nation was lately assuming the new denominational characterisation of 'Abrahamic', symbolically incorporating all three monotheistic religions claiming descent from the first covenant between God and Abraham. The presence of a Muslim imam along with a Protestant minister, a Catholic priest and a Jewish rabbi in public ceremonies in Washington, in state capitals, and in large urban centres has become routine. Among symbolic milestones in the process of public recognition one could mention the following: the first commissioned Islamic chaplain in the US Army was established in 1993 and in the US Navy in 1996; a Muslim symbol was displayed on the White House Ellipse in 1997; the Pentagon hosted its first Ramadan meal for Muslims in 1998; and on the first day of Ramadan in November 2000 the New Jersey legislature opened with a reading of the Qur'an by an imam. The Muslim public presence in official ceremonies and in inter-faith encounters has become even more prominent after the 9/11 terrorist attacks (Smith 1999). But simultaneously, one can also witness a mainly Protestant nativist backlash against Islam, which had actually begun before 9/11, but became exacerbated thereafter.[14]

The new anti-Muslim evangelical discourse has three main sources: (a) the militant pre-millennial Zionism among American evangelicals, who after the fall of the Soviet Union transferred the role, which the communist 'hordes' of the north and their Arab secular nationalist allies in the Middle East were supposed to play in their apocalyptic visions of the impending Armageddon, to all Muslim countries as enemies of Israel; (b) the missionary competition between Muslims and Christians (evangelicals and Pentecostals) throughout sub-Saharan Africa and in other parts of the world where one finds ethno-religious conflicts between Muslims and Christians, which adds to the evangelical frustration of being unable to preach openly the gospel of Jesus Christ in Muslim countries; and (c) the global 'War on Terror' after

---

[14] In addition to Cimino's (2003) paper, the following material draws heavily and freely upon personal conversations with Richard Cimino at the New School for Social Research.

9/11, which – notwithstanding the carefully phrased official disclaimers coming from the White House – prominent evangelical leaders such as Pat Robertson, Franklin Graham and Jerry Falwell have not hesitated to characterise openly as a 'crusade' and as an inevitable conflict between an essentially 'violent' Islam and the Christian West (Barisic 2002).

The most alarming manifestation of the emerging nativist Protestant anti-Muslim discourse is the series of blasphemous, defamatory tracts one finds in Christian bookstores, often written by Muslim converts to Christianity and resembling the old anti-popish tracts, which slander the Prophet Muhammad as a depraved sinner and discredit Islam as a false monotheistic and Abrahamic religion, which has pagan roots in the pre-Islamic worship of *Kaaba*.

The challenge confronting Islam in America is how to transform diverse immigrants from south Asia, who today constitute the largest and fastest growing group of Muslim immigrants, from Arab countries, and from west Africa into a single American Muslim *umma*. In this respect, the process of incorporation is not unlike that of different Catholic national groups into a single American Catholic church. The two options being debated today within Islamic communities across America, often put in terms of the Nation of Islam model versus the model of an assertive and powerful Jewish minority, reiterate some of the debates in nineteenth-century American Catholicism. At issue is whether Islam in America should be constructed as a segregated defensive subculture, protecting itself from corrosive Americanisation, or whether it should organise itself as a public self-assertive cultural option within American competitive multiculturalism. The threat of the Americanisation of Islam this would entail would be balanced by the opportunity of the Islamisation of America, which many Muslims view as an actualisation of Islam's universalism.

Owing to the still-growing Islamisation of the African American community, in a process that African American Muslims often depict not as conversion, but rather as reversion to a pre-slavery African Islam, the frequently contentious dialogue and dynamic interaction between African American and immigrant Muslims is bound to have a dramatic impact upon the transformation of American culture. It is still an open question which kind of internal denominational structure Islam in America is going to assume: whether it will succumb to what H. Richard Niebuhr called 'the evil of denominationalism', which he saw grounded in socioeconomic and ethno-racial divisions, or if it will organise itself into a national churchlike *umma*, able to bridge its internal ethno-linguistic and juridical-doctrinal divisions (Niebuhr 1929: 24). American Protestantism, Catholicism and Judaism represent in this respect alternative denominational models. American Islam is likely to develop its own distinct denominational pattern, while sharing some elements with all three. But if it is able to overcome in any way the pattern of congregational racial segregation that has plagued American Christianity, and to bridge the divide between immigrant and African American Muslims, it will have a significant impact upon American race relations.

The process of the Americanisation of Islam is already taking place, despite all the difficulties presented by internal debates, nativist resistance, and geopolitical conflicts. Islam is becoming not just a fast growing religion in America, but an American religion, one of the denominational alternatives of being religiously American. Moreover, Islam is destined to become, like Catholicism, an important public religion, which is likely to play a relevant role in American public debates in the future.

Conclusion

This chapter has tried to show that one of the most significant consequences of the new global patterns of transnational migration has been a dramatic growth in religious diversity on both sides of the Atlantic. The new immigrant religions, however, present significantly different challenges of integration in Christian/secular Europe and in Judeo-Christian/secular America, owing to the different histories of immigration and modes of immigrant incorporation, the different patterns of religious pluralism and the different types of secularism in both regions. Ultimately, religion in the United States constitutes a positive resource insofar as today, as in the past, religious associations and religious collective identities constitute one of the accepted avenues for immigrant incorporation and for mutual group recognition in the public sphere of American civil society. In Europe, by contrast, secularist world views and very different institutional patterns of public recognition through different forms of church–state relations make the incorporation of immigrant religions in the public sphere of European civil societies a more contentious issue.

7 | Muslims, religious equality and secularism

TARIQ MODOOD

There is an anti-Muslim wind blowing across the European continent.[1] One factor is a perception that Muslims are making politically exceptional, culturally unreasonable or theologically alien demands upon European states. My contention is that the claims Muslims are making in fact parallel comparable arguments about gender or ethnic equality. Seeing the issue in that context shows how European and contemporary is the logic of mainstream Muslim identity politics. I argue, additionally, that multicultural politics must embrace a moderate secularism and resist radical secularism.

Citizenship and national contexts

The same wind might be blowing across the whole continent, yet the landscape is not uniform. Of the three most populous western-European countries – (west) Germany, France and the United Kingdom – the former two have, in both absolute and relative terms, a larger foreign-born population and population of non-European origin than the UK. Yet issues of racial discrimination, ethnic identity and multiculturalism have less prominence in those two countries than in the UK. One aspect of this is that national debates on these topics have a lesser prominence, and that such debates are less frequently led by non-whites or non-Europeans, who are more the *objects of*, rather than *participants in*, the debates. Another aspect is the relative lack of data about ethnicity and religious communities, and consequently of research and literature. Yet this is not a simple matter of scale. Each

---

[1] The first half of this chapter borrows from and builds on Modood (2003a) (simultaneous publication in Modood (2003b)), and the second half borrows from and builds on parts of Modood and Kastoryano (2006). For a fuller elaboration of the perspective on which this chapter is based, see Modood (2007).

of the countries in the EU has a very different *conception* of what the issues are, depending upon its history, political culture and legal system.

The German experience is dominated by the idea that Germany is not a country of immigration, and so those newcomers who can show German descent are automatically granted nationality while the others are temporary guest workers or refugees; none are immigrants. Hence, out of its population of 80 million, Germany has 7 million without German citizenship. This includes about 2.5 million Turks and Kurds, some of whom are now third-generation Germans but who until recently were excluded from citizenship by German self-conceptions of nationality as *descent*. In contrast, France has a history of immigration that it has proudly dealt with by a readiness to grant citizenship. But it has a Republican conception of citizenship, which does not allow, at least in theory, any body of citizens to be differentially identified, for example as Arab.

In Germany, if you are of Turkish descent you cannot be German. In France, you can be of any descent but if you are a French citizen you cannot be an Arab. In each case, US-style – and now UK-style – composite identities like Turkish German, Arab French or British Indian are ideologically impossible. The giving up of pre-French identities and assimilation into French culture is thought to go hand in hand with the acceptance of French citizenship. If for some reason assimilation is not fully embraced – perhaps because some people want to retain pride in their Algerian ancestry, or want to maintain ethnic solidarity in the face of current stigmatisation and discrimination – then their claim to be French and equal citizens is jeopardised. The French conception of the Republic, moreover, also has integral to it a certain radical secularism, *laïcité*, marking the political triumph over clericalism. The latter was defeated by pushing matters of faith and religion out of politics and policy into the private sphere. Islam, with its claim to regulate public as well as private life, is therefore seen as an ideological foe, and the Muslim presence as alien and potentially both culturally and politically unassimilable – as evidenced, for example, in the ban on the Muslim headscarf, the *hijab*, in state schools, passed overwhelmingly by Parliament with very little discussion in January 2004.

The British experience of 'coloured immigration', in contrast, has been seen as an Atlanto-centric legacy of the slave trade, and policy and legislation were formed in the 1960s in the shadow of the US Civil Rights Movement, black power discourse and the inner-city riots in Detroit, Watts and elsewhere. It was, therefore, dominated by the idea of 'race', more specifically by the idea of a black–white dualism. It was also shaped by the imperial legacy, one aspect of which was that all colonials and citizens of the Commonwealth were 'subjects of the Crown'. As such they had rights of entry into the UK and entitlement to all the benefits enjoyed by Britons, from National Health Service treatment to social security and the vote. (The right of entry of course was successively curtailed from 1962 so that, while in 1961 Britain was open to the Commonwealth but closed to Europe, twenty years later the position was fully reversed.)

Against the background of these distinctive national contexts and histories, it is quite mistaken to single out Muslims as a particularly intractable and unco-operative group characterised by extremist politics, religious obscurantism and an unwillingness to integrate. Rather, the relation between Muslims and the wider British society and British state has to be seen in terms of the developing agendas of racial equality and multiculturalism. Muslims have become central to these agendas even while they have contested important aspects, especially the primacy of racial identities, narrow definitions of racism and equality, and the secular bias of the discourse and policies of multiculturalism. While there are now emergent Muslim discourses of equality, of difference and of, to use the title of the newsletter of the Muslim Council of Britain, 'the common good', they have to be understood as appropriations and modulations of contemporary discourses, and initiatives whose provenance lies in anti-racism and feminism.

While one result of this is to throw advocates of multiculturalism into theoretical and practical disarray, another is to stimulate accusations of cultural separatism and revive a discourse of 'integration'. While we should not ignore the critics of Muslim activism, we need to recognise that at least some of the latter is a politics of 'catching up' with racial equality and feminism. In this way, religion in Britain is assuming a renewed political importance. After a long period of hegemony, political secularism can no longer be taken for granted but is having to answer its critics; there is a growing understanding that the incorporation of Muslims has become the most important challenge of egalitarian multiculturalism.

British equality movements

The presence of new population groups in Britain made manifest certain kinds of racism, and anti-discrimination laws and policies began to be put into place from the 1960s. These provisions, initially influenced by contemporary thinking and practice in relation to anti-black racism in the United States, assume that the grounds of discrimination are 'colour' and ethnicity. Muslim assertiveness became a feature of majority–minority relations only from around the early 1990s; and indeed, prior to this, racial equality discourse and politics were dominated by the idea that the main post-immigration issue was 'colour racism'. One consequence of this is that the legal and policy framework still reflects the conceptualisation and priorities of racial dualism.

Till recently, it was lawful to discriminate against Muslims qua Muslims because the courts did not accept that Muslims were an ethnic group (though oddly, Jews and Sikhs were recognised as ethnic groups within the meaning of the law). While initially unremarked upon, this exclusive focus on race and ethnicity, and the exclusion of Muslims but not Jews and Sikhs, came to be a source of resentment. Muslims have had some limited indirect legal protection as members of ethnic groups such as Pakistanis or Arabs. Over time, groups like Pakistanis have become an active constituency within British 'race relations', whereas Middle Easterners tend to classify themselves as 'white', as in the census, and on the whole were not prominent in political activism of this sort, nor in domestic politics generally. One of the effects of this politics was to highlight race.

A key indicator of racial discrimination and inequality has been numerical under-representation, for instance in prestigious jobs and public office. Hence, people have had to be (self-)classified and counted; thus group labels, and arguments about which labels are authentic, have become a common feature of certain political discourses. Over the years, it has also become apparent through these inequality measures that it is Asian Muslims and not, as expected, African Caribbeans, who have emerged as the most disadvantaged and poorest groups in the country (Modood 1992; Modood *et al.* 1997). To many Muslim activists, the misplacing of Muslims into 'race' categories and the belatedness with which the severe disadvantages of the Pakistanis and Bangladeshis have come to be recognised mean that race relations are perceived at best as an inappropriate policy niche for Muslims, and at worst as a conspiracy to prevent the emergence of a specifically Muslim sociopolitical formation. To see how such thinking has emerged we need briefly to consider the career of the concept of 'racial equality'.

The initial development of anti-racism in Britain followed the American pattern, and indeed was directly influenced by American personalities and events. Just as in the United States the colour-blind humanism of Martin Luther King, Jr came to be mixed with an emphasis on black pride, black autonomy and black nationalism as typified by Malcolm X, so too the same process occurred in the UK (both these inspirational leaders visited Britain). Indeed, it is best to see this development of racial explicitness and positive blackness as part of a wider sociopolitical climate that is not confined to race and culture or non-white minorities. Feminism, gay pride, Québecois nationalism and the revival of a Scottish identity are some prominent examples of these new identity movements, which have become an important feature in many countries, especially those in which class politics has declined in salience; the emphasis on non-territorial identities such as black, gay and women is particularly marked among anglophones.

In fact, it would be fair to say that what is often claimed today in the name of racial equality, again especially in the English-speaking world, goes beyond the claims that were made in the 1960s. Iris Young (1992: 157) expresses well the new political climate when she describes the emergence of an ideal of equality based not just on allowing excluded groups to assimilate and live by the norms of dominant groups, but on the view that 'a positive self-definition of group difference is in fact more liberatory'.

Equality and the erosion of the public–private distinction

This significant shift takes us from an understanding of 'equality' in terms of individualism and cultural assimilation to a politics of recognition: to 'equality' as encompassing public ethnicity. This perception of equality means not having to hide or apologise for one's origins, family or community, and requires others to show respect for them. Public attitudes and arrangements must adapt so that this heritage is encouraged, not contemptuously expected to wither away.

These two conceptions of equality may be stated as follows:

- the right to assimilate to the majority/dominant culture in the public sphere, with toleration of 'difference' in the private sphere;
- the right to have one's 'difference' (minority ethnicity etc.) recognised and supported in both the public and the private spheres.

While the former represents a classical liberal response to 'difference', the latter is the view of the new identity politics. The two are not, however, alternative conceptions of equality in the sense that to hold one, the other must be rejected. Multiculturalism, properly construed, requires support for both conceptions. For the assumption behind the first is that participation in the public or national culture is necessary for the effective exercise of citizenship, the only obstacle to which are the exclusionary processes preventing gradual assimilation. The second conception, too, assumes that groups excluded from the national culture have their citizenship diminished as a result, and sees the remedy not in rejecting the right to assimilate, but in adding the right to widen and adapt the national culture, and the public and media symbols of national membership, to include the relevant minority ethnicities.

It can be seen, then, that the public–private distinction is crucial to the contemporary discussion of equal citizenship, and particularly to the challenge to an earlier liberal position. It is in this political and intellectual climate – namely, a climate in which what would earlier have been called 'private' matters had become sources of equality struggles – that Muslim assertiveness emerged as a domestic political phenomenon. In this respect, the advances achieved by anti-racism and feminism (with its slogan 'the personal is the political') acted as benchmarks for later political group entrants, such as Muslims. As I will show, while Muslims raise distinctive concerns, the logic of their demands often mirrors those of other equality-seeking groups.

Religious equality

So, one of the current conceptions of equality is a difference-affirming equality, with related notions of respect, recognition and identity – in short, what I understand by political multiculturalism. What kinds of specific policy demands, then, are being made by or on behalf of religious groups, and Muslim identity politics in particular, when these terms are deployed?

I suggest that these demands have three dimensions, which get progressively 'thicker' – and are progressively less acceptable to radical secularists.

No *religious discrimination*

The very basic demand is that religious people, no less than people defined by 'race' or gender, should not suffer discrimination in job and other opportunities. So, for example, a person who is trying to dress in accordance with their religion or who projects a religious identity (such as a Muslim woman wearing a *hijab*), should not be discriminated against in employment. Till the end of 2003 there was no legal ban on such discrimination in Britain. This is, however, only a partial 'catching-up' with the existing anti-discrimination provisions in relation to race and gender. For example, it initially did not extend to discrimination in provision of goods and services, and even now it does not create a duty upon employers to take steps to promote equality of opportunity.

Even-handedness in relation to religions

Many minority faith advocates interpret equality to mean that minority religions should get at least some of the support from the state that longer-established religions do. Muslims have led the way on this argument, and have made two particular issues politically contentious: the state funding of schools and the law of blasphemy. The government has agreed in recent years to fund a few (so far, seven) Muslim schools, as well as a Sikh and a Seventh Day Adventist school, on the same basis enjoyed by thousands of Anglican and Catholic schools and some Methodist and Jewish schools. (In England and Wales, over a third of state-maintained primary and a sixth of secondary schools are in fact run by a religious group, but all have to deliver a centrally determined national curriculum.)

Some secularists are unhappy about this. They accept the argument for parity but believe this should be achieved by the state withdrawing its funding from all religious schools. Most Muslims reject this form of equality in which the privileged lose something but the underprivileged gain nothing. More specifically, the issue between 'equalising upwards' and 'equalising downwards' here is about the legitimacy of religion as a public institutional presence.

Muslims have failed to get the courts to interpret the existing statute on blasphemy to cover offences beyond what Christians hold sacred, but some political support has been built for an offence of incitement to religious hatred, as has existed in Northern Ireland for many years, mirroring the existing one of incitement to racial hatred. (The latter extends protection to cover certain forms of anti-Jewish literature, but not anti-Muslim literature.) Indeed, such a proposal was in the Queen's Speech in October 2004, but was part of the raft of legislation that was abandoned to make way for the General Election of May 2005, before being reintroduced in the Queen's Speech in May 2005 and placed before Parliament in June. Despite the controversy that this has created, few people seem to have noticed how the law on race is already being stretched to cover religion so that anti-Muslim literature is becoming covered in the way that anti-Jewish literature has been covered for decades.[2]

Nevertheless, the government continued to have difficulties getting support for such legislation, not least from its own supporters, both inside and outside Parliament, where it especially provoked resistance from comedians, intellectuals and secularists, who feared that satire and criticism of religion were at risk (*The Sunday Times* 2004). Finally, Parliament passed a Bill in early 2006 to protect against incitement to religious hatred. Yet it was only passed after members of both houses of Parliament – supported by much of the liberal intelligentsia – forced

---

[2] The Crime and Disorder Act 1998 introduced the concept of a 'racially aggravated' offence, which covers not just the intention of an act but also its consequences. It relates primarily to acts of violence but also to amendments to the section of the Public Order Act 1986 that deals with threatening, abusive or insulting behaviour. So, the latter behaviour is not determined by intentions alone. Following 9/11, an Anti-Terrorism, Crime and Security Act was quickly passed and the phrase 'racially aggravated' extended to 'racially or religiously aggravated'. In 2003, the High Court upheld the conviction in the *Norwood* case, arguing that displaying a British National Party poster bearing the words 'Islam out of Britain' and 'Protect the British People' accompanied by a picture of the 9/11 attack on the Twin Towers amounted to an offence of causing alarm or distress. The High Court argued that evidence of actual alarm or distress was not necessary if it was determined that 'any right thinking member of society' is likely to be caused harassment, alarm or distress. It concluded, therefore, that the poster was racially insulting and, additionally, religiously aggravated. It seems then – though this is only on the basis of one case – that Muslims in Britain may have some legal protection against a version of incitement to religious hatred (for further details see *Norwood* v *DPP* [2003] All ER (D) 59, and CBMI (2002)).

the government to accept amendments that weakened its initial proposals. Unlike the incitement to religious hatred offence in Northern Ireland, and the incitement to racial hatred offence in the UK, mere offensiveness was not an offence, and moreover the incitement must require the *intention* to stir up hatred. Nevertheless, a controversy shortly after this Bill was passed showed that the media were beginning to voluntarily restrain themselves. This was the case with the Danish Muhammad cartoons affair, the cartoons being reprinted in several leading European newspapers but not by any major organ in Britain, suggesting there was a greater understanding in Britain about anti-Muslim racism and about not giving gratuitous offence to Muslims than in some other European countries (see Chapter 10).

Positive inclusion of religious groups

The demand here is that religion in general, or at least the category of 'Muslim' in particular, should be a category by which the inclusiveness of social institutions may be judged, as they increasingly are in relation to race and gender. For example, employers should have to demonstrate that they do not discriminate against Muslims by explicit monitoring of Muslims' position within the workforce, backed up by appropriate policies, targets, managerial responsibilities, work environments, staff training, advertisements, outreach and so on (FAIR 2002; CBMI 2002). Similarly, public bodies should provide appropriately sensitive policies and staff in relation to the services they provide, especially in relation to (non-Muslim) schools, social and health services; Muslim community centres or Muslim youth workers should be funded in addition to existing Asian and Caribbean community centres and Asian and black youth workers.

To take another case: the BBC currently believes it is of political importance to review and improve its personnel practices and its output of programmes, including its on-screen 'representation' of the British population, by making provision for and winning the confidence of women, ethnic groups and young people. Why should it not also use religious groups as a criterion of inclusivity and have to demonstrate that it is doing the same for viewers and staff defined by religious community membership?

In short, Muslims should be treated as a legitimate group in their own right (not because they are, say, Asians), whose presence in

British society has to be explicitly reflected in all walks of life and in all institutions; and whether they are so included should become one of the criteria for judging Britain as an egalitarian, inclusive, multicultural society. There is no prospect at present of religious equality catching up with the importance that employers and other organisations give to sex or race. A potentially significant victory, however, was made when the government agreed to include a religion question in the 2001 census. The question was voluntary but only 7 per cent did not answer it and so it has the potential to pave the way for widespread 'religious monitoring' in the way that the inclusion of an ethnic question in 1991 had led to the more routine use of 'ethnic monitoring'.

These policy demands no doubt seem odd within the terms of, say, the French or US 'wall of separation' between the state and religion, and may make secularists uncomfortable in Britain too. But it is clear that they virtually mirror existing anti-discrimination policy provisions in the UK. Moreover, Muslim assertiveness, though triggered and intensified by what are seen as attacks on Muslims, is primarily derived not from Islam or Islamism but from contemporary western ideas about equality and multiculturalism. While simultaneously reacting to the latter in its failure to distinguish Muslims from the rest of the 'black' population and its uncritical secular bias, Muslims positively use, adapt and extend these contemporary western ideas in order to join other equality-seeking movements. Political Muslims do, therefore, have an ambivalence in relation to multicultural discourses. On the one hand, as a result of previous misrecognition of their identity, and existing biases, there is distrust of 'the race relations industry' and of 'liberals'; on the other hand, the assertiveness is clearly a product of the positive climate created by liberals and egalitarians (Modood 2005). This ambivalence can tend towards antagonism as the assertiveness is increasingly being joined by Islamic discourses and Islamists. Especially, as has been said, there is a sense that Muslim populations across the world are repeatedly suffering at the hands of their neighbours, aided and abetted by the United States and its allies, and that Muslims must come together to defend themselves. There is a useful analogy with the black power movement here, not just in its internationalism, but one can say that as black nationalism and Afrocentrism developed as one ideological expression of black power, so, similarly, we can see political Islamism as a search for Muslim dignity and power.

A panicky retreat to a liberal public–private distinction

If the emergence of a politics of difference out of and alongside a liberal assimilationist equality created a dissonance, as indeed it did, the emergence of a British Muslim identity out of and alongside ethno-racial identities has created an even greater dissonance. Philosophically speaking, it should create a lesser dissonance, for a move from the idea of equality as sameness to equality as difference is a more profound conceptual movement than the creation of a new identity in a field already crowded with minority identities. But to infer this is to naively ignore the hegemonic power of secularism in British political culture, especially on the centre-left. While black and related ethno-racial identities were welcomed by, indeed were intrinsic to, the rainbow coalition of identity politics, this coalition is deeply unhappy with Muslim consciousness. While for some this rejection is specific to Islam, for many the ostensible reason is that it is a politicised religious identity. What is most interesting is that in this latter objection, if it is taken at its face value, the difference theorists, activists and paid professionals revert to a public–private distinction that they have spent two or three decades demolishing.

We thus have a mixed-up situation where secular multiculturalists may argue that the sex lives of individuals – traditionally, a core area of liberal privacy – are a legitimate feature of political identities and public discourse, and seem to generally welcome the sexualisation of culture, while on the other hand religion – a key source of communal identity in traditional, non-liberal societies – is to be regarded as a private matter, perhaps as a uniquely private matter. Most specifically, Muslim identity is seen as the illegitimate child of British multiculturalism. Indeed, the Rushdie affair made evident that the group in British society most politically opposed to (politicised) Muslims weren't Christians, or even right-wing nationalists, but the secular, liberal intelligentsia.[3]

Just as the hostility against Jews, in various times and places, has been a varying blend of anti-Judaism (hostility to a religion) and anti-Semitism

---

[3] The large Policy Studies Institute Fourth Survey found that nominal Christians and those without a religion were more likely to say they were prejudiced against Muslims than those Christians who said their religion was of importance to them (Modood 1997a: 134).

(hostility to a racialised group), so it is difficult to gauge to what extent contemporary British Islamophobia is 'religious' and to what extent 'racial'. Even before 11 September and its aftermath, it was generally becoming acknowledged that of all groups Asians face the greatest hostility today, and Asians themselves feel this is because of hostility directed towards Muslims (Modood 2005). These matters are not at all easy to disentangle and have hardly been researched at all, and anti-Muslim racism is only just beginning to be acknowledged by anti-racists. One has also to acknowledge that there must be analytical space for forthright criticism of aspects of Muslim doctrines, ideologies and practice without its being dismissed as Islamophobia – this being a parallel problem to, say, distinguishing anti-Zionism and anti-Semitism.

Is religious equality a lesser equality?

The multiculturalism or politics of difference that I have been advocating has four major implications for liberal citizenship. First, it is clearly a collective project and concerns collectivities and not just individuals. Second, it is not colour-/gender-/sexual-orientation-'blind', and so breaches the liberal public–private identity distinction, which prohibits the recognition of particular group identities so that no citizens are treated in a more or less privileged way or divided from each other.

Third, it takes race, sex and sexuality beyond being merely ascriptive sources of identity, merely categories. Race is of interest to liberal citizenship only because no one can choose their race and so should not be discriminated against on something over which they have no control. But if equality is about celebrating previously demeaned identities (e.g. in taking pride in one's blackness rather than in accepting it merely as a 'private' matter), then what is being addressed in anti-discrimination, or promoted as a public identity, is a chosen response to one's ascription. Exactly the same applies to sex and sexuality. We may not choose our sex or sexual orientation but we choose how to politically live with it. Do we keep it private or do we make it the basis of a social movement and seek public resources and representation for it?

Now Muslims and other religious groups are utilising this kind of argument, and making a claim that religious identity, just like gay identity, and just like certain forms of racial identity, should not just be privatised or tolerated, but should be part of the public space. In their case, however, they come into conflict with an additional fourth dimension of liberal citizenship that we can refer to as secularism: the view that religion is a feature, perhaps uniquely, of private and not public identity.

The response that woman, black and gay are ascribed, unchosen identities while being a Muslim is about chosen beliefs, and that Muslims therefore need or ought to have less legal protection than the other kinds of identities, is sociologically naive and a political con. The position of Muslims in Britain today is similar to the other identities of 'difference' as Muslims catch up with and engage with the contemporary concept of equality. No one chooses to be or not to be born into a Muslim family. Similarly, no one chooses to be born into a society where to look like a Muslim or to be a Muslim creates suspicion, hostility or failure to get the job you applied for. Though how Muslims respond to these circumstances will vary. Some will organise resistance, while others will try to stop looking like Muslims (the equivalent of 'passing' for white); some will build an ideology out of their subordination, others will not, just as a woman can choose to be a feminist or not. Again, some Muslims may define their Islam in terms of piety rather than politics – just as some women may see no politics in their gender, while for others their gender will be at the centre of their politics.

Those who see the current Muslim assertiveness as an unwanted and illegitimate child of multiculturalism have only two choices if they wish to be consistent. They can repudiate the idea of equality as identity recognition and return to the 1960s liberal idea of equality as colour-/sex-/religion- etc. blindness. Or they can argue that equality as recognition does not apply to oppressed religious communities, perhaps uniquely not to religious communities. To deny Muslims positive equality without one of these two arguments is to be open to the charge of double standards.

Hence a programme of racial and multicultural equality is not possible today without a discussion of the merits and limits of secularism. Secularism can no longer be treated as 'off-limits', or, as President Jacques Chirac said in a major speech in 2004, 'non-negotiable' (Cesari 2004: 166). Not that it is really a matter of being for or against secularism, but rather a careful, institution-by-institution analysis of how to draw the public–private boundary and further the cause of multicultural equality and inclusivity.

Secularism: different public–private boundaries in different countries

At the heart of secularism is a distinction between the public realm of citizens and policies, and the private realm of belief and worship. While all western countries are clearly secular in many ways, interpretations and the institutional arrangements diverge according to the dominant national religious culture and the differing projects of nation-state building, and thus make secularism a 'particular' experience.

For example, the United States has as its First Amendment to the Constitution that there shall be no established church; there is wide support for this and in the last few decades there has been a tendency among academics and jurists to interpret the church–state separation in continually more radical ways (Sandel 1994; Hamburger 2002). Yet, as is well known, not only is the USA a deeply religious society, with much higher levels of church attendance than in western Europe (Greeley 1995), but there is a strong Protestant, evangelical fundamentalism that is rare in Europe. This fundamentalism disputes some of the new radical interpretations of the 'no establishment clause', though not necessarily the clause itself, and is one of the primary mobilising forces in American politics: it is widely claimed that it decided the presidential election of 2004. The churches in question – mainly white, mainly in the south and mid-west – campaign openly for candidates and parties, indeed raise large sums of money for politicians and introduce religion-based issues into politics, such as positions on abortion, HIV/AIDS, homosexuality, stem-cell research, prayer at school and so on. It has been said that no openly avowed atheist has ever been a candidate for the White House and that it would be impossible for such a candidate to be elected. It is not at all unusual for politicians – in fact, for President George W. Bush, it was most usual – to publicly talk about their faith, to appeal to religion and to hold prayer meetings in government buildings. On the other hand, in establishment Britain, bishops sit in the upper chamber of the legislature by right and only the senior Archbishop can crown a new head of state, the monarch, but politicians rarely talk about their religion. It was noticeable, for example, that when Prime Minister

Table 7.1 *Religion vis-à-vis state and civil society in three countries*[a]

	State	Religion in civil society
England/Britain	Weak establishment but churches have a political voice	Weak but churches can be a source of political criticism and action
United States	No establishment	Strong and politically mobilised
France	Actively secular but offers top–down recognition	Weak; rare for churches to be political

[a] Adapted from Modood and Kastoryano (2006)

Blair went to a summit meeting with President Bush to discuss aspects of the Iraq war in 2003, the US media widely reported that the two leaders had prayed together. Yet, Prime Minister Blair, one of the most openly professed and active Christians ever to hold that office, refused to answer questions on this issue from the British media on his return, saying it was a private matter. The British state may have an established church but the beliefs of the Queen's first Minister are his own concern.

France draws the distinction between state and religion differently again. Like the USA there is no state church, but unlike the USA the state actively promotes the privatisation of religion. While in the USA, organised religion in civil society is powerful and seeks to exert influence on the political process, French civil society does not carry signs or expressions of religion. Yet the French state, contrary to the USA, confers institutional legal status on the Catholic and Protestant churches and on the Jewish Consistory, albeit carefully designating organised religions as '*cultes*' and not communities. We might want to express these three different national manifestations of secularism as in Table 7.1. So, what are the appropriate limits of the state? Everyone will agree that there should be religious freedom and that this should include freedom of belief and worship in private associations. Family too falls on the private side of the line but the state regulates the limits of what is a lawful family – for example, polygamy is not permitted in many countries – not to mention the deployment of official definitions of family in the distribution of welfare entitlements. Religions typically put a premium on mutuality and on care of the sick, the homeless, the elderly and so on. They set up organisations to pursue these aims, but so do states. Should there be a competitive or a co-operative relationship between these religious and state organisations, or do they have to ignore each other? Can public money – raised out of taxes on religious as well as non-religious citizens – not be used to support the organisations favoured by some religious taxpayers? What of schools? Do parents not have the right to expect that schools will make an effort – while pursuing broader educational and civic aims – not to create a conflict between the work of the school and the upbringing of the children at home but, rather, show respect for their religious background? Can parents, as associations of religious citizens, not set up their own schools and should those schools not be supported out of the taxes of the same parents? Is the school where the private (the family) meets the public (the state); or is it, in some Platonic manner, where the state takes over the children from the family and pursues its own purposes? Even if there is to be no established church, the state may still wish to work with organised religion as a social partner, as is the case in Germany, or to have some forum in which it consults with organised religion – some kind of national council of religions – as in Belgium. Or, even if it does not do that because it is regarded as compromising the principle of secularism, political parties, being agents in civil society rather than organs of the state, may wish to do this and institute special representation for religious groups as many do for groups defined by age, gender, region, language, ethnicity and so on. It is clear then that the 'public' is a multi-faceted concept and in relation to secularism may be defined differently than in relation to different dimensions of religion and in different countries.

We can all be secularists then, all approve of secularism in some respect, and yet have quite different ideas, influenced by historical legacies and varied pragmatic compromises, of where to draw the line between public and private. It would be quite mistaken to suppose that all religious spokespersons, or at least all political Muslims, are on one side of the line, and all others are on the other side. There are many different ways of drawing the various lines at issue. In the past, the drawing of them has reflected particular contexts shaped by differential customs, urgency of need and sensitivity to the sensibilities of the relevant religious groups (Modood 1994; 1997a). Exactly the same considerations are relevant in relation to the accommodation of Muslims in Europe today – not a battle of slogans and ideological over-simplifications.

Moderate secularism as an implication of multicultural equality

Multicultural equality, then, when applied to religious groups, means that secularism *simpliciter* appears to be an obstacle to pluralistic integration and equality. But secularism pure and simple is not what exists in the world. The country-by-country situation is more complex and, indeed, far less inhospitable to the accommodation of Muslims than the ideology of secularism – or, for that matter, the ideology of anti-secularism – might suggest (Modood and Kastoryano 2006). All actual practices of secularism consist of institutional compromises and these can, should be and are being extended to accommodate Muslims. The institutional reconfiguration varies according to the historic place of religion in each country. Today the appropriate response to the new Muslim challenges is pluralistic institutional integration, rather than an appeal to a radical public–private separation in the name of secularism. The approach that is being argued for here, then, consists of:

1. A reconceptualisation of equality from sameness to an incorporation of a respect for difference;
2. A reconceptualisation of secularism from the concepts of neutrality and the strict public–private divide to a moderate and evolutionary secularism based on institutional adjustments;
3. A pragmatic, case-by-case, negotiated approach to dealing with controversy and conflict: not an ideological, 'drawing a line in the sand' mentality.

This institutional integration approach is based on including Islam into the institutional framework of the state, using the historical accommodation between state and church as a basis for negotiations in order to achieve consensual resolutions consistent with equality and justice. As these accommodations have varied from country to country, it means there is no exemplary solution, for contemporary solutions too will depend on the national context and will not have a once-and-for-all-time basis. It is clearly a dialogical perspective and assumes the possibility of mutual education and learning. Like all negotiation and reform, there are normative as well as practical limits. Aspects of the former have been usefully characterised by Bhikhu Parekh as 'society's operative public values' (Parekh 2000: 267). These values, such as equality between the sexes, are embedded in the political constitution, in specific laws and in the norms governing the civic relations in a society. Norms, laws and constitutional principles concerning the appropriate place of religion in public life generally and in specific policy areas (such as schools or rehabilitation of criminals) consist of such public values and are reasoned about, justified or criticised by reference to specific values about religion/politics as well as more general norms and values in a society, such as fairness, or balance, or consensus and so on. I, therefore, recognise that the approach recommended here involves solutions that are highly contextual and practical but that they are far from arbitrary or without reference to values. While the latter are not static because they are constantly being reinterpreted, realigned, extended and reformed, nevertheless they provide a basis for dialogue and agreement.

An example is the development of a religious equality agenda in Britain, including the incorporation of some Muslim schools on the same basis as schools of religions with a much longer presence. It also includes the recommendations of the Royal Commission on the Reform of the House of Lords (2000) that in addition to the Anglican bishops who sit in that House by right as part of the Anglican 'establishment', this right should be extended to cover those of other Christian and non-Christian faiths. The same point can be made in relation to the fact that as early as 1974 the Belgian state decided to include Islam within its Council of Religions as a full member, or to the way that Muslims in the Netherlands have long had state-funded religious schools and television channels as a progressive step in that country's traditional way of institutionally dealing with organised religion: namely, 'pillarisation'.[4] Similarly, a 'Muslim community' is becoming recognised by public authorities in Germany by appealing to the historic German idea of a 'religious society' (*Religionsgesellschaft*).

---

[4] This principle, which recognised that Protestants and Catholics had a right to state resources and to some publicly funded autonomous institutions, officially ended in 1960. It is, however, still considered as a 'relevant framework for the development of a model that grants certain collective rights to religious groups' (Sunier and von Luijeren (2002)) in such matters as state funding of Islamic schools. So, the accommodation of Muslims is being achieved through a combination of mild pillarisation and Dutch minority policies.

Again, a series of French Interior Ministers have taken a number of steps to 'normalise' Islam in France by creating an official French Islam under the authority of the state in ways that make it identical to other faiths (for more on these cases, see Modood and Kastoryano (2006); also Cesari (2004)).

The recognition of Islam in Europe can, as some of these examples suggest, take a corporatist form, can be led or even imposed by the state in a 'top–down' way and can take a church or ecclesiastical model as its form. This may be appropriate for certain countries or at certain moments and could be – usually is – consistent with the conception of multiculturalism I have outlined. However, it would not be my own preference, for it would not represent the British multicultural experience and its potentialities at its best. A corporatist inclusion would require Muslims and their representatives to speak in one voice and to create a unified, hierarchical structure when this is out of character in Sunni Islam, especially the south Asian Sunni Islam espoused by the majority of Muslims in Britain, and of the contemporary British Muslim scene. Corporatism would very likely consist of state control of the French kind, with the state imposing its own template, plans, modes of partnership, and chosen imams and leaders upon Muslims. One mode of recognition is for the new minority faiths such as Islam to be represented in relation to the state by their spiritual leaders like the Anglican Church is by its bishops, or even, indeed, as the Catholic Church is in Britain. For while the Catholic Church is not an established church it has a clear relationship with the British, especially English, state (e.g. it is the single biggest beneficiary of state funding of faith schools) and it is its ecclesiastical hierarchy that is taken to be speaking for Catholics.

My own preference is for an approach that would be less corporatist, less statist and less churchy – in brief, less French. An approach in which civil society played a greater role would be more comfortable with there being a variety of Muslim voices, groups and representatives. Different institutions, organisations and associations would seek to accommodate Muslims in ways that worked for them best at a particular time, knowing that these ways may or ought to be modified over time, and that Muslim and other pressure groups and civic actors may be continually evolving their claims and agendas. Within a general understanding that there had to be an explicit effort to include Muslims (and other marginal and under-represented groups) different organisations – like my earlier example of the BBC – might not just seek this inclusion in different ways but would seek as representatives Muslims that seemed to them most appropriate associates and part-ners, persons who would add something to the organisation and were not merely delegated from a central, hierarchical Muslim body. The idea of numerical or 'mirror' representation of the population might be a guideline but it would not necessarily follow that some kind of quota allocation (a mild version of the corporatist tendency) would have to operate. Improvisation, flexibility, consultation, learning by 'suck it and see' and by the example of others, incrementalism and all the other virtues of a pragmatic politics in close touch with a dynamic civil society, can as much and perhaps better bring about multicultural equality than a top–down corporatist inclusion. 'Representation' here would mean the inclusion of a diversity of backgrounds and sens-ibilities, not delegates or corporate structures. Recognition, then, must be pragmatically and experimentally handled, and civil society must share the burden of representation.

While the state may seek to ensure that spiritual leaders are not absent from public forums and consultative processes in relation to policies affecting their flocks, it may well be that a Board of Jewish Deputies model of community representation offers a better illustra-tion of a community–state relationship. The Board of Deputies, a body independent of, but a communal partner to, the British state, is a federation of Jewish organisations that includes synagogues but also other Jewish community organisations, and its leadership typically consists of lay persons whose standing and skill in representing their community are not diminished by any absence of spiritual authority. It is most interesting that while at some local levels Muslim organisa-tions have chosen to create political bodies primarily around mosques (eg. the Bradford Council of Mosques), at a national level it is the Board of Deputies model that seems to be more apparent. This is certainly the case with the single most representative and successful national Muslim organisation, the Muslim Council of Britain (MCB), whose office-holders and spokespersons are more likely to be char-tered accountants and solicitors than imams. Most mosques in Britain are run by local lay committees, and the mullah or imam is a usually a minor functionary.[5] Very few of those who aspire to be Muslim

---

[5] The MCB's pre-eminence began to suffer from the mid-2000s, as it grew increasingly critical of the invasions of Iraq and of the so-called war on terror. The government started accusing it of failing to clearly and decisively reject

spokespersons and representatives have religious authority and are not expected to have it by fellow Muslims. So the accommodation of religious groups is as much if not more about the recognition and support of communities rather than necessarily about ecclesiastical or spiritual representation in political institutions. The state has a role here, which includes ensuring that Muslim civil society is drawn into the mainstream as much as it is to seek forms of representation within state structures.

In my preferred approach it would be quite likely that different kinds of groups – Muslims, Hindus and Catholics for instance, let alone women, gays and different ethnic minority groups – might choose to organise in different ways and to relate to key civic and political institutions in different ways. While each might look over its shoulder at what other groups are doing or getting and use any such precedents to formulate its own claims, we should on this approach not require symmetry but be able to live with some degree of 'variable geometry'. I am unable to specify what this degree of flexibility might be but it should be clear that sensitivity to the specific religious, cultural and socioeconomic needs in a specific time, place and political context is critical to multiculturalism. This indeterminacy leaves something to be desired but I hope it is evident that it can be a strength too. It also underlines that multiculturalism is not a comprehensive political theory but can and must sit alongside other political values and be made to work with varied institutional, national and historical contexts.

Conclusion

The emergence of Muslim political agency has thrown British multiculturalism into theoretical and practical disarray. It has led to policy reversals in the Netherlands and elsewhere, and across Europe has strengthened intolerant, exclusive nationalism. We should in fact be moving the other way and enacting the kinds of legal and policy measures that are necessary to accommodate Muslims as equal citizens

extremism and sought alternative Muslim interlocutors. With the realisation that no simple Muslim organisation was fully reflective of non-jihadi Muslims, the government seems to have readmitted the MCB back into the fold but now as only part of a plurality.

in European polities. These would include anti-discrimination measures in areas such as employment, positive action to achieve a full
and just political representation of Muslims in various areas of public
life, the inclusion of Muslim history as European history and so on.
Critically, I have been arguing that the inclusion of Islam as an
organised religion and of Muslim identity as a public identity are
necessary to integrate Muslims and to pursue religious equality. While
this inclusion runs against certain interpretations of secularism, it is
not inconsistent with what secularism means in practice in Europe.
We should let this evolving, moderate secularism and the spirit of
compromise it represents be our guide. Unfortunately, an ideological
secularism is currently being reasserted and is generating European
domestic versions of 'the clash of civilisations' thesis and the conflicts
that entails for European societies. That some people are today
developing secularism as an ideology to oppose Islam and its public
recognition is a challenge both to pluralism and equality, and thus to
some of the bases of contemporary democracy. It has to be resisted no
less than the radical anti-secularism of some Islamists.

8 | *Contemporary politics of secularism*

S. SAYYID

In an article on secularism and relativism, Akeel Bilgrami (2004: 174) writes:

It seems more and more urgent to declare oneself a secularist (and I hereby do so) in a time when wars are waged by a government dominated by thinking of the Christian Right, terror is perpetuated in the name of Islam, occupation of territories of continuously displaced population is perpetuated by a state constituted in explicitly Jewish terms and a beleaguered minority is killed in planned riots by majoritarian mobilization reviving an imagined Hindu glory.

It is possible to situate Bilgrami's intervention within the contemporary discourse on secularism.[1]

The logic of this discourse can clearly be seen from Bilgrami's quotation: a chain of equivalence is established between the Christian Right, Islamists, Hinduvata advocates and ultra-Zionists, as all exemplifying the menacing forces that are opposed by secularists. It is this logic that allows statements belonging to contemporary secularism to be produced, distributed and consumed even though it would be possible to point to many elisions and inconsistencies by which these statements and practices are put together in the first place. For example, to see in the Israeli occupation and repression of Palestinians

---

[1] By discourse, I mean a set of practices and statements constructed through a variety of sites that are identified not by reference to the same object, a shared style, a common set of concepts or persistent theme, but rather by a structured (i.e. non-random) relationship between statements and practices, and a frontier around which these practices and statements are arranged (Foucault 1974: 2; Hall 1992: 291–2). The point of analysing a discursive formation is not to find the 'real' truth hidden by various discontinuities in a specific discourse, but to examine the way in which a particular discourse relates to the institution of social order and identities (Lefort 1986). In this sense, the contemporary discourse on secularism constructs a world order in terms of a dichotomy between those who reject secularism and those who favour it.

a purely religious legitimacy, one would want the Zionist state to be justified in at least mainly Judaic, rather than Jewish, terms. Or is it really the case that the 'planned riots' of India are simply an offshoot of the expansion of Hinduvata, and were absent during the height of Nerhuvian (secular) hegemony? Is it also the case that the instances of large-scale violence (wars, 'terrorism', occupation and riots) are exclusive to religions? Could we not draw up another list in which starring roles in the perpetuation of great cruelty and violence would rightly go to secularist actors?

There is, however, another common thread suggested by Bilgrami – Islam and Muslims feature in all the cases he cites ('War on Terror', 'terrorism in the name of Islam', Zionist occupation and pogroms in India). This is not mere idiosyncrasy on his part. In this chapter, I want to explore the way in which secularism is deployed in relation to Muslims and Islam.

Secularism and the West

Secularism in its simplest and most widely circulated form calls for a de facto if not de jure separation between religion and politics. The forceful reassertion of Islam in the public sphere throughout the world is currently presented as one of the most significant challenges to the story of progressive global secularisation.[2] Recent debates in western plutocracies have focused on Muslim minorities as in need of secularisation. The overlaying of issues of secularisation with questions of how to include ethnically marked, often ex-colonial populations has helped to reinforce and, in some cases, reactivate discursive equivalences between national majorities, the current Westphalian world order and secularism. The 'problem' of Muslim minorities raises not only public policy questions about how to manage relations between a national majority and an ethnically marked 'minority' (Sayyid 2004; Hesse and Sayyid 2006), but also more general 'ideological' questions

---

[2] This is not to deny that, in recent years, secularism in the United States, at least, has been primarily discussed in terms of the separation of church and state, and largely in the context of cultural and political advances made by the Christian Right. It would be fair to say, however, that with the advent of the 'War on Terror' as the grammar of global governance, the discussion of secularism as a problem for the world is increasingly inflected through Islamicate examples and instances.

about the extent to which the 'final vocabulary' (Rorty 1989: 73) of the western enterprise is adequate to the task of including Muslims and, at the same time, preventing the subversion of that enterprise.

Secularism is presented as one of the key achievements of western cultural formations. Its supposed benefits can be grouped into three broad headings. First, there is a set of *epistemological* arguments based around the claim that without secularism there can be no scientific progress, and without scientific progress there could be no technological advances. In this sense, secularism as an epistemological category rather than a social one can be described as denoting a shift from an episteme centred on God to one centred on Man (*sic*). The core of the argument is that secularism delegitimates the claims of religious authorities to control the production of knowledge, and creates the conditions for the rejection of ontological claims found in sacred narratives in favour of a scientifically approved ontology.

A second cluster of arguments emphasises the *civic benefits* of secularism. It argues that secularism is necessary to ensure peace and social harmony and to prevent religious passions from getting out of hand. By separating religion and confining it to the private sphere, secularism prevents differences in religious opinions from becoming the source of conflicts that would engulf a society's public space. Religious differences become matters of individual taste and therefore have little impact upon the organisation of social life at large. In addition, secularism prevents contending groups from making appeals to supernatural forces as a way of reinforcing their positions, and keeps all parties on a level playing field in which debate cannot be short-circuited by such appeals.

Third, it is argued that secularism presents the necessary precondition for the *exercise of democracy*, which, following Lefort's (1986: 279) useful understanding, is based on keeping the space of power empty. The removal of God allows the space of power to be emptied. On this account, democracy is government that is ultimately based on the idea of the 'sovereignty of the people' – regardless of how this idea is expressed in reality. (For example in Britain it is Parliament that is sovereign, not the people; however, the power of Parliament derives from the people.) Popular sovereignty seems to preclude any place for the idea of a sovereign God or sovereign priesthood.

Thus, the benefits of secularism help to define modernity itself. Modernity, of course, remains a narrative about western exceptionality (Sayyid 2003 [1997]: 101–2), thus secularism becomes a marker of western identity. The epistemological, civic and democratic arguments for secularism are formulated as part of a narrative of western exceptionality. Therefore, the articulation of a Muslim subject position within the context of the ethnoscapes of western countries presents a peculiar challenge to western identity. Muslims come to represent anti-secularism simply because the designation of Muslim is interpreted as referring to a religious subject position. The emergence of this subject position within the public spaces of western plutocracies, therefore, seems to erode the divide that secularism seeks to institutionalise. The reactivation of a translocal Muslim consciousness has the effect of bringing to the fore the counterfactual nature of Islam vis-à-vis the West (e.g. Davies 2006: 203–5). Thus, the lack of secularism in Islam is contrasted with the presence of secularism in the West, where this contrast helps to confirm the necessity and importance of secularism if a civilisation is to prosper. In contrasting western and Islamicate civilisations, advocates of secularism find Islam wanting, and that deficiency is partly explained by suggesting that the failure of secularism to be established in the Islamicate world doomed Islam to failure. Islam, however, does not only exist as a mere counterhistory; it also circulates among Muslims as a marker of distinct historical and cultural formations in its own right, and, as such, the attempt to present the benefits of secularism as of universal significance founders. In other words, the shift from western to Islamicate societies seemingly undermines the universal claims for secularism.

Secularism and Muslims

It is increasingly the case that Muslim communities appear as the most prominent groups of people who seemingly do not accept the claims of secularism.[3] Partly, this is due to the way in which western history and Islamicate history have different things to say about the necessity of secularism or otherwise. Specifically, the applicability of the three main arguments for secularism and their relevance for Muslims can be challenged by focusing on the experience of autonomous Islamicate

---

[3] Of course, this is not to deny that some Muslims accept the claims of secularism. In fact, in the wake of the global dirty war, many Muslim organisations have emerged in western plutocracies that advocate secular or moderate Islam, e.g. Progressive Muslims and Muslims for Secular Democracy. It is fair to say, however, that many more Muslims are critical of aspects of secularism.

cultural formations: that is, those cultural formations that existed prior to the colonial transformation of the planet.

The problem with the claims made on behalf of secularism is that they are very often conducted through a discourse of 'westernese': that is, western historical developments are seen as having universal relevance. Thus secularism in the West is not seen as a contingent development arising out of the specific history of the West, but as a necessary condition arising out of the unfolding of history itself. Secularism becomes then a necessary stage that all cultural formations have to pass through if they are to progress towards modernity. There are, however, good reasons for questioning whether the three major arguments made for the benefit of secularism have a general significance that extends beyond societies and cultures that trace their genealogy to Europe.

The epistemological case for secularism rests upon a conflict between science and church – a conflict symbolised by the trials of Galileo. The absence of an organised church made such clear demarcations between the authority of religion and science difficult to draw within Islamicate societies. More importantly, perhaps, the epistemological case for the benefits of secularism rests on the assumption that the understanding of the Divine in Islamic and Christian discourses is homologous.

Christological and Islamicate discourses on the Divine should not be seen as essential or foundational, since differences in reflection on the Divine indicate contingent conversations within diverse hermeneutic traditions, and not the uncovering of specific essences that are 'hard-wired' within Christianity or Islam. Nevertheless, it may be useful to point to the different positions on the nature of divinity that can be teased out once all proper qualifications have been made concerning the complexity of the topic and the diversity of opinions about it. For example, many of the early Christian sectarian disputes often had a Christological dimension, such as the controversies between those who accepted the interpretations of the Council of Chaledon, and those who did not, such as the Arians, Nestorians and Monophysites. The dominance of this Chaledonian interpretation helped produce a conception of the Divine and the mundane in which both seemingly occupy the same plane. The conjoining of human and Divine spheres as described through the category of incarnation, in which Divine and human fuse in the body of Christ, helped to sustain a perspective in which human endeavour could be seen as potentially competing with the Divine. In other words, the Divine and the human come to be locked in a zero-sum game. As a consequence science and religion continually collide.

In hegemonic Islamic interpretations, the distinction between the Divine and the human cannot be bridged. Islamic reflections on the nature of the Divine have been fairly consistent in maintaining the gap between human and Divine spheres, a gap that is wide and permanent. Therefore, no human enterprise can appropriate or displace the centrality of the Divine, since the human and Divine can be said to exist in distinct ontological realms that cannot be conflated. Thus, all human attempts to know cannot bridge the gap between the human and Divine. Human knowledge cannot become a replacement for narratives of Divine causality, since such narratives describe things that cannot strictly speaking occupy the same ontological space.

The case for secularism as necessary for civic peace is largely based on extrapolating from the European experiences of the wars of the Reformation and Counter-Reformation to make a general point about the relationship between civic peace and depoliticisation of religious belief. (It is important to bear in mind that conflict between the forces of Reformation and Counter-Reformation was an internal conflict; the incompatibility between the two positions was a product of the process of polemicisation that led to the conflict and was not due to prior incommensurability. It could be argued that incommensurability can, in many circumstances, act like a fire-break and help dampen conflict by limiting the space of a common ground. After all, without a common ground there cannot be a battlefield.)

The hundred years of religious wars between Reformation and Counter-Reformation have no serious analogue in Islamicate history. Perhaps the closest approximation is the conflict between the Fatimids and Abbassids; however, the infrastructural capacity of neither the Abbassid nor the Fatimid political order was sufficient to produce such an intensive form of violence as experienced in the hundred-year wars of religion in Europe.[4] This does not mean that Islamicate societies were immune to sectarian warfare, but rather that sectarian

---

[4] To be sure, there are many other cases in which conflict between the various groupings within Islamicate history took a decidedly sectarian turn. The point, however, is that the centuries-long struggle between Protestants and Catholics is not the best template by which to understand the formation and disputation of sects within an Islamicate context.

conflict was never on such a scale or intensity that Muslims had to draw the conclusion that civic peace is only possible if religion is confined to the private sphere. Indeed, if anything, the very opposite suggests itself: the retreat of religion from the public sphere in Islamicate history has been most often associated with the breakdown of civic peace. The oft admired secularist order in Turkey, for example, was imposed from the top upon an exhausted, war-weary population. The compulsory and coercive secularism of the Turkish Republic was not a response to the demands of the Turkish masses but proceeds rather from the authoritarian project of the Kemalists to westernise Turkey (Sayyid 2003 [1997]). Secularism in the context of Islamicate communities has often meant de-Islamisation, and has for the most part been imposed either by colonial regimes or Kemalist governments. Such projects have all served to increase rather than reduce social conflict. Empirically, the scale and intensity of violence in Muslim countries that have been ruled by avowedly secular regimes has been such that it would not inspire much confidence in the association between secularism and civic peace.

The argument that secularism is a necessary precondition for any political system of popular sovereignty ignores the multiplicity of possible ways in which popular sovereignty can be finessed: for example, diverse constitutional monarchies, or even the suggestion by Mawdudi and others, who re-described popular will as vice-regal rather than sovereign. In other words, the sovereignty of the Divine is an elaboration of the centrality of God to the cosmos, but cannot be a practical sovereignty in the sense suggested by Carl Schmitt (that 'the sovereign is who decides upon the exception'), if for no other reason than because the idea of a monotheistic version of the omnipotent and omniscient God does not allow for the Divine to have any exception.[5] The argument that Islamists enter a logical cul-de-sac when they advocate popular sovereignty without abandoning the notion of sovereignty of God has been most elegantly argued by Olivier Roy (1994). Using the example of the Islamic Republic of Iran, Roy contends that there is a logical contradiction at the heart of the political system established by Imam Khomeini, in which legitimacy of the regimes is based on both democratic and theocratic principles. The logical

---

[5] There are of course other reasons, including the difficulty of actually knowing what a particular Divine decision is.

contradiction that Roy sees, however, is a reflection of his assumption that the nature of the Divine and its relationship to human agency must function in an Islamicate context as it does in western history.

It would seem that the meaning of secularism is perhaps to be found in its inclusion within westernese. Precisely because the articulation of a global Muslim subjectivity contributes to the provincialisation of Europe's final vocabulary, it threatens to reveal the Plato-to-NATO sequence as a hegemonic, historiographical convention rather than history itself. In the context of Muslims living in western plutocracies, the staples of the 'immigrant' imaginary become strained, as categories such as religion, minority, 'race' etc. are seen more and more as part of the Plato-to-NATO sequence rather than descriptions of objectivity (Sayyid 2004). This suggests that the validity of this sequence rests upon the exercise of coloniality. Coloniality is not to be understood merely in the sense of colonialism, but rather refers to the logic of governmentality that not only supports specific forms of historical colonialism but continues to structure a planetary hierarchy in terms of a distinction between West and the non-West (and its various cognates) beyond the formal institutionalisation of colonialism (Mignolo 2005: 7; Hesse and Sayyid 2006).

Secularism and India

An effort to circumvent some of the objections about the ethnocentric nature of the arguments for secularism is to try and broaden the applicability of secularism. Secularism is broadened *diachronically* to argue that it is not a Westphalian invention, and *synchronically* to argue that it has non-European cognates. The historical broadening consists of finding instances of political structures that are not of the Westphalian family. This means having to show that empires, the most durable pre-nation-state political structures, were secular, and that Muslimistan, in particular, has its own inherent secularism. Such a view is bolstered by reference to various *ahadith* that demonstrate that the Prophet (*pbuh*) himself made a distinction between decisions and actions made as a consequence of Divine revelations, and those based on the application of human knowledge and reason. Such a division, however, becomes more problematic in the post-Prophetic context, since it would confine the religious to the receipt of Divine revelations, and if Muslims were to accept this division, it would follow that by definition everything in the post-Prophetic era would be secular. Thus, division between the secular and religious would collapse as the secular, for all intents and purposes, would colonise the religious. Such a position could only be sustained by a circular reasoning, in which the division between religious and secular must be articulated by the hegemony of secularism. Religion, in other words, becomes a category generated by secularism. Secularism, of course, has its own history within the western Enlightenment. Thus, attempts to expand its temporal reach can only be sustained by presenting the reading of this particular history of the West as the history of the world. Rather than making the case for non-Eurocentric antecedents for secularism, then, the introduction of the religious–secular divide into the historiography of other societies only further reinscribes the supremacy of westernese. An approach in which a conception of secularism culled from European history is then applied to non-European cases, and which (not surprisingly) finds serious anomalies, is not adequate. Such an approach reinforces the idea of secularism as essentially European.

Another way of getting around the European parochialism of secularism is to make the case for secularism in non-western societies. Indian secularism seems to provide an example of such a possibility, as Rajeev Bhargava well elaborates (Chapter 4).[6] Of course, it could be argued that Indian secularism has clear western roots. Modern India, as an heir to the British Raj, 'internalised' many of the practices of colonial governance, including the manner in which the populations of the region were represented and regulated through the idea of distinct religious communities (Inden 1990; King 1999; Mandair 2006). It is also the case that Nehru's emphasis on secularism for India – as a means of dealing with the religious question in the context of the Pakistan movement – reflects a western perspective. As Judith Brown (2000) points out, Nehru mainly knew India from Indology. The genealogy of secularism in India, however, is not what I want to discuss, except to say that the description of an Indian secularism as distinct from western secularism is a complicated claim. I propose to bracket it for the purpose of the argument I am developing here.

---

[6] It is important to remind oneself that the West is not a geographical category as such; the non-western character of societies cannot be simply read as a reflection of such geographical identification.

Indian (liberal-elite) political rhetoric has made considerable play upon the centrality of secularism in India's public life. It is suggested that the durability of Indian democracy, its relative civic peace (give or take the various 'insurgences' in Kashmir, Nagaland, Punjab etc.) and, since the days of 'Shining India', its rapid economic growth, all point to the way in which the promotion of secularism provides beneficial effects even in a society as apparently different from western Europe as India. This, then, would seem to offer an example of secularism in a non-western context being able to provide the benefits that are claimed for it in the context of western historical development. India's prosperity, democracy and civic peace seem to be associated with the commitment of India's ruling elite to secularism. If secularism can be said to work in India, then it may be possible to restore its universal claims.

One way of understanding Indian secularism is to see it in the context of the Partition of the British Raj. The story of south Asia since 1947 is often presented as a study in contrasts, in which one of the successor states to the British Raj is presented as a confessional state and the other as secular. This India–Pakistan comparison, which is such a staple of much south Asian historiography, also doubles up as an argument for secularism and its universal validity. Indian secularism, in other words, circulates as a marker of the distinctive character of India vis-à-vis Pakistan (especially so within the Nehruvian discourse, which was hegemonic in India for at least the first forty years after its formation), in which India as a democratic and normal state is contrasted with Pakistan as an Islamic and failed state.

Currently, secularism in India is presented as the means of preserving the Nehruvian discourse under threat from the advocates of Hinduvata. But given the way in which the massacres during partition are commonly associated with violence unleashed primarily by religious passions, secularism is considered essential to preserving civic peace in India, primarily in defusing tensions between the Hindu majority and Muslim minority. Secularism in India, then, essentially manages the relationship between a Muslim minority and the nation-state majority. Other issues also enter the ambit of Indian secularism, but it is the management of Muslim populations that is of central concern.

Indian secularism (along with Indian democracy), however, coexists with an institutionalised system of communal violence in which the primary victims tend to be Muslims (Brass 2003). Secularism allows Hindu–Muslim violence to be represented as exceptional rather than intrinsic to contemporary India (Asad 2003: 8). Paul Brass's (2003: 377–80) careful analysis of Hindu–Muslim violence, and the institutionalised riot system thorough which it is exercised, would suggest that the discourse of Indian secularism has not so much defused the violence but rather worked to render it largely invisible.[7] It could be argued that secularism in India, along with 'planned riots', is part of the institutional ensemble by which Muslims in India are disciplined and domesticated.

The underlying assumption behind attempts to equate secularism with civic peace and dialogic possibilities is that religion is dangerous because its ability to incite hostility is unparalleled. Thus, secularism actually operates as a name for the commitment to anti-dogmatism. Why should religious passions, however, be considered more violent than other passions? The response to such questioning usually takes the form that if someone thinks that they are on 'a mission from God' they are unlikely to be dissuaded by objections on more mundane grounds, nor are they likely to see themselves as participants in 'ideal communicative' dialogue. This response, however, is not really about religion, but about claims that a higher authority is validating one's position. This higher authority, moreover, does not have to take the form of God or gods, it can take (and has taken) the name of History, or Science, or Reason.

Secularism and indifference

So far I have discussed the case for secularism largely in relation to claims made on its behalf. I have suggested that most of these claims are not as strong as it is sometimes suggested. It seems that the two most prominent cases of secularism – western and 'Indian' – are currently deployed in relation to the emergence of a Muslim identity. In the remainder of the chapter, I would like to suggest another take on the relationship between Muslim identity and secularism.

Are Muslims religious? Or, to be more precise, does being a Muslim mean being a member of a religious community? At one level the answer is obvious and to ask this question seems rather odd. The obviousness of

---

[7] The homology with racism and western plutocracies is worth noting: racism continues to be presented as an exceptional state of affairs rather than something intrinsic to the current western order (Hesse 2004).

the answer, however, rests upon an understanding of religion that sees it as a 'natural' term; that is, where religion is deemed to be about God or gods (Stark and Finke 2000). This would include all faiths with the possible exception of some branches of Buddhism. It would also exclude systems of thought like Marxism or Positivism (despite Comte's best efforts) since they are not centred on divine being(s). What kind of subject position labours under the designation 'Muslim' is a question that vexed the earliest Muslim community.

Following the death of the Lord of Medina, many of the various groups that had given him allegiance refused to give allegiance to Abu Bakr as the head of the Islamicate state. They did not reject Islam but simply felt that their practice of Islam did not entail having to pay tribute to Medina. This position was not acceptable to the leadership of the Islamic state, who could not imagine a Muslim who did not belong to the Islamicate polity; in other words, for them, Muslims did not simply constitute a community of faith bound by common spiritual practices and beliefs, but also members of a political community expressed through rites of political belonging (giving *baya*, paying tribute, accepting the authority of the officers of the state etc). In 757 CE, however, when the Muslim province of Andalusia refused to accept the new Caliphal authorities in Baghdad and thus refused to give *baya* or pay tribute, most Muslims continued to accept that the Muslims of al-Andalus were still Muslims and part of the *umma*. It came to be accepted that the boundaries between the *umma* and the Caliphate did not have to be congruent (Sayyid 2006). This oscillation between Muslims denoting a polity as well as a congregation suggests that the articulation of Muslim identity cannot simply be reduced to a religious identity. Muslim denotes a multicultural, transnational subject position in which the Enlightenment-inspired split between what constitutes the proper religious sphere and what constitutes the proper secular sphere is not so clear-cut.

Islam is certainly not alone in not organising the sense of selfhood of its subjects along a secular–religious divide. Hindus and ancient Romans, among others, similarly made little distinction between religious duties and obligations, and other forms of identification. Today this is most clearly expressed in the case of Jewish identity, which continues to refer to ethnicity as well as a set of religious beliefs and practices. In the Jewish case, notions of 'racial' identity seemingly trump notions of identity derived from Judaism: in other words, claims of Jewish descent are sufficient to confer a Jewish identity, without necessitating an acceptance or observation of practices that characterise Judaism.

Muslims are multi-lingual, multicultural subjects; so to what extent can we speak of a unified Muslim identity? Clearly, the dominant markers by which collective identities (nationality, class, 'race') are often expressed would seem to exclude as significant a Muslim subject position (Sayyid 2000: 39). Muslims do, however, share the possibility of telling stories about themselves: stories that begin with the revelations received from the Prophet and continue with the addition of many discursive threads through time to create a tapestry that can be represented as distinct, with its own system of signifying practices. Individual Muslims are often thrown into this complex web, or choose to become part of it so that the many aspects of their biographies resonate with a privileged meaning within this historical sequence. From the names they take, or are given, to the way they comport themselves, the story that begins with the Archangel Gabriel speaking to a forty-year-old merchant in Mecca, through the formation of the Islamic state in Medina, the circulation of the Qur'an and the expansion of the Islamicate order to embrace a large part of the Earth's surface, helps situate those who call themselves Muslims. This situating can take many forms, from uncritical affirmation, to total rejection fuelled by self-loathing, through all kinds of positions in between and at various stages in one's biography.

The articulation of a Muslim identity, however, points to a historical community. And for a variety of contingent and specific reasons the history of this community has come today to embody a counter-history to the dominant Plato-to-NATO sequence. As such, the articulation of a Muslim subject position becomes political in two senses of the term. First, it is political in that it occurs as an interruption of the dominant discourse, and its emergence draws attention to the 'ignoble' institutionalisation of the dominant discourse. Second, by interrupting the dominant discourse it subverts the mechanism that exists for transforming political antagonisms into cultural differences, and thus it is political in the sense that it is caught up in a field sustained by the distinction between friends and enemies.

The current debate about secularism within western plutocracies takes place in the context of mobilisations of Muslims in the name of Islam. The potential for Muslims to generate transnational mobilisations puts into crisis one of the major building blocks of the Westphalian system, which produces ethnicised minorities in opposition to a national majority by drawing up boundaries that construct certain populations as national majorities and others as ethnicised minorities. As a consequence, the articulation of a Muslim subject position is not merely international, in that Muslims can be found in many nation-states; it is also *diasporic*, in that the scattering of Muslims continues to take place in contexts of de-territorialised political subalternity (Sayyid 2000). These mobilisations continue to be seen and to be constituted as problematic for a host of reasons, including the shift in power that they signal between national majorities and their ethnicised minorities, and between coloniality and post-colonial effects.

In this current context, then, secularism becomes a means of dealing with the articulation of Muslim identity. So while the literature on secularism tends to focus on its merits, what is decisive about it is not the benefits that may or may not accrue from its endorsement, but rather that its endorsement becomes an affirmation of westernese. The various citizenship tests, the attacks on the veil, the demands that Muslims conform to western (i.e. secular) values, and so on can all be read as arising from the way in which the quest for a Muslim autonomy implicitly (and, in some cases, explicitly) challenges the Plato-to-NATO sequence and undermines the legitimacy of westernese. Secularism is deployed not to ensure civic peace or epistemological advances, but rather to maintain western historiographical hegemony. The current debate about secularism, in other words, turns less on its avowed concern with separating religion from politics but rather on that with the depoliticising of Muslims. Secularism as a discursive regime deals not with 'objective reality' but with a specific constructed version of its object. It generates the Muslims as the permanently transgressive subject, whose 'religious essence' is constantly being undermined by temptations of the political. Consequently, Muslim politics become either a purely empirical designation or an illegitimate articulation. The proper Muslim is religious – where religion is a sign of pre-modern episteme. It follows that the Muslim who is political is not properly a Muslim. Being political means being modern; it also means being a people with History. Secularism, by establishing the boundary between the religious and the political, also becomes another means of policing the boundary between the pre-modern and modern, and the western and non-western.

9 | *Muslims in the West and their attitudes to full participation in western societies: some reflections*

ABDULLAH SAEED

The resurgence of political Islam in the mid twentieth century, the Iranian Revolution of 1979 and the terrorist attacks of recent decades have ignited a debate in the West that had been dormant for some time. Some western commentators, such as the Oriana Fallaci (2002), have argued that there is a fundamental divide between 'Muslim' values and 'western' values. They project an image of an Islam that is violent, fanatical and extremist, and intent on destroying western civilisation. For them, Muslims are engaged in a struggle for global dominance, control and subjugation of the religious 'Other'. Their views are reflected by numerous journalists, commentators and politicians: Le Pen in France, Jörg Haider in Austria and the late Pim Fortuyn in the Netherlands; Hiryse Ali also in the Netherlands, for example. Similarly there are certain Muslims who argue that Islam and the West are on a collision course and there is no way that a coexistence is possible. While this is one view among Muslims there are others for whom such a simplistic view of coexistence is highly problematic.

Although this debate about Islam and the West is a broad one, my interest is in the Muslims living in the West. Part of this debate is the view held by many in the West that even those Muslims who are *citizens* of western states, and who have made the West their home, somehow are not prepared to coexist with the religious Other or are incapable of doing so for Islamic legal/theological reasons. Given the current alarm over Muslim terrorism (as we have seen in 9/11, Bali, Jakarta, Madrid and, more recently, London), some in the West argue that the Muslim presence in the West is a great concern. Others go even further and argue that Muslims in the West are a serious threat to western societies and that they should be countered by various decisive actions. For them, Muslims cannot be loyal citizens of a western nation-state because their loyalty is to Islam.

200

They are seen as a type of 'fifth column', quietly existing until the opportunity arises to challenge the secular nation-state – even violently – and to change it.

In this chapter I would like to explore one aspect of the debate in the West about Islam: how Muslims in the West think about the ability or otherwise of Muslims to coexist with non-Muslims in a western secular environment. I will use the term 'the West' in a rather restricted way to refer to a cultural-geographical entity primarily focused on western Europe, North America and Australia. I argue that Islam in the West, like Islam in the 'Muslim world', is a diverse and complex phenomenon that defies the single conception of Islam so prevalent today. I also argue that, contrary to what many believe, many Muslims in the West *are* coming to terms with western social, cultural and political environments, at least at a pragmatic level. That is, they are comfortable with modern western political and social values such as democracy, human rights, gender and religious equality, and the separation of religion and state. Of course, this shift in thinking was forced upon Muslims living in the West by circumstances and the need to survive in a new environment. Nevertheless, their adaptation was facilitated by the high degree of flexibility within the Islamic tradition, be it in law, ethics or theology, as well as by an environment in the West in which freedom of religion is important. While this is a positive development, there are disturbing trends among certain sections of Muslim communities in the West, who argue strongly that coexistence between Muslims and others in the West is both impossible and undesirable. Between the two extremes, however, there are many voices.

Islam in the West: an overview

Contrary to the popular notion that Islam in the West is a recent phenomenon mostly of the twentieth century, Islam, from its inception in the seventh century CE, has been part of the Christian West and the western psyche. Islam's interaction with the West occurred, first, through confrontation with the Christian Byzantine Empire in the seventh century; second, with the Muslim conquest of the Iberian peninsula and the subsequent 800 years of Muslim rule; third, though the Crusades of the late eleventh to the thirteenth centuries; and fourth, through the Ottoman conquests of Eastern Europe. More recently, the colonialism of the nineteenth and twentieth centuries and the migration of large numbers of Muslims to western countries have formed large communities of Muslim minorities.

Interaction between Muslim and western societies has not always been confrontational. At times, there was mutual respect and inter-action for the benefit of both sides: caliphs, sultans and emirs exchanged gifts with the emperors and kings of Europe. From the beginning, Muslims and Christians in the West engaged in trade between the Muslim world and Christian Europe despite wars and papal decrees not to engage in trade with the 'infidel' Muslims. There were diplo-matic relations and the transfer of knowledge, Greek philosophy and mathematics being a famous example. In many cases, conflict and the invasion of territory was not the result of religious difference; often it was for political or economic gains. This long view of history is both useful and dangerous; useful in that we can see that crises occur and are resolved, but dangerous in that memory can lead to generalisa-tions and also perpetuate grievances. We should not make the gene-ralisation that the interaction between the Muslims and Christians in Europe was always negative and hostile.

Although the Muslim presence in the West is not new, significant permanent Muslim populations in western Europe, the United States, Canada and Australia are relatively recent, particularly in the post-colonial era. This presence is no small matter, as Timothy Savage (see below) in his research highlights, although the figures given here should be taken with some caution as reliable data are difficult to get. In Europe, it is believed, there are approximately 23 million Muslims, making up nearly 5 per cent of the population. Approximately 50 per cent of Muslims in western Europe were born there. The Muslim birth rate in Europe is, in some European countries, higher than that of non-Muslims, and as a result Muslim communities in certain European countries are significantly younger than the non-Muslim population. In France, for example, one-third of France's five million Muslims are under the age of 20, compared to 21 per cent of the French population as a whole. In Germany, one-third of Germany's four million Muslims are under the age of 18 (compared to 18 per cent of the German popu-lation) (Savage 2004: 28).

Migration and birth rate have been the major factor in the increase of Muslim population in Europe. Conversion to Islam is only a minor one, making up less than 1 per cent of all Muslims in Europe. Accord-ing to Savage (2004: 28), '[f]rom this low base, however, conversions could develop as a new and potentially significant source not only of the growth of the Muslim presence in Europe but also of its voice and visibility'. One estimate cited is that Muslims will comprise at least 20 per cent of the European population by 2050. Savage (2004: 28) even predicts that one-quarter of France's population could be Muslim by 2025. While many scholars might consider these figures to be indeed off the mark and alarmist, such figures increase the fear that the West is facing a threat to its existence. This also implies other challenges for western governments, not only in Europe but also in North America and Australia. As Savage (2004: 38–9) says: 'The increasing Muslim presence in Europe has reopened debates on several issues: the place of religion in public life, social tolerance in Europe, secularism as the only path to modernity, and Europe's very identity.' One of the ways European countries respond to this 'Muslim factor' is by 'effectively nationalizing, if not secularizing, Islam'. Savage adds, 'These governments are trying to foster nationally oriented Islams subordinate to the state as well as European norms stretching back to the Treaty of Westphalia, the Enlightenment, and Napoleonic rule.' These measures include providing imams with education in local languages and culture, building mosques with local finance to avoid investment from Arab sources, restricting the wearing of the *hijab* (Islamic headscarf), and virtually 'shoehorning Muslim organizations into structures that correspond to national objectives, such as Belgium's Central Body for the Islamic Religion' (Savage 2004: 41).

The policy, however, has so far not been highly successful, as often governments have favoured certain groups of Muslims over others, and have taken measures that have come to be too sensitive (as is the case of the headscarf in France) and thus alienated a large part of the Muslim communities. Such efforts at nationalising or secularising Islam have had a negative impact on the emergence of a fully western form of Islam. A western form of Islam must come from within the Muslim community rather than be imposed by a national government. It should be an authentic response from the Muslims themselves as the governments' involvement in matters – involving religious practice – often backfires.

Different views on the nature of Islam: Islam is not necessarily one

Much of the fear of Muslims in the West is based on the belief that Islam is an indivisible whole: that Muslims all over the world form a single, homogeneous community with the same beliefs, values, practices and institutions. According to this view, regardless of where they come from, Muslims are all the same. That they come from many ethnic, linguistic, cultural or theological, spiritual or legal backgrounds, is often disregarded. While this view is quite popular in the West and much of the popular imagination in the West often relies on this view of Islam and Muslims, others argue for a more nuanced view. They argue that such a simplistic and essentialist notion of what Islam is, and who Muslims are, is fundamentally flawed. These critics argue against labelling all Muslims in a negative manner on the basis of the actions of certain groups among Muslims.

The reality of Islam and Muslims is quite different. Wherever Muslims live in the West, from France to the United States to Australia, their communities are diverse. No single voice or culture is dominant. What the American Muslim scholar Aminah McCloud (2003: 159) says about the United States applies to Muslims elsewhere in the West:

The American Muslim community is at once a mosaic, and a tattered quilt. Orthodox, heterodox, Sunni, Shi'i, and Sufi all make claims of Islam in the United States. Because there is no official or state-sponsored Islam, all find sanctuary and voice. Exiled princes and authors, refugees, and asylum seekers from the Muslim world jockey for a platform to represent Islam along with first, second, and third generation converts of African and European American descent. The cacophony of voice raised is dynamic, if sometimes deafening. The variety of discourses is as wide as the many ethnicities in the Muslim community.

It is also assumed that all Muslims in the West are believers: fully practising, 'committed' Muslims. Again, this view is highly misleading. Muslims are like any other religious community. There are those who are committed, practising and deeply religious. Equally there are those who are simply nominal or 'cultural' Muslims. Tariq Ramadan (1999) observes that, in Europe, probably half of Muslims are nominal Muslims. The same would most likely apply to elsewhere in the West.

Can Muslims live under non-Muslim rule? Juristic analysis of the pre-modern period

A legalistic debate on full participation of Muslims in western societies usually begins with questions along the lines of: can Muslims live under non-Muslim rule? Can a Muslim be fully Muslim without sharia?

As for Muslims living under 'non-Muslim rule', the Qur'an saw the Muslim presence among non-Muslims in Mecca (610–22 CE) as normal during the time of the Prophet. It was only after the Prophet established a 'Muslim' territory in Medina following his migration from Mecca that the Qur'an asked Meccan Muslims to migrate to Medina (Qur'an 2:218, 4:89) as a way to consolidate and strengthen the Muslim community. This instruction was not a specific command to migrate from a 'non-Muslim' to a 'Muslim' territory as such. On a number of occasions, the Qur'an indicates that what matters is not whether Muslims live in non-Muslim areas but whether in such areas they are free from oppression and persecution. The Prophet encouraged Muslims to flee persecution in Mecca and seek refuge with a Christian ruler in Abyssinia. When his teaching spread across Arabia, the Prophet accepted that individual Muslims would live among and sometimes be 'ruled' by pagans, and Christians under the 'rule' of their non-Muslim tribes.

Pronouncements in the Qur'an and the practice of the Prophet provided the basis for the classical Muslim jurists (*fuqaha*) to debate the issue of a Muslim's residence under non-Muslim rule. Moreover, early in the development of Islamic law in the seventh and eighth centuries CE, the jurists were interpreting such texts in the light of the sociopolitical situation of their own time. The most apparent 'fact' at the time was the existence of a powerful caliphate ruling in the name of Islam, under which Muslims as a whole formed a community and in which Islam remained supreme. Non-Muslims were not seen as equal to Muslims and residence in non-Muslim territories was seen as problematic.

Malik (d. 769), who represents the strictest school of law with regard to Muslim residence under non-Muslim rule, stated that Muslims should not reside in non-Muslim territories. Malik also disapproved of Muslims travelling to non-Muslim lands even for business. This position was adopted by Maliki jurists and has been maintained until the early modern period, particularly in North Africa. While Malikis tended to be the strictest with regard to Muslim residence under non-Muslim rule, the other schools of law such as Shafi'i, Hanbali, Hanafi and the Shi'a were more lenient and flexible. For instance, Tabari (d. 923), a commentator on the Qur'an, believed that the ability to practise religion is the key determinant in any discussion on the permissibility of Muslim residence. For Shafi'i (d. 820), Muslims may reside in non-Muslim territories if there is no fear that they may be enticed away from their religion. For him it was the practical dangers for one's religion that were the main consideration. The Hanafi jurist Shaybani (d. 805) argued that Muslims were not obliged to migrate from a non-Muslim to a Muslim territory. Abu Hanifa (d. 767) believed that non-Muslim territory should not be a permanent place of residence for Muslims. For Shi'a, in some cases, it might even be better to reside in a non-Muslim territory because that territory might be free from persecution and oppression. (Abou El Fadl 1994: 134–5).

Among the ideas that dominated the thinking of jurists on the question of residence was that by residing under non-Muslim rule, they would inadvertently be strengthening the 'enemy', that they might be acquiring certain undesirable values and norms from non-Muslims, and that they would be compromising the notion of the supremacy of Islam over other religions. While some form of social interaction with non-Muslims was unavoidable, a strict separation at least at a theological-legal level was seen as important, doubtless justifying such positions on selected Qur'anic and *hadith* texts that appear to emphasise the supremacy of Islam.

This politico-military dominance of Islam and Muslims suffered a battering from the eleventh century CE onwards. This is evident in the case of the Christian reconquest of Spain and the Mongol invasion of the eastern parts of the Muslim world. In both cases, Muslims came under direct non-Muslim rule on a large scale, leading to extensive debates among Muslim jurists on how Muslims in those contexts should live. Some jurists accommodated the changed reality into their thought and argued that Muslims should accept non-Muslim rule, while others, such as the Malikis in North Africa, argued for migration of Muslims from Spain to Muslim lands.

From pre-modern debate to contemporary reality: Muslims in a new environment

Even though the jurists have proposed a variety of views on the issue, Muslims have been living under non-Muslim rule for centuries. But living as citizens in the West is relatively new. On the whole, Muslim *residence* in the West is largely a phenomenon of the late nineteenth and twentieth centuries. Today, these Muslims are subject to each country's constitution and laws. Usually, no concession is given to religious communities to govern aspects of their lives according to their religious or traditional laws (except in some aspects of family law). Citizenship requires commitment to the institutions of the State. State involvement in religious matters is minimal and usually there is a separation of church and state.

Nor is there clear guidance in Islamic law or ethics for these citizens of the West, except some general principles and a few indirect cases or precedents from which they have to construct what is appropriate for them. Thus Muslims in the West are attempting to find new answers to new problems. Many early juristic views do not seem to be particularly helpful in the present context. Given that Islamic law was developed as the supreme law in the lands where Muslims ruled, Muslim jurists did not address in sufficient detail the case of Muslims living permanently as minorities under non-Muslim rule. The natural state of affairs, from the point of the view of the jurists, was Muslim rule over Muslims, and the legal system was to be based on 'Islamic law'. Any other situation was simply seen as an exception and did not warrant developing an edifice of law for such an exception.

For Muslims in the West today, however, the exception has become the norm. Muslim minorities exist in all countries in the West and the numbers are increasing. In the pre-modern period it was relatively easy for religious communities – even if they were minorities – to function as a single entity and unit under a different system of rule. This was because of the way religious communities were treated in many great empires where freedom to practise their religion under the guidance of their religious leaders was given, as was the case with the Ottoman millet system. Religious communities were considered independent entities with their own norms, rules and laws. In the modern period, the emergence of nation-states based on the idea of common citizenship has changed that situation dramatically.

Four trends of Islam in the West: participation and isolationism

Observers of Muslim presence in the West propose many ways in which one can classify, categorise and discuss Muslims in the West. I would like to identify four trends that are based on the following criteria:

- The relationship of Muslims in the West to a particular land, nation or country. I call this the 'national dimension'.

- The extent to which Muslims emphasise tradition and past interpretations of the religion (and literal reading of the sacred texts of Islam). I call this the 'traditional dimension'.
- The extent to which Muslims are activists in projecting their particular brand of Islam and are influenced by certain twentieth-century Muslim thinkers and movements. I call this the 'ideological dimension'.
- The extent to which Muslims have an anti-western bias or consider themselves part of western society. I call this the 'approach-to-the-West dimension: isolationism vs. participation'.

A range of views exists among Muslims as far as their attitudes to western societies is concerned: Muslims living in the West but hostile to the West, Muslims living in the West grudgingly and with no interest in being part of western society, Muslims living in the West with some admiration for its values but undecided as to whether they want to be full members of the society, and Muslims who are 'western' by virtue of where they were born and live and have no difficulty in being western and Muslim.

Based on the above, we may classify Muslims in the West into four trends. The first three trends are part of the broad category of 'isolationists' or 'semi-isolationists', while the fourth trend comprises 'participants':

(i) Ethno-national/traditionalist/non-ideological/isolationist;
(ii) Transnational/semi-traditionalist/ideological/semi-isolationist;
(iii) Transnational/traditionalist/non-ideological/isolationist;
(iv) Indigenous/non-traditionalist/non-ideological/participant.

Most readers probably would have no difficulty in understanding the first three categories. The fourth, however, may be seen as improbable and even a contradiction in terms. Can a Muslim be fully western, American, European or Australian? I will argue, however, that it is the fourth trend that is, or is becoming, one of the most important trends in Muslim communities, mainly at a pragmatic level.

Isolationists

(i) Ethno-national/traditionalist/non-ideological/isolationist

This represents the form of Islam that early migrants brought to the West when they arrived in places like the United States, France, the

United Kingdom and Australia from the Middle East, north Africa, the Indian sub-continent and southeast Asia from the nineteenth century onwards. They brought with them their legal schools and local understandings of what it means to be Muslim, such as in dress and the role of women in society, and in foods and customs. In the United Kingdom, it was the cultural norms from the Indian sub-continent that predominated. In France, it was Algerian and later other north African norms. In Australia it was initially the Afghans, Turks and the Lebanese. In the United States, it was largely the norms of Arab migrants from the Middle East. Given that specific legal schools dominated the thinking of Muslims with regard to what was islamically acceptable, the earliest settlers brought a conception of Islam that was highly legalistic and traditionalist. This legalism and traditionalism continues to dominate much of the thinking in significant Muslim circles in the West.

These traditionalists argue for a strict following of the 'authorised' interpretations of their particular legal school. Where possible, they prefer to be as faithful to the literal reading of the ethical-legal texts of Islam. This form of Islam is characterised by a huge diversity of expression as it is largely ethnically based, coloured by Islam from 'back home'. Its focus is primarily on basic rituals such as prayer and fasting, as well as on Islamic practices brought from places of origin. Many of this generation established institutions such as mosques, basic teaching facilities for religious instruction and Islamic centres, and procured facilities such as halal meat as well as space for Muslim cemeteries. They are often 'isolationist' in their attitude to the host country and have little interest in local issues: politics, economic or legal.

(ii) Transnational/semi-traditionalist/ideological/ semi-isolationist

This trend was introduced into the West in the twentieth century by two groups of Muslims: the first being students from the Arab world, who were influenced by the thought of the Muslim Brotherhood, and from the Indian sub-continent, who were influenced by Jamaat-i-Islami; and the second being Muslim activists who had to flee the Arab world because of their association with the Muslim Brotherhood movement.

This form of Islam was attractive to a large number of the young, many of whom were university students, as it presented a more 'modern' and 'activist' form of the creed. For instance, those who were influenced by the Muslim Brotherhood had an activist agenda; they targeted the youth, organising study circles, emphasising the need to be involved in the development of the community and pursuing an agenda of propagation of Islam (*da'wa*). They were among the most vocal opponents of assimilation and played an important role in establishing Muslim student organisations on university campuses. In the United States since the 1970s, for instance, they have continued to play an important role in Muslim intellectual and social life to this day.

In the early 1970s their message tended to be defensive and apologetic and emphasised a distinct Muslim identity vis-à-vis the 'western'. Purists in this group viewed the West in negative terms, focusing on its alleged moral failings and emphasising the positives of Islam. Their slogan was 'Islam is a way of life'. They were antagonistic to what they considered to be modern *jahiliyya* (akin to pre-Islamic norms), whether in nationalism, communism or capitalism. They believe Islam has a solution for all problems of our time. They emphasise Islamisation of every aspect of life, from economics to politics to law. They are keen to develop institutions such as 'Islamic banks' and stress Islamic dress; in short, more Islamisation. Their message is simple and they are good at marketing their views. They believe their brand of Islam is 'modern' in outlook and compatible with modern life. These semi-traditionalists essentially follow the traditionalists but present the ethico-legal content of Islam in a modern garb. However, they do this without asking fundamental questions about the relationship that the ethico-legal content of the Qur'an may have to its socio-historical context or about the interpretations of that ethico-legal content that were made in the following generations. They package the ethico-legal content in a somewhat 'modern' idiom often within an apologetic discourse. Overtime, many in this camp moved away from their 'isolationist' rhetoric and began to argue for full 'participation'.

(iii) *Transnational/traditionalist/non-ideological/isolationist*

One trend that is making its mark in the West is a form of Islam that appeared in the West in the late 1980s and into the 1990s. Heavily influenced by the Salafi trends that are closely connected with Hanbali-Wahhabi literalism and financed by sources in the Arabian Gulf, they made a significant foray into the West. They established a large number of mosques and centres, media outlets, and a presence on university campuses.

This brand of Islam neglects Islam's diversity and the intellectual and creative richness of its past. The differences among Muslims, the breadth of scholarship, the philosophy, the theology, the exegesis and the enormously rich debates among Muslims are not particularly attractive to them. They want an Islam that remains unquestioned by scholarly inquiry or threatened by 'unconventional' interpretation. Simplistic answers are provided by symbols and literal interpretation rather than by intellectual inquiry. As such, these figures consider Islam to be a fixed entity, unchanging throughout history.

While not all members of this trend are hostile to the West, some have expressed radical views, with a clear indication that their purpose is to 'change' western societies. Quite often without any regard to what they can or cannot do in these societies, they argue for replacing the so-called 'man-made' laws in the West with Islamic ones – which they consider to be directly sanctioned by God. They make use of history, from the Crusades to the nineteenth-century domination of Muslims by colonial powers and the Israel–Palestine problem, in agitating for a struggle against the West. This sub-group of radicals has few active participants but, unfortunately, with their slogans and attitude, they tend to get media attention and their rhetoric is taken by many in the West as representative of the views of the entire Muslim community.

Many of these hard-line isolationists have developed an ideology that is fanatical and extremist. As far as their view of western societies is concerned, it can be described as follows:

They see American society [for example] as immoral, sexually decadent, greedy, and exploitative of the weak at home and abroad. Philosophically, they do not appreciate the value of freedom and tolerance; ideologically, they disagree with democracy as a means of political governance. For them, democracy is an institution that legitimizes basic instincts of humanity and is an affront to divine laws. They describe the American system as *kufr* (a system against the laws of Allah or the Islamic Sharia) and reject it totally. (Khan 2003: 189)

This ideology sees a permanent conflict between Muslims and non-Muslims (in particular Christians and Jews) that has to be overcome, the establishment of an Islamic caliphate ruled by a caliph where sharia is implemented as the solution to the problems of the Muslims

today and Muslims who do not share its view as collaborators or
'modernists' whose views should be rejected. Some have resorted to
militant-jihadi-style anti-western activities.

Participants

(iv) Indigenous/non-traditionalist/non-ideological/Participant

This trend among Muslims in the West is becoming quite common.
It has no historical precedent, no clear-cut methodology to deal with
Islamic law, no established grand narratives or writings. It is purely a
product of a fusion of Islam with the West, western environment and
western values. In the USA, the UK, Canada and Australia its primary
language is English, in France it is French, and in Germany it is German.
Its frame of reference is the local environment. It is multi-national and
multicultural in its orientation.

Its adherents are actively negotiating Islam within the context of the
local culture. They are developing strategies to deal with the question
of integration and adaptation without assimilation. For these Muslims
in the West, Australia, for example, is not a foreign country but their
home. Culturally and intellectually they do not identify with their
parents' or grandparents' place of origin (overseas). Any distant memory
their parents may have of another distant home is irrelevant for them.

At the level of religious discourse, they are dealing with areas such
as rethinking Islam; Muslim identity, Islamic norms and values in the
western context, *itjihad* and the reinterpretation of key Islamic texts,
citizenship, functioning in a secular environment, and what it means
to be *both* western and Muslim. Their familiarity with the institutions,
culture, values, norms and history of the western country they find
themselves in makes them an important intermediary between Muslims
and non-Muslim mainstream western society. They are not necessarily
attached to particular theologians, religious leaders or foreign imams.
They do not want to be affiliated with a particular transnational
movement or legal or theological school.

The influence of the western environment on the Participants is
unmistakable in how these Muslims perceive 'religion'. For them, Islam
is a 'private' phenomenon within the secular environment. There is no
emphasis on the political dimension of Islam, such as establishing an

Islamic state or adopting Islamist slogans like 'Islam is a religion and a state'. For these Muslims in the West, Islam is centred on one's relationship with God and with other human beings. Islam is not seen as an ideological tool or a comprehensive system of law and politics, although it is important to add that these Muslims are not detached from politics; participating in the political process of their countries is seen as following the commands of the Qur'an to participate in community life and development.

This privatisation of religion, so to speak, is a significant development, in which religion has become less dominated by law, politics, ideology or local orthodoxies. Consequently, a more enlightened, liberal and indigenous Islam is in the making. Given that Muslims in this category are not bound by particular legal or theological schools of Islam, they free themselves from earlier theological-juristic opinions held by a particular school. They do not see it as necessary to be labelled Hanafi, Shafi'i, Maliki, Salafi, Sunni or Shi'i. For them, the label 'Muslim' is sufficient.

These Muslims are also assertive in how they approach the textual traditions of Islam. They believe it is possible to read the foundation texts of Islam in translation, for example. This is a major shift from the long-held belief that one has to read the Qur'an in Arabic to understand its meaning, and that translations should not be relied upon. They are willing to accept intermediaries between the individual and the texts.

Participant Muslims reject the idea that one cannot be fully Muslim unless one is ruled by 'Islamic law', not secular law. They do not make a sharp distinction between Islamic law and secular law in their daily lives. Provided laws support notions such as justice, equity, equality and public interest, these Muslims will respect those laws as Islamic in intention or essence.

Participant Muslims argue that even in the so-called Islamic countries, for example Malaysia or Indonesia, most of the laws in force in the country are not necessarily based on the foundation texts of Islam: the Qur'an and *hadith*. Many of the laws in place are not very different from the laws in force in western countries. Although, these western laws might be labelled secular, to Participant Muslims they are not un-Islamic so long as they are in accord with Islamic values. Thus from the Participants' point of view, the distinction between so-called secular laws and Islamic laws is blurred.

Participant Muslims take abiding by the laws in the countries of which they are citizens seriously, and consider that as part of being obedient to God. Respect and obedience to the local laws (regardless of whether the the authorities are Muslim or not) was also emphasised by classical Muslim jurists in their writings. Difficulties primarily arise if laws prohibit fundamental Islamic beliefs or practices such as prayer, fasting and *zakat*. In this context, even the laws that permit things like gambling, prostitution or alcohol are not considered problematic as such laws do not oblige Muslims to engage in those practices.

Relying on a range of concepts and taking into consideration their circumstances in the West, Participant Muslims reject pre-modern concepts such as *dar al-harb* and *dar al-islam*, which divide the world into 'us' and 'them', the world of Islam and the world of the infidel. They believe that such labels are obsolete in discussing today's political entities, such as nation-states, membership of which is not based on religious affiliation. Tariq Ramadan, a theoretician of what he calls 'European Islam' (Ramadan 1999), argues there are five fundamental rights that are secured in European/western societies: the right to practise Islam, the right to knowledge, the right to found organisations, the right to autonomous representation and the right to appeal to law. Where these rights exist, he argues, that place should be considered an 'abode of Islam'.

For the Participant Muslims, citizenship is a contract, the terms of which Muslims are obliged to honour, including obeying all the laws in force in the country, paying taxes and contributing to the well-being of the country. As far as social relations are concerned, Muslims must deal with all people, regardless of their faiths, on the basis of honesty, trustworthiness and justice (Ramadan 1999: 162–73).

Concluding remarks

These 'Participant' Muslims represent what I refer to as 'the emerging western tradition of Islam'. This strand of Islam is coming to terms with a range of new issues, including democracy, human rights, gender equality, secular law, freedom of expression and religion, and equality before the law. It exists in practice but it is only recently that Muslims in the West have started to develop methodological tools and principles to provide an intellectual foundation for this approach. It is a product of the fusion of Islam with the western environment, and western liberal-democratic values. It has been most visible since the 1990s through the writings of a number of Muslim scholars based in the West, such as Ramadan (1999), Bassam Tibi (2002) and Muqtedar Khan (2003).

This 'western Islam' (or western tradition of Islam) is being driven mostly by the indigenisation of Islam in the West. It is espoused mostly by second- or third-generation Muslims, other indigenous Muslims and converts to Islam from other systems of belief. Many professional and middle-class Muslims also belong to this strand. Its frame of reference is the local environment of the West and its inspiration comes from that context. This western tradition of Islam is challenging traditional understandings of a range of important issues in order to suit the social, cultural, political and intellectual context of Muslims in the West.

In relation to Participant Muslims and with particular reference to American Muslims, the American Muslim scholar, Muqtedar Khan (2003: 176) says:

[T]he American Muslim identity ... is rapidly emerging. Political as well as historical forces are constructing it. The interplay between American values and Islamic values and mutual reconstitution of each other is leading to a liberal understanding of Islam more in tune with dominant American values such as religious tolerance, democracy, pluralism, and multicultural and multi-religious co-existence.

Participant Muslims are contributing to Islamic thought in a significant way. Their work will most likely lead to a rethinking of existing approaches, methods and principles in jurisprudence, Qur'anic exegesis and Islamic ethics. This work in the West should not be seen as a marginal, irrelevant exercise for Muslims. Its implications on the Muslim world are great. Although, as an intellectual discourse, it is still in the early stages, it is making its mark on the wider Muslim discourse in the area of reform of Islamic law and thought.

10 Liberal democracy, multicultural citizenship and the Danish cartoon affair

GEOFFREY BRAHM LEVEY AND
TARIQ MODOOD

Few cases in recent years have more vividly illustrated the political and theoretical conundrum that is the subject of this book than the Danish cartoon controversy. On 30 September 2005, the Danish right-of-centre newspaper *Jyllands-Posten* published twelve editorial cartoons under the heading 'The face of Muhammad'. The purpose, the newspaper explained, was to join the debate about criticism of Islam and self-censorship. Danish Muslim groups protested immediately, but within a few months the controversy had grown into a significant conflagration of peaceful and violent demonstrations, and worse, across Europe, Asia and the Middle East. Many news outlets decided that the proper and, perhaps, safer course was to forgo reprinting the cartoons, even as a news story. Other outlets decided that democracies were being intimidated and that free speech and fundamental liberties warranted defence by republishing the offending material. Scholars also vigorously debated the case (e.g. Modood *et al.* 2006).

In this concluding chapter, we wish to step back from the heat of the public controversy, but also from the mode (and perhaps mood) of the earlier academic exchanges, to consider the episode from the broader historical and political compass of this volume. Specifically, we want to ask whether the Danish cartoon affair might not be viewed as a vehicle for rethinking and perhaps reconfiguring some of our longstanding assumptions about liberal democracy and its capacities to accommodate cultural difference. The public and academic debates have tended to frame the Danish cartoon affair in one of two ways: as a clash between liberal-democratic and pre-liberal or illiberal religious values, or, alternatively, as a question of whose position in the debate

216

is most consistent with liberal-democratic values. We begin, instead, from the unremarkable assumption (albeit one curiously missing in the debate) that in principle, and especially in practice, liberal-democratic values conflict, not only *between* liberalism and democracy, but also *within* liberalism and democracy. We will argue that cases like the Danish cartoon affair present liberal democracies with choices not only about whether to invite or permit, or censor or censure, certain kinds of provocative images but also, more fundamentally, about which liberal-democratic principles and conceptions of these principles they emphasise and when. In making such choices, appeals are typically made to considerations beyond 'mere' fidelity to liberal-democratic norms. In cases like the Danish cartoon controversy, the choice, we shall argue, is also about whether and how best to make multicultural democracies work.

We will begin with a brief account of the Danish cartoon controversy. There are many different aspects to this case, and our concern is to identify those aspects that bear on what we consider to be the main issues. We will argue that the Danish cartoons encompass not one, but three, distinct problem areas: the representation of Muhammad and the status of religious commitments, attacks on a religion or religions, and attacks on a religious group or groups. Our discussion then turns to examining how liberal-democratic values and multicultural citizenship relate to each of these cases.

The Danish cartoons

The origins of this affair lie in the difficulties that the Danish writer, Kare Bluitgen, had in finding artists to illustrate his children's book on the Prophet Muhammad.[1] An author who wished to increase knowledge about Muhammad among Danish schoolchildren would surely have known about the prohibition observed by most Muslims on images of the Prophet (and other revered figures), so his search for an illustrator is odd. In any case, he failed to find anyone to undertake this task. He believed that illustrators were reluctant to provide images as they feared reprisals, including violence, from Muslim extremists.

---

[1] For an account of the events we primarily rely on the timeline given in the Wikipedia entry: http://en.wikipedia.org/wiki/Jyllands-Posten_Muhammad_cartoons_controversy.

At some point this became known to Flemming Rose, the cultural editor of the largest newspaper in Denmark, *Jyllands-Posten*, who resolved to challenge what he saw as religious censorship by intimidation. He asked forty cartoonists to draw cartoons of Muhammad (Klausen 2006b), with the intention of publishing as many as he could together: a form of collective security in the breach of an Islamic taboo. Twelve accepted the commission and, on 30 September 2005, twelve cartoons of Muhammad were published in the paper, with an editorial by Rose.

Before considering the cartoons themselves, one should know something about the paper, *Jyllands-Posten*. Ulf Hedetoft (2006: 2), a Danish professor specialising in migration studies, describes it as: 'ideologically close to the ruling political majority ... fully in line with the peculiar kind of Danish Islamophobia and anti-immigrant scepticism that has come to dominate public debates (and has undergirded government policies) within the last few years, if not for much longer'. It was, however, a paper that respected the religious sensitivities of its conservative readership; as we discuss below, on at least one recent occasion the newspaper had declined to publish a cartoon of Christ on the grounds that it would offend the majority of its readers.

The twelve cartoons were not all of a type. As Erik Bleich (2006: 18) usefully explains, two of the cartoons are quite benign or even positive:

One of these cartoons – apparently penned by someone pragmatically interested in the job as a children's book illustrator – is a straightforward image of Muhammad as a shepherd-figure ... [another is] of a schoolboy clad in standard-issue Western youth garb who has written on the chalkboard "The editorial team of *Jyllands-Posten* is a bunch of reactionary provocateurs." This is expressly not a picture of the prophet and therefore does not contravene religious prohibitions. Rather, it is an immigrant child who is both cheeky and savvy enough to thumb his nose at the media.

On the other hand, most of the cartoons are of Muhammad and offer a negative portrayal, with several associating him with violence, and there are two that Bleich thinks should be banned as they constitute an incitement to racial hatred. The one that gave the most offence, and was the most widely portrayed in news reports, is of Muhammad with a bomb in his turban, with a lit fuse, and the *shahadah* or Islamic creed written on the bomb.

On 9 October, the Islamic Society in Denmark demanded that *Jyllands-Posten* apologise to all Muslims and withdraw the cartoons, and five days later up to 5,000 people staged a peaceful demonstration outside the Copenhagen office of the newspaper. Violence, however, also began to enter the picture as two of the cartoonists went into hiding after receiving death threats. Shortly afterwards, the controversy was internationalised as an Egyptian newspaper published six of the cartoons and ambassadors from ten Muslim countries requested a meeting with the Danish Prime Minister, Anders Fogh Rasmussen. He refused to meet them, however, or to distance himself from the cartoons on the grounds of respecting freedom of speech. The controversy continued to spread internationally, drawing in various governments and organisations from Muslim countries, as well as newspapers in non-Muslim countries, some of which reprinted some of the cartoons.

The action that probably did most to publicise the cartoons in the Muslim world, and to create a diplomatic crisis, was the tour in the Middle East of a delegation of imams from the Islamic Society in Denmark. It is said that they muddied the waters, for their dossier 'did not simply enclose the twelve cartoons published in *Jyllands-Posten* when engaging the Arab League. They added three others, genuinely grotesque caricatures (showing pedophilia, sodomy, and the prophet represented as a porker), to bolster their campaign portfolio' (O'Leary 2006: 25). It is this lobbying that is thought to have led, in late January 2006, to various governments from the Muslim world recalling their ambassadors from Denmark and with some initiating a boycott of Danish products. Efforts were then made by *Jyllands-Posten* and the Danish government to show understanding of the hurt caused, but as they fell short of an apology for the original publication or the limiting of future publications, the situation escalated. There were violent scenes in some Muslim cities, a number of Danish embassies were attacked and the building housing the embassy in Damascus was stormed and set alight (though most of the damage was done to two other national embassies in the building). Several demonstrators were killed in Muslim countries (presumably by the security forces), but many were also killed in mob violence as the controversy was picked up by hostile Christians and Muslims in Nigeria. Many western governments expressed solidarity with Denmark, as did many western newspapers in reproducing the cartoons. Some papers, though (as in Britain), refused to do so on the grounds that they are of a poor quality, merely give offence, and that the right to freedom of speech has to be balanced by socially responsible journalism. While calm, diplomatic relations and trade were ultimately restored, it is fair to say that the rights and wrongs of publishing the cartoons remain a live issue.

We take it as given that the violence exhibited in the aftermath of the cartoons at some of the demonstrations, the burning of churches and the attacks on Danish embassies, and so on, are unacceptable. We also acknowledge that certain groups may have embellished or exploited the cartoons saga for political purposes. However, unlike some, we think the fact that it took time and various organised campaigns by activists before Muslim publics were made aware of the publications is neither here nor there, for that is generally how matters are publicised and protests mobilised. What is clear is that the real cartoons and their reproduction in numerous western newspapers offended many Muslims. For us, then, the case poses two key questions of interest. First, should the Muhammad cartoons have been commissioned and published by *Jyllands-Posten* (or any responsible outlet)? Second, what response does their publication warrant, if any?

In addressing these questions, it is necessary, we suggest, to distinguish between three problematic aspects of the cartoons. Each of these aspects is contained in the image of Muhammad with a lit bomb in his turban and the *shahadah* inscribed on the bomb. For convenience, our discussion will mainly focus on this image. The first problematic aspect that this cartoon emblematically contains is the representation of Muhammad. Such representation per se involves neither the vilification of, nor incitement against, Islam or Muslims; rather it involves a perceived breach of a well-known Islamic injunction. It raises the questions of the appropriate jurisdiction of religious law in liberal democracies and of the respect that may be owed those who abide by such law. The second problematic aspect in the cartoon is the suggestion that *Islam* is violent and dangerous. We do not claim that the cartoonist intended this image to target Islam as opposed to Muslims, only that the two targets are analytically separate and separable, and that different implications attend each situation. The third problematic aspect presented in the cartoon is thus precisely the targeting of Muslims as violent and dangerous.

In our view, this aspect is the most serious among the three; we shall argue that it constitutes a form of racism.

It is well to note a fourth possible interpretation of the Muhammad-and-bomb cartoon: namely, as meaning to depict how Islam has been hijacked by extremists, who have become a violent force in the world today. This, indeed, is how Flemming Rose says he interpreted this cartoon when it first reached his desk (Rose 2006). The trouble with this gloss is that if a picture paints a thousand words, then a cartoon like the one being considered is bound to be reduced to a few predictable sentences. Even if Rose correctly caught the cartoonist's meaning, the associations in the image are so obviously open to being misinterpreted as an attack on either Islam or Muslims, or both, that neither the cartoonist nor, especially, the editor is much let off the hook.[2] Accordingly, we shall not pursue this alternative interpretation here.

Liberty, equality and fraternity

In his Foreword to this volume, Charles Taylor invokes the Tricolour values of liberty, equality and fraternity to elaborate three important meanings or ambitions of secularism. The Tricolour also presents a convenient way to explore how liberal-democratic principles variously apply and conflict in the cartoon affair.

On one side, 'liberty' sanctions maximally free and unfettered speech. Even allowing for the usual hedges of excluding incitement to violence, treason and vilification, those who defend the in-principle right to publish even offensive material and who reject its subsequent censure do so first and foremost in the name of liberty. On the other side, 'fraternity' would seem to prioritise instead the welcoming acceptance, consideration and inclusion of others. 'Equality', as we see it, is a more relative value. Following Dworkin (1978: 125), it can be understood as 'equal treatment', involving equal measures of a particular good, or

---

[2] Kurt Westergaard, the cartoonist who depicted the Prophet Muhammad with a bomb in his turban, has indeed stated that he meant his cartoon to be a protest against terrorism and not against Islam, and in March 2008 threatened to sue the Dutch politician Geert Wilders for using his cartoon in an anti-Islam film. Without a hint of irony, Westergaard is reported as stating: 'I will not accept my cartoon being taken out of its original context and used in a completely different one' (*BBC News* 2008).

'treatment as an equal', where all parties are shown equal concern and respect. Understood as equal treatment, the principle of equality can figure in support of either or both liberty and fraternity: one can test it according to how other religious creeds, individuals and groups must endure the 'rough and tumble' of democratic politics in the name of liberty; one can also test it according to how consideration is granted to particular parties, sparing them some of the barbs of 'liberty as usual'. Understood as treatment as an equal, equality may well sanction *disparate* treatment out of consideration for pressing background circumstances and other social goals.

Let us now examine how these principled possibilities play out when applied to the three most problematic representations furnished by the Danish cartoon controversy identified above: the very representation of Muhammad, the identification of Islam with violence and terrorism, and the identification of Muslims with violence and terrorism.

The representation of Muhammad

Discussions of the Danish cartoon affair usually acknowledge the particular hurt that representing Muhammad causes Muslims, but treat this aspect as entailing essentially the same provocation and posing the same question of acceptability as the image of Muhammad and the bomb. There is reason, however, for considering the 'representational issue' separately.

The depiction of Muhammad has long been something of a taboo in most Islamic communities, and even though it has not been universally shared by Muslims (images of the Prophet are found in western Asia, especially among some Shi'ites), the convention appears to have hardened in more recent times (Akram 2006). Muslims the world over are thus genuinely shocked and affronted when they come across images that violate the taboo. Yet, unlike the cartoons of Muhammad with the bomb and some others, the representation of Muhammad does not per se involve a derogatory characterisation of either Islam or Muslims; nor does it, in and of itself, constitute incitement to religious hatred. Rather, the offence is both in the perceived breach of the religious taboo, and in the insult or lack of respect shown Muslims that the breach is taken to imply. We say 'perceived' breach advisedly: several commentators have pointed out that the Islamic injunction against depicting Muhammad lacks clear Qur'anic authority (*BBC*

News 2006a). As Islam scholar Clive Kessler (2006: 30) points out, the injunction would in any case be addressed specifically to *Muslims*: the 'Prophet Muhammad never declared that there should and could never be pictures of himself, by anybody. It was not in his power, and probably not (and could hardly have been) in his imagination, ever to issue such an edict.' Some of the shocked reaction to the cartoon images among Muslims may have been mediated by a belief that the taboo also applied to non-Muslims. But doubtless much of the upset was also mediated by the perceived insult that, though non-Muslims may not be bound by the taboo on representing Muhammad, a major Danish newspaper did not respect the Muslim community enough to refrain from engaging in an obviously provocative act.

So the representation of Muhammad presents us essentially with two issues: the breaching of religious edict, and its implied lack of respect for a particular community. Let us examine each issue in turn.

The breaching of the religious taboo raises the question of the appropriate jurisdiction of religious law. Transgressions of this taboo are seen as blasphemous in the eyes of the faithful. On the other hand, secular liberal societies are not usually in the business of prescribing religious law, at least not without serious qualification – and for good reason. 'Blasphemy' is derived from the Greek meaning 'speaking evil'. In the Judeo-Christian tradition, it includes 'all verbal offences against sacred values' or, as it was put in the seventeenth century, 'treason against God' (Hassan 2006: 121). There is no exact equivalent in Islam of the Judeo-Christian notion of blasphemy. However, Islamic law proscribes insulting Allah, the Prophet Muhammad or the divine revelation. As Riaz Hassan (2006: 122) explains,

From the perspective of Islamic law acts of blasphemy can be defined as any verbal expression that gives grounds for suspicion of apostasy. Blasphemy also overlaps with infidelity (kufr), which is the deliberate rejection of Allah/ God and revelation. In this sense expressing religious opinions at variance with standard Islamic views could easily be looked upon as blasphemous.

Clearly, the compass of what people of faith might find offensive based on the dictates of their religion is comprehensive, and leaves little room for deviation and diversity in a multi-faith and multicultural society. Liberty for everyone, not least among people of faith, would be imperilled. Precisely for this reason, the legal offences of what are commonly called 'blasphemous libel' and, more recently, 'religious hatred' do not generally seek to protect religious sensibilities simply as the faithful themselves pronounce it. Rather, as we discuss in the next section, these laws tend to be much more narrowly focused on prohibiting material that aims to vilify, denigrate or incite hatred of religion or religious groups.

Thus, even *if* the edict against representing Muhammad happened also to apply to non-Muslims, it would not or, at least, should not carry legal endorsement in a free society. A free and secular society means, if it means anything, that individuals should not be made to observe religious injunctions, whether or not they are believers or members of the faith communities concerned.

Now, one test of this liberty principle is the degree to which it enjoys equal protection of the laws, as the Americans call it, or what we have called equal treatment. Suffice it to say that the secular principle of freedom from religious law is generally upheld in liberal democracies, even where religious sensibilities may be especially challenged. Western liberal democracies do not, for example, proscribe the consumption of pork or beef out of consideration for the sacred beliefs, and often deeply felt repulsion, of Jews and Hindus. And, of course, several religious practices have been outlawed in liberal democracies, including polygamy, and some kosher and halal ritual slaughtering (e.g. in Norway, Denmark and Sweden), regardless of the sensibilities of their religious adherents. Yet there are exceptions to this side of the secular rule. In India, cows remain sacred in most places of the country, where beef is not available for consumption, even for those who do not share Hindu belief (Kolanad 2001: 62–4). In Israel, there are laws requiring separate male and female seating on buses servicing Orthodox religious neighbourhoods (Harel 2007).

What, then, of blasphemy laws? For many people, the fundamental problem with such laws is their abridgement of free speech and thus that they exist. However, given their persisting enactment in many democracies, there is no doubting that a major problem with these laws is their often-discriminatory protection of only Christianity. In some places, such as Britain, this discrimination is expressly defined in the laws; in other places, it is a function of how a 'generic' blasphemy law is interpreted and applied by the courts. In either case, such privileging scarcely serves equal protection of the laws, especially where the beneficiary is the dominant faith in the society, as against vulnerable, minority faith communities. Just such a concern has been raised over the equal protection of Denmark's blasphemy law – Article 140 of the Criminal Code – which allows for a fine or up to four months of imprisonment for 'any person who, in public, ridicules or insults the dogmas or worship of any lawfully existing religious community' (Danish Immigration Service n.d.). The Danish scholar Jytte Klausen (2006a) notes that while a Danish (and Lutheran) public prosecutor dismissed a complaint against the Muhammad cartoons on the grounds that they did not obviously constitute blasphemy, all Danish blasphemy cases concern images of Jesus, with one delaying a film about his sex-life for some fourteen years. There may be reason, here, to differentiate between the cartoons that simply represent Muhammad from those that portray him in disparaging or disrespectful ways (something that Klausen does not consider). Much depends on whether Danish courts have found against even benign images or stories of Jesus; then, even the representation of Muhammad might qualify prima facie as constituting blasphemy under the Act.

Overall, then, the weight of liberal-democratic practice is against legally prescribing the observance of religious injunctions, although exceptions remain, while, in the case of blasphemy, the laws rarely coincide with the religious definitions of it. This much, of course, is unsurprising, since liberalism emerged precisely in opposition to the church or religion dictating politics. However, it does serve to underscore that the principle of equality as equal treatment is not really at issue regarding the *legality* of acts that depict Muhammad. Even given the exceptions to the rule of the non-enforcement of religious injunctions, legal recourse or remedy is not an appropriate response to acts like those of *Jyllands-Posten* in depicting Muhammad. The exception, as just noted, would be if similar, non-demeaning images of other religious icons had been found, in Denmark, to constitute blasphemous libel (although the better outcome would be if no such images were actionable). So far, this has not been proved. The act of merely representing Muhammad in cartoon form displays rather a lack of sensitivity, respect and civic consideration; it is not a case of demeaning a religious community, hate speech or incitement to violence. Still, context is everything. One can imagine cases where the mere depiction of Muhammad might constitute hate speech: for example, if streets in a Muslim neighbourhood were adorned with posters of Muhammad's image under cover of darkness. The *Jyllands-Posten* case is different. If the editors erred and are deserving of rebuke for representing

Muhammad in their paper, then it is for what they did or failed to do at the level of respect.

And regarding respect, the first point worth making concerns liberty and fraternity. A sense of fraternity might well temper the value on liberty, and thus the willingness to engage in acts that one knows to be an affront to the religious sensibilities of some among one's neighbours or fellow citizens. There is nothing in the store of liberal-democratic values that precludes such consideration, and much in them that would encourage it. To this extent, *Jyllands-Posten* seems to have assumed that the self-censorship of some publications and artists in refraining from reproducing Muhammad's image was a failure to stand up for liberal-democratic values, when such restraint was just as likely to have been a working expression of them.

The second point concerns equal treatment, and potentially much more than that. As emerged in February 2006, a few years prior to their Muhammad cartoons feature, the editors at *Jyllands-Posten* had declined to publish some cartoons depicting Jesus Christ (*Spiegel Online* 2006). It is uncertain just how satirical or benign these cartoons were; one report suggests they portrayed the Ascension of Jesus (Klausen 2006a). At the time, the responsible *Jyllands-Posten* editor, Jens Kaiser, wrote to the cartoonist explaining their rejection as follows: 'I don't think the readers of *Jyllands-Posten* would be pleased with the drawings. I think they would cause an outrage. That's why I won't use them.' When confronted with this email in 2006, the same editor claimed that his remarks were simply a polite way of communicating rejection; the real reason was that the 'cartoons were just bad' (*Spiegel Online* 2006). However, in another statement, Kaiser suggests that the difference between the two cases is that his paper commissioned illustrators to do the Muhammad cartoons, whereas the Jesus cartoons were sent unsolicited (reported in Klausen 2006c). Regarding Muhammad, then, the editors deliberately set out to be provocative; regarding Jesus, they did not think of doing so.

Or did they? Flemming Rose, the editor who commissioned the Muhammad cartoons, contends that *Jyllands-Posten* had previously published a cartoon, by the same cartoonist that sketched the image of Muhammad with a bomb for a turban, showing 'Jesus on the cross having dollar notes in his eyes and another with the star of David attached to a bomb fuse' (Rose 2006). So let us make our point carefully. What is certain is that *if* the newspaper rejected the Jesus cartoons out of concern for the sensibilities of its readers at the time, then such action would seriously throw into question Rose's defence of the Muhammad cartoons in terms of the importance of unbridled free speech and of separating the secular from the sacred. For then his paper would have acted in a spirit of fraternity over and above liberty in respect of another religious community when its sensibilities were on the line. In doing this for one religious community and not the other, he and his newspaper would have ended up compromising not only their own principles of liberty and equality, but of fraternity as well.

Our third point concerns equality in the sense of treatment as an equal. On this account, equality is honoured by showing equal respect and concern to all parties involved. Doing so may recommend equal treatment, but it also may recommend disparate or special treatment once the background circumstances of the parties and broader social goals are taken into account. It is worth noting that something like this version of equality can be glimpsed at work even in *Jyllands-Posten*'s justification for publishing the Muhammad cartoons. Rose argued not, or not only, that Danish Muslims should be treated the same for the sake of the principles of equal treatment and liberal democracy, but also for the sake of Danish Muslims themselves:

The cartoonists treated Islam the same way they treat Christianity, Buddhism, Hinduism and other religions. And by treating Muslims in Denmark *as equals* they made a point: We are integrating you into the Danish tradition of satire because you are part of our society, not strangers. The cartoons are including, rather than excluding, Muslims. (Rose 2006; emphasis added)

We do not wish to make too much of this implied sense of concern for Muslims in *Jyllands-Posten*'s actions, since so much else in their public statements on why they did what they did emphasises the incompatibility of special consideration with 'contemporary democracy and freedom of speech' (Rose 2005).[3] We simply note that this version of liberal equality (and a rather coercive version of integration) makes an appearance in their defence, and underscores again how the newspaper and everyone else has a choice in how they understand and apply liberal-democratic values.

---

[3] 'The modern, secular society is rejected by some Muslims. They demand a special position, insisting on special consideration of their own religious feelings. It is incompatible with contemporary democracy and freedom of speech, where you must be ready to put up with insults, mockery and ridicule' (Rose 2005).

The newspaper, after all, *could* have taken into account the well-being of Danish Muslims and reached diametrically opposite conclusions regarding what action best served their interests and integration. It *could* have shown equal respect and concern by noting that the prevailing situation is one in which Muslims in general are being marginalised, disproportionately targeted and made vulnerable. It *might* have considered showing solidarity with the Muslim community. At the very least, it *could* have concluded that, in such circumstances, insisting on a lesson in free speech and equal treatment by going out of one's way to cause offence is likely to be received as another poke in the eye rather than as a kind invitation to integrate.

So, on the question of representing Muhammad given Muslim sensitivities, there is a range of possible and competing ways of interpreting, applying and thus defending liberal-democratic values. In assessing *Jyllands-Posten*'s actions, we have tended to stress the force of 'equality', in its dual conceptions, and 'fraternity'. But one could consistently invoke 'liberty' and 'equal treatment' in support of robust free speech; part of *Jyllands-Posten*'s problem, here, is its apparent inconsistency. However, insofar as the newspaper believed that liberal-democratic values, *as such*, warranted publication of the images, we hope we have said enough to show why this belief is mistaken (cf. Hansen 2006a, and O'Leary 2006). However, we suggest that other considerations and commitments, beyond liberal-democratic values, also play a decisive part in shaping people's positions on the representational issue.

Jyllands-Posten seems to hold the view that culturally diverse immigrants are fine as long as all the onus of adjustment falls on the immigrants, and none on Danish society and its political institutions. Jutland has long been a culturally homogeneous and religiously fervent region, comparatively, and the newspaper has 'always minded the religious and political sensitivities of its readership, the Lutheran farmers and the provincial middle class' (Klausen 2006c). In contrast, our view is that multicultural democracies can only work, or work well, where there is some mutual adjustment between immigrants and the host society. A great deal of the adjustment does and will inevitably fall on the immigrants. And some of the practices they may bring – such as forced marriages, female genital mutilation and honour killings – will rightly be deemed non-negotiable and subject to the law. Yet, there are many aspects of immigrant and minority cultures to which the host society could adjust itself that would genuinely assist the integration process. Often these adjustments need only be made at an informal level, beyond the purview of the law. Taking into account the well-known sensitivities of Muslims by refraining from producing deliberately provocative images of Muhammad seems, to us, like a perfect example of just such an informal adjustment in the interests of multicultural integration.

There is a model worth building on here, to which Rose himself alludes. As he puts it, 'When I visit a mosque, I show my respect by taking off my shoes. I follow the customs, just as I do in a church, synagogue or other holy place' (Rose 2006). Yet Rose misunderstands the force of this example. He is right that believers cannot simply expect non-believers to observe such customs, beyond the holy places, also in 'the public domain', and can certainly not expect this as a matter of legal enforcement or from political intimidation. But he is wrong to think that beyond the mosque or church or synagogue we are – or should treat each other as – *only* liberal democrats. First, such an assumption is unlikely to produce a successful and harmonious multicultural democracy, as the Danish cartoon case well illustrates. Second, the assumption is manifestly false. Most people *do* take into account the values and sensitivities of their neighbours where these may be affected by one's actions. *Jyllands-Posten* itself endorsed this sentiment when it declined the Jesus cartoons. As in the holy places, relations of respect in the public spaces turn on knowing who one's fellow citizens are and what they value, and of taking this into account. As Anas Osman, an American Muslim and investment banker, reminded Flemming Rose, 'It's not censorship to be considerate of others' (*International Herald Tribune* 2006).

Islam as a violent creed

What, then, of the cartoon read as an attack on Islam as a creed? As before, we are not suggesting that the cartoon depicting Muhammad with a fused bomb for a turban *was* meant to target Islam as a faith rather than Muslims as a group, only that it should be considered as a possibility. The inscription of the *shahadah* on the bomb lends this interpretation some credence. Some may object that an attack on Islam is just an attack on Muslims as well. Doubtless those who strongly identify with the faith are likely to feel as if they themselves are being maligned. Nevertheless, targeting a faith should not be

automatically conflated with targeting its adherents. Denunciation of
Israel and Zionism, core sites of contemporary Jewish identity, need
not be anti-Semitic or attacks on Jews, as such (Klug 2003, 2004b).
Neither is denunciation or pillorying of Islam necessarily an attack on
Muslims. Of course, in both cases the targeting of the doctrine or the
state may well be a veiled or even overt attempt to target their
adherents. But this is an empirical question that requires careful sifting
of the details of the case; analytically, it is imperative not to define one
as the other a priori.

So, what follows, regarding liberal-democratic values, *had* the
cartoon of Muhammad and the bomb been meant as a statement
about Islam?

It should be clear that 'liberty' sanctions criticism of religion, religions and specific religious practices. That the cartoon's association of
Islam as sanctioning violence or terrorism, on this reading, may be ill
informed and false does not, by itself, count as an argument that
printing such material should not be permitted, or should be subject to
penalties if it is. Assaults on sacred beliefs and practices – whether
from rival theologies, artistic license, simple misinformation or the
deliberately satirical – are part and parcel of free speech in liberal
democracies. That is why the musicals and film versions of *Jesus
Christ Superstar* (1970, 1973) and *Godspell* (1971, 1973), Martin
Scorsese's film *The Last Temptation of Christ* (1988) (based on Nikos
Kazantzakis's 1960 novel), and Mel Gibson's *The Passion of the
Christ* (2004) were rightly allowed to see the light of day unfettered by
law, despite upsetting and being vigorously opposed by various religious groups. That is why Monty Python's *The Life of Brian* (1979)
and the novel and film adaptation of *The Da Vinci Code* (2003, 2006)
were also rightly aired despite presenting parodies or false accounts of
church history and upsetting particular groups.

The nature of the attack is, however, of critical importance. The
progression from the blasphemous libel provisions of old to the religious hatred provisions enacted by some liberal democracies today is
instructive here. As recognised by English law, the criminal offence of
blasphemous libel protects against the publication of material that
subjects 'God or Christ, the Christian religion, the Bible, or some
sacred subject' to scurrility, vilification or abuse, and thus 'lead[s] to a
breach of the peace' (Law Commission 1985). The first recorded case
of blasphemous libel was in 1676, and involved material calling Jesus
Christ a bastard and whoremaster (Gilchrist 1997). From this point,

the state increasingly took over from the church as the chief prosecutor of charges of blasphemy. As previously noted, blasphemy laws are often problematic in their discriminatory privileging of Christianity. However, such laws are scarcely improved by extending them to include other faiths.

Even confined to Christianity, the crime of blasphemous libel has waned to the point of near universally recognised obsolescence. Where once it was the church that sought to prosecute against blasphemy, and then the state, in the twentieth century the cases increasingly involved individuals or groups bringing action against other individuals or groups, and few of these succeeded. The last successful prosecution for blasphemy in England was in 1977, while there have been no prosecutions, successful or otherwise, in the United States since 1969 (Hassan 2006: 121). In Australia, where blasphemous libel is generally treated as a common law offence, its status is uneven across jurisdictions. In the state of Victoria, for example, prior to the 1990s, the last attempt to prosecute blasphemy as a common law offence in the state was in 1919. In 1997, the Roman Catholic Archbishop of Melbourne brought action under the blasphemy provisions to suppress the National Gallery of Victoria exhibiting the controversial artwork *Piss Christ* (discussed below). In that case, Justice Harper ventured the view that blasphemous libel was an anachronism (Gilchrist 1997). Another state, Queensland, excised blasphemy from its criminal code as far back as 1899, arguing that these provisions of English law were 'manifestly obsolete or inapplicable to Australia' (quoted in Law Reform Commission of New South Wales 1992). In Denmark, the cases also have been sporadic and mostly counter-productive (Klausen 2006c). In short, blasphemy has 'become almost impossible to prove, and it is not clear what it is protecting' (Coleman and White 2006: 4).

The move to religious hatred laws in some jurisdictions reflects a wish to avoid the inefficacy (and Christian-centricity) of blasphemy laws. They do this by substantially narrowing the definition of the offence. In particular, such laws seek to extend the widely supported need in contemporary democracies for an offence of incitement to racial hatred, to an offence that covers incitement to religious hatred and group defamation as well. The United Kingdom's Racial and Religious Hatred Act 2006 is a case in point. The religious hatred provisions of the Act provide that: 'A person who uses threatening words or behaviour, or displays any written material which is threatening, is guilty of an offence if he intends thereby to stir up religious hatred.' Freedom-of-speech concerns have been protected in two ways: first, by outlawing only 'threatening' words and behaviour, and not those that are merely critical, abusive or insulting; and, second, by requiring that persons can be prosecuted only if they intend to stir up hatred, and not if they are merely reckless (*BBC News* 2006b). Many people, including one of us (Modood), believe that the 'intention' requirement – which is very difficult to prove and not part of the racial hatred legislation – is unfortunate in overly diluting the protection afforded religious groups. Yet even without this condition, it would not be a simple matter for religious hatred laws to prohibit an ambiguous image like that of Muhammad and the turban-bomb, which some will seek to defend as political criticism or satire of a religion or a particular interpretation of a religion, and not of Muslims as a group.[4]

It is clear, then, that short of incitement to hatred, religion will remain subject to the 'rough and tumble' of life in liberal democracies. The record suggests that whatever the historical demonisation of Islam and Muhammad in medieval Christianity, today Islam is being subjected to forms of irreverence that have been honed on Christian

---

[4] The first case heard under the Australian state of Victoria's Racial and Religious Tolerance Act 2001 is very interesting in this respect. The Islamic Council of Victoria brought an action in a representative capacity, under the Act, against two pastors from Catch the Fire Ministries for allegedly inciting religious hatred against Victorian Muslims. The Act states that 'A person must not, on the ground of the religious belief or activity of another person or class of persons engage in conduct that incites hatred against, serious contempt for, or revulsion or severe ridicule of, that other person or class of persons.' The Act excludes a person's motive in engaging in such conduct as irrelevant. It also deems 'irrelevant whether or not the race or religious belief or activity of another person or class of persons is the only or dominant ground for the conduct, so long as it is a substantial ground.' However, the Act also provides that no contravention occurs where a person is engaged, 'reasonably and in good faith', in publication, discussion or debate for 'any genuine academic, artistic, religious or scientific purpose' or 'in the public interest'. In December 2004, in a controversial decision, the Victorian Civil and Administrative Tribunal found the two pastors guilty of inciting religious hatred against Muslims. In December 2006, the Victorian Supreme Court upheld the appeal against the Tribunal's decision. A key finding of the appellate court was that the Tribunal had failed to draw a distinction between hatred of the beliefs of a particular religion and the hatred of persons holding those beliefs. Earlier in 2006, Equal Opportunity Victoria chief executive, Dr Helen Szoke, suggested that it would be unlikely that the state's Racial and Religious Tolerance Act would prohibit the *Jyllands-Posten* cartoons (*The Age* 2006).

targets, usually by ex-Christians. The Messiah, the Last Supper, the Resurrection, the Ten Commandments, the Pope, and God Himself, among many other sacred images, have been variously mocked, maligned and misrepresented in legions of cartoons, songs, shows and other media. While some regret this trend and think it has gone too far, it is fair say that what we have today is 'blasphemy' as an art form, and not merely blasphemy as minority dissent from a powerful, authoritarian Christianity. Perhaps the most celebrated and pertinent case is, of course, Salman Rushdie's unflattering portrait of Islam in his 1988 novel, *The Satanic Verses*. But Islam is far from being singled out in this respect, even if the mocking of Islam brings into play distinctive and powerful contexts.

Take pop diva Madonna, for example, who is something of a serial and equal-opportunity offender in religious affairs. In 1989, she had Catholic leaders crying 'blasphemy' over her video for the hit song 'Like a prayer', which featured burning crosses, religious icons crying blood and her seducing a black Jesus (*CBC News* 2006). More recently, her album *Confessions on a Dance Floor* (2005) had some observant Jews upset. It included a song titled 'Isaac', which referred to the sixteenth-century Jewish mystic and founder of Kabbalah, Isaac Luria. For some time, Madonna, a lapsed Catholic, has been a devotee of Kabbalah. But that scarcely mattered to the custodians of Luria's tomb and seminary in the northern Israeli town of Safed, who accused her of breaking a taboo. 'There is a prohibition in Jewish law against using the holy name of our Master, the Sage Isaac, for profit', the seminary's director, Rabbi Rafael Cohen, was reported as saying in the Israeli newspaper, *Ma'ariv* (*Sydney Morning Herald* 2005). A year later and Madonna was in the news for staging a mock crucifixion during her *Confessions Tour* performance in Rome, a stone's throw from the Vatican. 'It is disrespectful, in bad taste and provocative', Father Manfredo Leone from Rome's Santa Maria Liberatrice church said. 'Doing it in the cradle of Christianity comes close to blasphemy' (*CBC News* 2006). As it happens, on this occasion Muslim and Jewish leaders showed their religious solidarity by also publicly condemning Madonna for her poor taste and judgement.

Even more provocative than artists and entertainers exploiting or parodying religious themes are the attempts to portray religious images in base and confronting ways. Andres Serrano's *Piss Christ* (1987), a photograph of a crucifix submerged in the artist's own urine, is perhaps the best-known example. Understandably, it offended many Christians.

When the item was exhibited at the National Gallery of Victoria in Australia in 1997, the exhibit had to be closed prematurely after two youths vandalised the glass display by taking a hammer to it (Gilchrist 1997). Another modern art exhibit, *Sensation: Young British Artists from the Saatchi Collection*, caused controversy when it debuted at New York's Brooklyn Museum. The exhibit included an image of the Virgin Mary smeared in elephant dung. Then New York Mayor, Rudolph Giuliani, considered this to be an obscenity and sought to have the exhibit closed on pain of withdrawing public funding. Such an attempt at censorship in liberal New York itself became controversial; however, many New Yorkers demonstrably shared his point of view.[5]

All religions, not only Islam, are thus subject to the provocations thrown up by life in liberal democracies. Indeed, it could be said that what has happened in the West is that the viciousness we associate with political satire has been extended to bring religion to the level of profane politics. Consider, for example, the extraordinary cartoon war that almost derailed Indonesian and Australian relations, sparked by Australia's decision to grant temporary protection visas to forty-two West Papuans in early 2006. It is worth remembering that Indonesia is the world's most populous Muslim country. The initial salvo, on the front page of the *Rakyat Merdeka* newspaper (27 March 2006), depicted the Australian Prime Minister and Foreign Minister as copulating dingos, with the former saying 'I want Papua Alex! You try to play it.' Days later, the editorial cartoon in the weekend edition of *The Australian*, the national 'quality' broadsheet newspaper, depicted a character resembling Indonesia's President Susilo Bambang Yudhoyono as a tail-wagging dog mounting a West Papuan with a bone through his nose, and saying 'Don't take this the wrong way ...' (Figure 1).

Indeed, despite, or perhaps because of, the gross offensiveness and inflamed tensions these cartoons caused in both those countries, we believe the Indonesian Embassy in Canberra hit exactly the right note in its protest:

[T]hese cartoons are malicious, tasteless and are detrimental to the effort to improve the relationship between Indonesia and Australia ... While I acknowledge the freedom of the media in Indonesia and Australia and

---

[5] See www.artsjournal.com/issues/Brooklyn.htm.

Figure 1 Bill Leak, 'No offence intended', *The Weekend Australian*, 1 April 2006. © Newspix/News Ltd/3rd Party Managed Reproduction and Supply Rights. Reproduced with permission.

respect its independence from government interference, I believe there is a responsibility from the media to be sensitive and attentive to the consequences of their actions (Embassy of the Republic of Indonesia 2006).[6]

Similarly, in the case of offences to religious sensibilities, the appropriate response can only be more free speech or 'speaking back' (Gelber 2002). As Bleich (2006) observes, it is curious that some liberals who defended the free speech rights of *Jyllands-Posten* to publish material like the Muhammad cartoons should also condemn the demonstrations that erupted around the world in protest against them. As we argued earlier in relation to the representational issue, a sense of fraternity or solidarity with those offended, or likely to be, would clearly recommend that one refrain from engaging in, or

---

[6] For his part, Indonesia's President drew on the Danish cartoon affair to address his country's media: 'It's my responsibility, taking lessons from the Muhammad cartoons, to say to the Indonesian media, "Let's be more proper, don't go beyond the limits. Let's express the people's emotions, nationalism, dignity and honour in a more correct way"' (translated; *ABC Online* 2006).

patronising, acts that are disrespectful, or else voice one's dismay where they do occur. And if one is not ordinarily inclined towards such feelings of solidarity, then showing equal respect and concern by allowing for the present vulnerabilities of Muslims and a need to smooth their integration, might lend the inclination encouragement.

As for the religious, short of remonstrating and demonstrating, the only other suitable response to such perceived offences is to be found within religion itself. As Rabbi Cohen of the Isaac Luria seminary in Israel wisely recognised, beyond registering his complaint against Madonna, there was nothing further for him or political authorities to do about the matter: 'This is an inappropriate act, and one can only feel pity at the punishment that she [Madonna] will receive from Heaven' (*Sydney Morning Herald* 2005).

Muslims as terrorists and dangerous

The previous discussion assumed for the sake of argument that the cartoon of Muhammad and the turban-bomb was intended or may reasonably be read as a comment on Islam as a faith rather than on Muslims. Yet, the cartoon can also plausibly be read as a comment on Muslims (and no doubt was). Since we argue that this difference matters regarding how the decision to publish such a cartoon should be judged, let us now turn to the more serious offence of targeting Muslims rather than Islam.

Jytte Klausen (2006a) suggests that another of the cartoons in the series is clearly 'anti-Semitic' in the following terms:

For brevity's sake, let's do a 'veil of ignorance' test and consider the cartoon depicting the Prophet as an old man with a blood-dripping sword and two pretty and young women in face-veils standing behind. We know they are pretty because of their big eyes and the form of their bodies suggested by the cartoonist. And please note the bushy eyebrows and the Semitic nose attributed to Mohamed. Then replace the sword with a trunk full of money and replace the turban with skullcap. What do you get? You get a classic Nordic or German anti-Semitic cartoon of Jews from the 1930s.

We view this cartoon differently from Klausen in some of the details. For one thing, we are at a loss to see any blood dripping from the old Prophet's sword. Second, we read the big eyes of the veiled women as signifying awareness and a ready openness to the world in contrast to their Prophet-master, who keeps them in veils and who is portrayed with a blindfold. Still, Klausen has a point about the phenotyping of Muhammad with a bulbous nose and bushy eyebrows, and the negative stereotyping implicit in the sword vis-à-vis the women. While the overall image and message may not come close to the crude, anti-Semitic *Stürmer* cartoons of the Nazi era (see Rosenthal 2006), the representation is strongly suggestive of a comment on Muslims as much as on Islam.[7] As noted, we think the same might be said also of the turban-bomb cartoon, notwithstanding the inclusion of the Islamic creed in that image. The main point is that, in our view, an attack on Muslims as a group marks a brush with racism. It invites, in a way that the previously discussed cases of the 'mere' representation of Muhammad and an attack on Islam as a creed do not, the possible justification of legal action under religious and/or racial hatred laws.[8]

The laws proscribing Holocaust denial, as found in many European countries, are instructive in this respect. Some people suggest that such laws show that religious sensibilities in general, and Muslim sensibilities in particular, are not treated as seriously as Jewish sensibilities. One can argue the merits and demerits of proscribing free speech in the case of Holocaust denial, a debate that became even more pressing with the conviction and imprisonment in Austria of the British writer David Irving in early 2006. The stated complaints about the privileged legal treatment of Holocaust denial, however, need to be disentangled.

It is true, as canvassed in the previous section, that religion is not protected in the way that the facticity of the Holocaust is. However, this applies to Judaism as much as to any other religion. Holocaust denial and the laws proscribing it have nothing to do with religion. Nor do they have anything to do with the protection of Jews' feelings or

---

[7] A third cartoon – of a thin and quizzical-looking Muhammad figure with short horns emerging from his turban – is also ambiguous. On the one hand, the horns might be taken as a sign of demonisation following the widespread medieval Christian representation of Moses with horns, typically used to signify the ignonimy and dishonour of the Jews for rejecting Jesus Christ the Messiah. On the other hand, the horns from a turban might be suggestive of honour and integration, since there is an ancient Egyptian tradition, and Hebrew biblical suggestion, in which a horned Moses signifies rays of light and nobility, a tradition that finds its echo among the Vikings, where helmeted horns represent men of high rank. On the multiple meanings of the horned Moses in history, see Mellinkoff (1970).

[8] Again, we are aware that the very ambiguity of the image does not make prohibition easy, either as a matter of principle or in practice.

sensibilities, as such. The laws are silent on cartoonists who liken the Israelis to the Nazis, for example. Nor do such laws exist for the sake of protecting historical truth; there are no laws against people claiming that World War II did not happen, for example, or that France beat Italy in the 2006 World Cup. Holocaust denial laws can only be understood and justified, we suggest, as an act of fraternity and solidarity with groups, principally Jews, who were mercilessly murdered by the Nazis, and whose remnants today face the added trauma of being told by neo-Nazis and others that they either imagined this horror or invented it for material gain. Such laws say: 'Your people were mass-murdered then; we will take measures, even at the cost of some of our liberty, to ensure that you are not assailed, of all things, with your own people's murder now.' Holocaust denial laws thus protect a group or groups from hatred and incitement that exploit a particular historical travesty; they do not protect a religion or a culture or even those groups' broader sensibilities. While they have little relevance to the protection of religions, they are akin to religious and racial hatred laws that aim to protect *groups* from hatred and incitement against them.

The first challenge to our contention that a few of the Danish cartoons are suggestive of negative stereotyping and demonisation of Muslims is that we fail to allow for the medium of cartoonery. The stock-in-trade of cartoons is, after all, caricature. The features of subjects are invariably exaggerated in ridiculous ways, and associations are graphically and necessarily stretched to make a point in the space of a picture. We readily concede these points about the craft of cartooning, but suggest that cartooning, no less than other forms of speech and expression, is governed by appropriate limits. We think caricature is one thing, and negative stereotyping quite another. Caricaturing football hooligans, for example, carries no implication – and no chance of implying – that all football fans are hooligans. The contrary perception is too widely appreciated and entrenched.

Negative stereotyping, however, trades on and reinforces prejudice. It can work in two ways: via a process of induction and a process of deduction. Brian Klug (2004a: 20) nicely captures the difference in describing anti-Semitism:

The logic of anti-Semitism does not work like this: 'The Rothschilds are powerful and exploitive, hence Jews in general are.' But more like this: 'Jews are powerful and exploitive, just look at the Rothschilds.' In other words, anti-Semites do not generalize from instances. They are disposed to see Jews in a certain negative light, which is why I call their prejudice 'a priori.'

What we are now witnessing in the treatment of Muslims in the West is the shift from inductive to deductive negative generalisations about them. Inductive negative stereotyping can be seen clearly in the security policies of 'racial profiling', where security services concentrate their attention on people who look or behave a certain way based on the activities of Islamists. Deductive negative stereotyping is evident or at least strongly suggested in the two Danish cartoons under consideration. Klug's (2003: 6) definition of anti-Semitism on this score applies with equal force to these images of Muslims:

It would be more accurate (if cumbersome) to define the word along these lines: a form of hostility towards Jews as Jews, in which Jews are perceived as something other than what they are. Or more succinctly: hostility towards Jews as *not* Jews. For the 'Jew' towards whom the antisemite feels hostile is not a *real* Jew at all. Thinking that Jews are really 'Jews' is precisely the core of anti-Semitism.

Thinking of or picturing Muslims as really 'Muslims' is similarly the core of Islamophobia.

There is, however, a second challenge to our claim that some of the cartoons are racist: Muslims are a religious group, not a race; *ergo* they cannot be the victims of racism. For example, political scientists Russell Hansen (2006a,b) and Brendan O'Leary (2006) argue, in the context of the Danish cartoon affair, that talk of Muslims as suffering racism is inappropriate, for, insofar as they suffer racism, it is not qua Muslims. Similarly, in the aftermath of the Christmas 2005 beach riots in Sydney – images of which were beamed around the world – many commentators claimed that the attack by 'Anglo-Australians' on Muslim Australians could not be racism because the spur was a perception that Muslims were not adequately abiding by Australian norms, not the colour of their skin or their physical appearance (see Levey and Moses 2008).

There is no question that there is a complex of issues currently defining the Muslim experience. How Muslims are perceived today is both connected to how they have been perceived and treated by European empires and their racial hierarchies, and by Christian

Islamophobia and the Crusades in earlier centuries. The images, generalisations and fears have both continuity and newness to them. Moreover, these perceptions and treatments overlap with contemporary European/white people's attitudes and behaviour towards blacks, Asians, immigrants and so on. The perception and treatment clearly have a religious and cultural dimension, but equally clearly they have a phenotypical dimension. Given a number of images – cartoons – of people and asked to pick out a Muslim, most people would have a go and not reply 'but I do not know what any of these people believe', just as if they were asked to identify Jews they would have a go (though perhaps less so today than in the past given that Jews are becoming de-racialised or normalised as 'white' in many parts of the West). In the Sydney riots, 'Anglo-Australians' attacked as presumptively Muslim anyone who was of 'middle-Eastern appearance', not simply those who wore Islamic clothing.

It is true that 'Muslim' is not a (putative) biological category in the way that 'black' or 'south Asian' (aka 'Paki') or Chinese is. Nor does 'Muslim' carry the same kind of ethno-national marker of identity as does 'Jew'. Yet focusing on these differences misses what is common to the process of racialisation of any group. Consider, first, the Jewish case. The centuries-long Christian persecution of the Jews was grounded in their religious beliefs and distinctive customs; acceptance of Christ could put an end to their misery. Traditional Judeo-phobia became 'anti-Semitism' – a virulent and lethal biologically based prejudice – only in the nineteenth century, as Jews sought fully to integrate in western Europe. Jews were racialised as outsiders precisely when they sought to become insiders or full members. The prejudice against them transmuted from a damning theological disputation to the blood in their veins, where what they believed or did or how they looked was immaterial. In understanding racism, what is key, here, is not that 'blood' was invoked to exclude or condemn all Jews, but the targeting of all members of the Jewish group simply by virtue of their membership. It should not be forgotten that Bosnian Muslims were 'ethnically cleansed' by people who were phenotypically, linguistically and culturally the same as them. The ethnic cleanser, unlike an inquisitor, wasted no time in finding out what people believed, if and how often they went to a mosque and so on: rather, their victims were simply 'ethnically' identified as Muslims.

Or take the case of people of south Asian origin, locally called 'Asians' (and less pleasant monikers), who comprise the most numerous non-whites in the UK. It has been argued that even before the rise of a distinct anti-Muslim racism there was an anti-Asian racism and that it was distinct from anti-black racism in having distinct stereotypes (if one was unintelligent, aggressive, happy-go-lucky and lazy, the other was 'too clever by half', passive, worked too hard and did not know how to have fun (Modood 1997b)). Moreover, if in the case of black people the stereotypes appealed to some (implicit) biology, to IQ, physical prowess, sense of rhythm, sexual drive and so on, none of the main stereotypes about Asians even implicitly referred to a scientific or folk biology. The stereotypes all referred to Asian cultural norms and community structures – to gender roles and norms, patriarchy, family authority and obligations, arranged marriages, religion, work ethic and so on. Notwithstanding the phenotypical appearances, anti-Asian racism is predominantly a form of cultural racism.

The most violent form of racism that Asians in Britain have experienced is random physical attacks in public places, 'Paki-bashing'. We have not seen any analysis of this phenomenon that refers to any biological beliefs held by the perpetrators. Interviews with the pool of people from which the perpetrators come – young working-class white males, especially 'skinheads' – and others in their neighbourhoods accuse Asians not of a deficient biology but of being aliens, of not belonging in 'our country', of 'taking over the country' and so on (Back 1993; Bonnett 1993; Cohen 1988; Modood 2005). That is, things of which the Nazis accused the Jews (in addition to not having the right blood).

Once we break with the idea that (contemporary) racism is only about biology, then we should be able to see that cultural and religious groups also can be racialised; that Muslims can be the victims of racism qua Muslims as well as qua Asians or Arabs or Bosnians. We suggest that precisely this process of racialisation – albeit so far at a much lower level of violence – is taking place in western Europe and indeed most parts of the West. The stereotypical targeting of Muslims in cartoons qualifies as a part of it.[9]

---

[9] For an extended discussion on the racialisation of Muslims, see Modood (2006a, b).

Conclusion

The Danish cartoon affair is typically construed as a clash between Muslim sensibilities on the one hand, and liberal-democratic values on the other. We have suggested that the affair has many more sides to it than that; it includes also a conflict within the value set of liberal democracy. We have argued that the publication of the Muhammad cartoon series entails three different possible types of offence: the deliberate depiction of Muhammad despite a well-known Muslim objection to such representation, the criticising or mocking of Islam as a creed and the stereotypical targeting of Muslims. Regarding the first two cases, we have observed that the principle of liberty does not require deliberately causing offence to people, while equality and fraternity might actually work to check any such inclination. However, we acknowledge that honouring liberty and a version of equality also means that people are entitled to cause offence in these ways without legal restriction or penalty. We have argued that the third type of offence – the targeting of Muslims through hostile stereotypes – is different. The attempt to target, denigrate and thus exclude members of a cultural group simply by virtue of their membership is a form of racism. It breaches the liberal-democratic values of liberty, equality and fraternity. It legitimately falls – or should fall – within the terms of racial or religious hatred legislation. In sport, 'playing the man and not the ball' is considered a foul and an actionable offence. So should it be in the relations among liberal-democratic citizens.

Episodes like the Danish cartoon affair present liberals with choices. There are choices to be made about what liberty, equality and fraternity mean. There are choices about which meaning and which value should assume priority, and under what conditions. And there are choices about how these meanings and values apply to the details of specific cases. Making these kinds of choices will necessarily be informed by a host of considerations beyond the values in question. We suggest that a key consideration in this respect is the pragmatic question of how best to make multicultural democracies work. As the essays in this book have variously shown, governing values require interpretation, and some interpretations can end up frustrating rather than serving effective governance. Whether the challenge is religion or ethnic diversity, or Islam or Muslims, liberal-democratic principles will be of little help if they cannot meet the challenge.

References

ABC Online. 2006. 'Yudhoyono calls for calm over Papuan visas', PM Program, 3 April, www.abc.net.au/pm/content/2006/s1607498.htm.

Abou El Fadl, K. 1994. 'Legal debates on Muslim minorities: between rejection and accommodation', *Journal of Religion and Ethics* 22: 127–62.

Ackerman, B. 1989. 'Why dialogue?', *Journal of Philosophy* 86: 5–22.

Ahmed, I. 1987. *The Concept of an Islamic State: An Analysis of the Ideological Controversy in Pakistan*. London: Frances Pinter.

Akram, A. 2006. 'What's behind Muslim cartoon outrage: Muhammad's image', *San Francisco Chronicle*, 11 February.

Archard, D. 2001. 'Political disagreement, legitimacy, and civility', in B. v. d. Brink (ed.), *Civic Virtue and Pluralism,* special issue of *Philosophical Explorations* 4: 207–23.

Asad, T. 2003. *Formations of the Secular: Christianity, Islam and Modernity*. Palo Alto, CA: Stanford University Press, pp. 494–526.

   2006. 'Trying to understand French secularism', in H. de Vries and L. E. Sullivan (eds.), *Political Theologies: Public Religions in a Post-Secular World*. New York: Fordham University Press.

Audi, R. 1989. 'The separation of church and state and the obligations of citizenship', *Philosophy & Public Affairs* 18: 259–96.

   1991. 'Religious commitment and secular reason', *Philosophy & Public Affairs* 18: 66–76.

   1993. 'The place of religious argument in a free and democratic society', *San Diego Law Review* 30: 677–701.

   1997. 'The state, the church, and the citizen', in Weithman (ed.), pp. 38–75.

Austin, G. 1972. *The Indian Constitution: Cornerstone of a Nation*. New Delhi: Oxford University Press.

Back, L. 1993. 'Race, identity and nation within an adolescent community in south London', *New Community* 19: 217–33.

Bader, V. 1984. 'Habermas' theorie van het communicatieve handelen als legitimiteitstheorie', *Krisis* 16: 71–93.

   1988. 'Macht of waarheid?', *Kennis en Methode* 12: 138–57.

   1991. *Kollectives Handeln*. Opladen: Leske & Budrich.

243

1999. 'Religious pluralism, secularism or priority for democracy?', *Political Theory* 27: 597–633.

2003a. 'How to make policy-advising by (social) scientists and philosophers more democratic and effective?' Paper presented at Ethics and Public Policy International Conference, Utrecht, 15–16 May.

2003b. 'Religions and states: a new typology and a plea for nonconstitutional pluralism', *Ethical Theory and Moral Practice* 5: 55–91.

2003c. 'Religious diversity and democratic institutional pluralism', *Political Theory* 3: 265–94.

2007. *Secularism or Democracy? Associational Governance of Religious Diversity*. University of Amsterdam Press.

Barber, B. 1988. *The Conquest of Politics*. Princeton University Press.

Barisic, S. 2002. 'Pat Robertson describes Islam as a violent religion that wants to dominate'. Associated Press, 22 February.

Baubérot, J. 2000. *Histoire de la laïcité française*. Paris: Presses Universitaires de France.

2005. 'La loi de 1905 est plus qu'une loi', in Y.-C. Zarka (ed.), *Faut-il reviser la loi de 1905? La séparation entre religions et l'Etat en question*. Paris: Presses Universitaires de France, pp. 105–31.

Bauböck, R. (ed.). 1994. *From Aliens to Citizens: Redefining the Status of Immigrants in Europe*. Aldershot: Ashgate.

Bauböck, R., A. Heller and A. R. Zolberg (eds.). 1996. *The Challenges of Diversity: Integration and Pluralism in Societies of Immigration*. Aldershot: Ashgate.

Bauböck, R. and J. Rundell (eds.). 1998. *Blurred Boundaries: Migration, Ethnicity, Citizenship*. Aldershot: Ashgate.

Baynes, K. 1992. *The Normative Grounds of Social Criticism: Kant, Rawls, and Habermas*. State University of New York Press.

BBC News. 2005. 'US chastity ring funding attacked', 17 May, http://news.bbc.co.uk/2/hi/americas/4553721.stm.

2006a. 'Q&A: depicting the prophet Muhammad', 2 February, http://news.bbc.co.uk/2/hi/middle_east/4674864.stm.

2006b. 'Q&A: religious hatred law', 1 February, http://news.bbc.co.uk/1/hi/uk/3873323.stm.

2006c. 'Straw's veil comments spark anger', 5 October, http://news.bbc.co.uk/1/hi/uk_politics/5410472.stm.

2007. '"Chastity ring" girl loses case', 16 July, http://news.bbc.co.uk/2/hi/uk_news/6900512.stm.

2008. 'Cartoonist to sue over Islam film', 28 March, http://news.bbc.co.uk/2/hi/europe/7318733.stm.

Behme, T. 2002. 'Pufendorf's doctrine of sovereignty and its natural law foundations', in I. Hunter and D. Saunders (eds.), *Natural Law and*

Civil Sovereignty: Moral Right and State Authority in Early Modern Political Thought. Basingstoke: Palgrave, pp. 43–58.

Bellah, R. 1967. 'Civil religion in America', *Daedalus* 96: 1–21.

Benhabib, S. 1986. *Critique, Norm, and Utopia: A Study of the Foundations of Critical Theory*. New York: Columbia University Press.

1992. 'Models of public space: Hannah Arendt, the liberal tradition, and Jürgen Habermas', in C. Calhoun (ed.), *Habermas and the Public Sphere*. Cambridge, MA: MIT Press, pp. 73–98.

2002. *The Claims of Culture: Equality and Diversity in the Global Era*. Princeton University Press.

Bettinson, C. 1989. 'The *Politiques* and the *Politique* party: a re-appraisal', in K. Cameron (ed.), *From Valois to Bourbon: Dynasty, State and Society in Early Modern France*. University of Exeter Press, pp. 35–50.

Bhargava, R. 1998a. 'Introduction', in Bhargava (ed.), pp. 1–30.

(ed.). 1998b. *Secularism and Its Critics*. New Delhi: Oxford University Press.

1998c. 'What is secularism for?', in Bhargava (ed.), pp. 486–542.

2004. *Inclusion and Exclusion in South Asia: The Role of Religion*. Background paper for Human Development Report, UNDP.

2007. 'The distinctiveness of Indian secularism', in T. N. Srinavasan (ed.), *The Future of Secularism*. Delhi: Oxford University Press, pp. 20–58.

Bilgrami, A. 2004. 'Secularism and relativism', *Boundary* 31: 173–96.

Billington, R. A. 1938. *The Protestant Crusade, 1800–1860: A Study of the Origins of American Nativism*. New York: Macmillan.

Bleich, E. 2006. 'On democratic integration and free speech: response to Tariq Modood and Randall Hansen', in Modood *et al.*, pp. 17–22.

Bohman, J. 2003a. 'Deliberative toleration', *Political Theory* 31: 757–79.

2003b. 'Reflexive public deliberation', *Philosophy and Social Criticism* 29: 85–105.

Bonnett, A. 1993. *Radicalism, Anti-Racism and Representation*. London and New York: Routledge.

Bowen, J. 2004. 'Muslims and citizens: France's headscarf controversy', *Boston Review* 29 (February/March): 31–5.

2006. *Why the French Don't Like Headscarves*. Princeton University Press.

Brass, P. R. 2003. *The Production of Hindu–Muslim Violence in Contemporary India*. Seattle and London: University of Washington.

Brink, B. v. d. 2002. 'Politischer Liberalismus und ziviler Perfektionismus', *Deutsche Zeitschrift für Philosophie* 6: 907–24.

Brown, J. 2000. *Nehru: Profiles in Power*. London: Longman.

Brubaker, R. 2001. 'The return of assimilation? Changing perspectives on immigration and its sequels in France, Germany, and the United States', *Ethnic and Racial Studies* 24: 531–48.

Caplan, J. 1988. *Government without Administration*. Oxford: Clarendon Press.

Casanova, J. 1994. *Public Religions in the Modern World*. Chicago: University of Chicago Press.

1998. 'Between nation and civil society: ethno-linguistic and religious pluralism in Ukraine', in R. Heffner (ed.), *Democratic Civility*. New Brunswick, NJ: Transaction, pp. 203–28.

2001. 'Civil society and religion: retrospective reflections on Catholicism and prospective reflections on Islam', *Social Research* 68: 1041–80.

2006. 'Religion, secular identities, and European integration', in P. Katzenstein and T. Byrnes (eds.), *Religion in an Expanding Europe*. Cambridge University Press, pp. 65–90.

CBC News. 2006. 'Religious leaders protest Madonna's glittery concert crucifixion', 3 August, www.cbc.ca/arts/story/2006/08/03/madonna-concert-protest.html.

Cesari, J. 2004. *When Islam and Democracy Meet: Muslims in Europe and in the United States*. New York: Palgrave Macmillan.

Chandhoke, N. 1999. *Beyond Secularism: The Rights of Religious Minorities*. New Delhi: Oxford University Press.

Chatterjee, P. 1998. 'Secularism and toleration', in Bhargava (ed.), pp. 345–79.

Chicago Tribune. 2002. 'Christians, Jews still predominate', 29 January.

Christin, O. 1997. *La paix de religion: l'autonomisation de la raison politique au XVIe siècle*, Paris: Seuil.

Cimino, R. 2003. 'Evangelical discourse on Islam after 9/11'. Paper presented at the Association for the Sociology of Religion annual meeting (August), Atlanta.

Cohen, J. L. and A. Arato 1992. *Civil Society and Political Theory*. Cambridge, MA: MIT Press.

Cohen, N. W. 1992. *Jews in Christian America: The Pursuit of Religious Equality*. New York: Oxford University Press.

Cohen, P. 1988 'The perversions of inheritance: studies in the making of multi-racist Britain', in P. Cohen and H. S. Bains (eds.), *Multi-Racist Britain*. London: Macmillan.

Cohen, R. (ed.). 1995. *The Cambridge Survey of World Migration*. Cambridge University Press.

Colas, D. 1997. *Civil Society and Fanaticism: Conjoined Histories*, trans. A. Jacobs. Stanford University Press.

Coleman, E. B. and K. White. 2006. 'Negotiating the sacred in multicultural societies', in E. B. Coleman and K. White (eds.), *Negotiating the Sacred: Blasphemy and Sacrilege in a Multicultural Society*. Canberra: ANU E Press, pp. 1–12.

Colemann, J. 1997. 'Deprivatizing religion and revitalizing citizenship', in Weithman (ed.), pp. 264–90.

Commission on British Muslims and Islamophobia (CBMI). 2002. *Response to the Commission on Racial Equality's Code of Practice*. London: The Commission.

Connolly, W. E. 1995. *The Ethos of Pluralization*. Minneapolis: University of Minnesota Press.

    1999. *Why I Am Not a Secularist*. Minneapolis: University of Minnesota Press.

    2005. *Pluralism*. Durham, NC: Duke University Press.

Crouzet, D. 1991. *Les guerriers de Dieu: La violence au temps des troubles de religion*, 2 vols. Seysell: Editions Champ Vallon.

    1997. *La sagesse et le malheur: Michel de L'Hospital, Chancelier de France*. Seysell: Editions Champ Vallon.

Curry, T. J. 1989. 'Church and state in seventeenth and eighteenth century America', *Journal of Law and Religion* 7: 261–73.

Dalin, D. G. (ed.). 1993. *American Jews and the Separationist Faith: The New Debate on Religion in Public Life*. Washington, DC: Ethics and Public Policy Center.

Danish Immigration Service. n.d. 'A7 solemn declaration: criminal offences', www.nyidanmark.dk/resources.ashx/Resources/Blanketter/ Erklaeringer/2006/A7-erklaering_UK.doc.

Davie, G. 1994. *Religion in Britain since 1945: Believing without Belonging*. Oxford: Blackwell.

    2000. *Religion in Modern Europe: A Memory Mutates*. Oxford University Press.

Davies, N. 2006. *Europe, East and West*. London: Jonathan Cape.

Davis, D. B. 1960. 'Some themes of countersubversion: an analysis of anti-Masonic, anti-Catholic, and anti-Mormon literature'. *Mississippi Valley Historical Review* 47: 205–24.

Denzer, H. 1972. *Moral philosophie und Naturrecht bei Samuel Pufendorf: eine geistes- und wissenschaftliche Untersuchung zur Geburt des Naturrechts aus der Praktischen Philosophie*. Munich: C. H. Beck.

Deveaux, M. 2005. 'A deliberative approach to conflicts of culture', in A. Eisenberg and J. Spinner-Halev (eds.), *Minorities within Minorities*. Cambridge University Press.

Dewey, J. 1927. *The Public and Its Problems*. Athens: Swallow Press.

Diaz-Stevens, A. M. and A. M. Stevens-Arroyo. 1998. *Recognizing the Latino Resurgence in US Religion*. Boulder, CO: Westview.

Dolan, J. P. 1985. *The American Catholic Experience*. Garden City, NY: Doubleday.

Dolan, J. P. and A. F. Deck (eds.). 1994. *Hispanic Catholic Culture in the United States*. Notre Dame, IN: University of Notre Dame Press.

Dolan, J. P. and J. R. Vidal (eds.). 1994. *Puerto Rican and Cuban Catholics in the United States, 1900–65*. Notre Dame, IN: Notre Dame University Press.

Dommelen, E. van. 2003. *Constitutionele Rechtspraak vanuit rechtsfilosofisch perspectief*. Tilburg: Boom Juridische Uitgevers.

Döring, D. 1993. 'Säkularisierung und Moraltheologie bei Samuel von Pufendorf', *Zeitschrift für Theologie und Kirche* 90: 156–74.

Douglass, R. B. 1994. 'Liberalism after the good times: the "end of history" in historical perspective', in R. B. Douglass and D. Hollenbach (eds.), *Catholicism and Liberalism: Contributions to American Public Philosophy*. Cambridge University Press, pp. 100–26.

Dreitzel, H. 1988. 'Der Aristotelismus in der politischen Philosophie Deutschlands im 17. Jahrhundert', in E. Keßler, C. H. Lohr and W. Sparn (eds.), *Aristotelismus und Renaissance: In memoriam Charles B. Schmitt*. Wiesbaden: Otto Harrassowitz, pp. 163–92.

2001a. 'Das christliche Gemeinwesen', in H. Holzhey and W. Schmidt-Biggemann (eds.), *Die Philosophie des 17. Jahrhunderts, Band 4: Das heilige Römische Reich deutscher Nation, Nord- und Ostmitteleuropa*. Basel: Schwabe, pp. 673–93.

2001b. 'Naturrecht als politische Philosophie', in H. Holzhey and W. Schmidt-Biggemann (eds.), *Die Philosophie des 17. Jahrhunderts, Band 4: Das heilige Römische Reich deutscher Nation, Nord- und Ostmitteleuropa*. Basel: Schwabe, pp. 836–48.

2003. 'The reception of Hobbes in the political philosophy of the early German Enlightenment', *History of European Ideas* 29: 255–89.

Dworkin, R. 1978. 'Liberalism', in S. Hampshire (ed.), *Public and Private Morality*. Cambridge University Press, pp. 113–43.

Ebaugh, H. R. and J. S. Chafetz (eds.). 2000. *Religion and the New Immigrants*. Walnut Creek, CA: AltaMira.

Eberle, C. J. 2002. *Religious Conviction in Liberal Politics*. Cambridge University Press.

Eck, D. L. 2002. *A New Religious America: How a 'Christian Country' Has Become the World's Most Religiously Diverse Nation*. San Francisco: Harper.

Eisenach, E. J. 2000. *The Next Religious Establishment*. Lanham, MD: Rowman & Littlefield.

Eisenberg, A. N. 2002. 'Accommodation and coherence: in search of a general theory for adjudicating claims of faith, conscience, and culture', in R. Shweder, M. Minow and H. R. Markus (eds.), *Engaging*

Cultural Differences: The Multicultural Challenge in Liberal Democracies. New York: Russell Sage Foundation, pp. 147–64.

Elshtain, J. B. 1994. 'Catholic social thought, the city, and liberal America', in R. B. Douglass and D. Hollenbach (eds.), *Catholicism and Liberalism: Contributions to American Public Philosophy*. Cambridge University Press, pp. 151–71.

Embassy of the Republic of Indonesia. 2006. 'Embassy denounces leak', *The Australian*, 5 April.

Esposito, J. 2007. 'America's Muslims: issues of identity, religious diversity, and pluralism', in T. Banchoff, ed., *Democracy and the New Religious Pluralism*. Oxford University Press, pp. 133–50.

Evans, C. 2001. *Freedom of Religion under the European Convention on Human Rights*. Oxford University Press.

Fallaci, O. 2002. *The Rage and the Pride*. New York: Rizzoli.

Ferrara, A. 2002. 'Public reason and the normativity of the reasonable', *Deutsche Zeitschrift für Philosophie* 6: 925–43.

Ferrari, S. and A. Bradney (eds.). 2000. *Islam and European Legal Systems*. Aldershot: Ashgate.

Fetzer, J. S. and J. C. Soper. 2005. *Muslims and the State in Britain, France, and Germany*. Cambridge University Press.

Fish, S. 1997. 'Mission impossible', *Columbia Law Review* 97: 2255–333.

Foley, E. 1992. 'Tillich and Camus, talking politics', *Columbia Law Review* 92: 954–83.

Foreign and Commonwealth Office. 2006. *Muslims of Britain*. London: FCO.

Forst, R. 2006. ' "To tolerate means to insult": toleration, recognition, and emancipation', in B. v. d. Brink and D. Owen (eds.), *Power and Recognition*. Cambridge University Press, pp. 215–37.

Forum Against Islamophobia and Racism (FAIR). 2002. *A Response to the Government Consultation Paper, 'Towards Equality and Diversity: Implementing the Employment and Race Directives'*. London: FAIR.

Foucault, M. 1974. *The Archaeology of Knowledge*. London: Tavistock.

1977. *Discipline and Punish: The Birth of the Prison*, trans. A. Sheridan. London: Allen Lane.

1991. 'Governmentality', in G. Burchell, C. Gordon and P. Miller (eds.), *The Foucault Effect: Studies in Governmentality*. London, Harvester Wheatsheaf, pp. 87–104.

2003. '*Society Must be Defended': Lectures at the Collège de France 1975–76*, ed. M. Bertani and A. Fontana, trans. D. Macey. New York: Picador.

Frankenberg, G. and U. Rödel. 1981. *Von der Volkssouveränität zum Minderheitenschutz*. Frankfurt am Main: EVA.

Freedman, J. 2004. 'Secularism as a barrier to integration? The French dilemma', *International Migration* 42: 5–27.

Galston, W. 2002. *Liberal Pluralism*. Cambridge University Press.

  2003. 'Jews, Muslims and the prospects for pluralism', *Daedalus* 132: 73–7.

Gauchet, M. 1994. 'L'Etat au miroir de la raison d'Etat: la France et la Chrétienté', in Y.-C. Zarka (ed.), *Raison et déraison d'Etat*. Paris: Presses Universitaires de France.

  1998. *La religion dans la démocratie*. Paris: Gallimard.

Gelber, K. 2002. *Speaking Back: The Free Speech versus Hate Speech Debate*. Amsterdam: John Benjamins.

Geuss, R. 2002. 'Liberalism and its discontents', *Political Theory* 30: 320–38.

Gilchrist, K. 1997. 'God does not live in Victoria', *Art Monthly* (December), www.artslaw.com.au/Publications/Articles/97Blasphemy.asp.

Glazer, N. and D. P. Moynihan. 1963. *Beyond the Melting Pot: The Negroes, Puerto Ricans, Jews, Italians, and Irish of New York City*. Cambridge, MA: MIT Press.

Gray, J. 2000. *Two Faces of Liberalism*. Cambridge: Polity Press.

Greeley, A. M. 1972. *The Denominational Society: A Sociological Approach to Religion in America*. Glenview, IL: Scott, Foresman.

  1995. 'The persistence of religion', *Cross Currents* 45 (Spring): 24–41.

  2003. *Religion in Europe at the End of the Second Millennium: A Sociological Profile*. New Brunswick, NJ: Transaction.

Greenawalt, K. 1988. *Religious Convictions and Political Choice*. New York: Oxford University Press.

  1995. *Private Consciences and Public Reasons*. Oxford University Press.

Gutmann, A. 1987. *Democratic Education*. Cambridge University Press.

  2003. *Identity in Democracy*. Princeton University Press.

Gutmann, A. and D. Thompson. 1990. 'Moral conflict and political consensus', *Ethics* 101: 64–88.

  1996. *Democracy and Disagreement*. Cambridge, MA: Belknap Press.

Habermas, J. 1989. *The Structural Transformation of the Public Sphere: An Inquiry into a Category of Bourgeois Society*, trans. T. Berger. Cambridge, MA: MIT Press.

  1990. *Discourse Ethics. Notes on a Program of Philosophical Justification*. Cambridge, MA: MIT Press.

  1995. 'Reconciliation through the public use of reason: remarks on John Rawls's political liberalism', *Journal of Philosophy* 92: 109–131.

  1996. *Between Facts and Norms: Contributions to a Discourse Theory of Law and Democracy*, trans. W. Rehg. Cambridge, MA: MIT Press.

  2001. *Glauben und Wissen*. Frankfurt am Main: Suhrkamp.

2006. 'Religion in the public sphere', *European Journal of Philosophy* 14: 1–25.

Hadaway, K., P. L. Marler and M. Chaves. 1993. 'What the polls don't show: a closer look at US church attendance', *American Sociological Review* 58: 741–52.

Haddad, Y. Y. (ed.). 2002. *Muslims in the West: From Sojourners to Citizens.* New York: Oxford University Press.

Hall, S. 1992. 'The West and the rest: discourse and power', in S. Hall and B. Gieben (eds.), *Formations of Modernity.* Cambridge: Polity Press, pp. 275–331.

Hamburger, P. 2002. *Separation of Church and State.* Cambridge, MA: Harvard University Press.

Hamilton, C. 1995. *Family, Law and Religion.* London: Sweet and Maxwell.

Hammerstein, N. 1986. 'Universitäten – Territorialstaaten – gelehrte Räte', in R. Schnur (ed.), *Die Rolle der Juristen bei der Entstehung des modernen Staates.* Berlin: Duncker & Humblot, pp. 687–735.

Hanafi, H. 2002. 'Alternative conceptions of civil society: a reflective Islamic approach', in Hashmi (ed.), pp. 56–75.

Hansen, R. 2006a. 'The Danish cartoon controversy: a defence of liberal freedom', in Modood *et al.*, pp. 7–16.

2006b. 'Free speech, liberalism and integration: a reply to Bleich and Carens', in Modood *et al.*, pp. 42–51.

Harel, A. 2007. 'Regulating modesty-related practices', *Journal of Law & Ethics of Human Rights* 1: 213–36.

Hashmi, S. H. (ed.). 2002. *Islamic Political Ethics: Civil Society, Pluralism, and Conflict.* Princeton University Press.

Hassan, R. 2006. 'Expressions of religiosity and blasphemy in modern societies', in E. B. Coleman and K. White (eds.), *Negotiating the Sacred: Blasphemy and Sacrilege in a Multicultural Society.* Canberra: ANU E Press, pp. 119–30.

Heckel, M. 1983. *Deutschland im konfessionellen Zeitalter.* Göttingen: Vandenhoeck & Ruprecht.

1984. 'Das Säkularisierungsproblem in der Entwicklung des deutschen Staatskirchenrechts', in G. Dilcher and I. Staff (eds.), *Christentum und modernes Recht: Beiträge zum Problem der Säkularisation.* Frankfurt am Main: Suhrkamp, pp. 35–95.

1989a. 'Säkularisierung: staatskirchenrechtliche Aspekte einer umstrittenen Kategorie', in K. Schlaich (ed.), *Martin Heckel Gesammelte Schriften: Staat, Kirche, Recht, Geschichte,* 4 vols. Tübingen: J. C. B. Mohr, 1989–97, Vol. 2, pp. 773–911.

1989b. 'Zur Entwicklung des deutschen Staatskirchenrechts von der Reformation bis zur Schwelle der Weimarer Verfassung', in K. Schlaich (ed.), *Martin Heckel Gesammelte Schriften: Staat, Kirche, Recht, Geschichte*, 5 vols. Tübingen: J. C. B. Mohr, Vol 1, pp. 366–401.

Hedetoft, U. 2006. 'Denmark's cartoon blowback'. *Open Democracy*, 1 March, www.opendemocracy.net/faith-europe_islam/blowback_3315.jsp.

Herberg, W. 1960. *Protestant–Catholic–Jew*. Garden City, NY: Doubleday.

Herbermann, C. G. *et al.* (eds.). 1913. *The Catholic Encyclopedia: An International Work of Reference on the Constitution, Doctrine, Discipline, and History of the Catholic Church*, 17 vols. New York: Encyclopedia Press, Vol. 14.

Hertzberg, A. 1989. *The Jews in America: Four Centuries of an Uneasy Encounter*. New York: Simon & Schuster.

Hervieu-Léger, D. 2004. 'Religion und sozialer Zusammenhalt'. *Transit: Europäische Review* 26: 101–19.

Hesse, B. 2004. 'Im/plausible deniability: racism's double conceptual bind', *Social Identities* 10: 9–29.

Hesse, B. and S. Sayyid. 2006. 'Narrating the postcolonial political and the immigrant imaginary', in N. Ali, V. S. Kalra and S. Sayyid (eds.), *A Postcolonial People: South Asians in Britain*. London: Hurst, pp. 13–31.

Higham, J. 1988. *Strangers in the Land: Patterns of American Nativism, 1860–1925*, 2nd edn. New Brunswick, NJ: Rutgers University Press.

  1999. 'Instead of a sequel; or, How I lost my subject', in C. Hirschman, P. Kasinitz and J. de Wind (eds.), pp. 383–9.

Hinrichs, C. 1971. *Preußentum und Pietismus: der Pietismus in Brandenberg-Preußen als religiös-soziale Reformbewegung*. Göttingen: Vandenhoeck & Ruprecht.

Hirschman, A. 1981. *The Passions and the Interests*. Princeton University Press.

Hirschman, C., P. Kasinitz and J. de Wind (eds.). 1999. *Handbook of International Migration: The American Experience*. New York: Russell Sage Foundation.

Hollenbach, D. S. J. 1993. 'Contexts of the political role of religion: civil society and culture', *San Diego Law Review* 30: 877–901.

  1994. 'A communitarian reconstruction of human rights: contributions from Catholic tradition', in R. B. Douglass and D. Hollenbach, (eds.), *Catholicism and Liberalism: Contributions to American Public Philosophy*. Cambridge University Press, pp. 127–50.

  1997. 'Politically active churches', in Weithman (ed.), 297–306.

Holmes, S. 1988. 'Jean Bodin: the paradox of sovereignty and the privatisation of religion', in J. R. Pennock and J. W. Chapman (eds.), *Religion, Morality and the Law*, Nomos 30. New York University Press, pp. 5–45.

Holmes, S. 1995. *Passions and Constraint: On the Theory of Liberal Democracy*. University of Chicago Press.

Hunter, I. 1994. *Rethinking the School: Subjectivity, Bureaucracy, Criticism*. Sydney: Allen & Unwin.

2001. *Rival Enlightenments: Civil and Metaphysical Philosophy in Early Modern Germany*. Cambridge University Press.

2004a. 'Christian Thomasius on the right of Protestant princes regarding heretics', *Eighteenth-Century Thought* 2: 39–98.

2004b. 'Conflicting obligations: Pufendorf, Leibniz and Barbeyrac on civil authority', *History of Political Thought* 24: 670–99.

2005. 'Kant's *Religion* and Prussian religious policy', *Modern Intellectual History* 2: 1–27.

Huntington, S. P. 1996. *The Clash of Civilizations and the Remaking of World Order*. New York: Simon & Schuster.

2004. *Who Are We? The Challenges to America's National Identity*. New York: Simon & Schuster.

Husserl, E. 1970. *The Crisis of European Sciences and Transcendental Phenomenology*, trans. D. Carr. Evanston: Northwestern University Press.

Inden, R. 1990. *Imagining India*. Oxford: Blackwell.

International Herald Tribune. 2006. 'After fury over cartoons, an attempt at dialogue', 12 July.

Israel, J. 2006. *Enlightenment Contested: Philosophy, Modernity, and the Emancipation of Man 1670–1752*. Oxford University Press.

Ivers, G. 1995. *To Build a Wall: American Jews and the Separation of Church and State*. Charlottesville: University Press of Virginia.

Jacobsohn, G. J. 1993. *Apple of Gold: Constitutionalism in Israel and the United States*. Princeton University Press.

2003. *The Wheel of Law*. Princeton University Press.

Jasso, G., D. S. Massey, M. R. Rosenzweig and J. P. Smith. 2003. 'Exploring the religious preferences of recent immigrants to the United Sates: evidence from the New Immigrant Survey pilot', in Y. Y. Haddad, J. I. Smith and J. L. Esposito, (eds.), *Religion and Immigration: Christian, Jewish, and Muslim Experiences in the United States*. Walnut Creek, CA: AltaMira.

Jefferson, T. 1982. 'A draft of a bill for establishing religious freedom', in E. S. Gaustad (ed.), *A Documentary History of Religion in America: To the Civil War*. Grand Rapids: Eerdmans, pp. 259–61.

Jelen, T. and C. Wilcox (eds.). 2002. *Religion and Politics in Comparative Perspective: The One, the Few and the Many*. New York: Cambridge University Press.

Juergensmeyer, M. 1994. *New Cold War? Religious Nationalism Confronts the Secular State*. Berkeley and London: University of California Press.

Kant, I. 1970a. 'An answer to the question: "What is Enlightenment?"', in H. Reiss (ed.), *Kant: Political Writings*. Cambridge University Press, pp. 54–60.

1970b. 'On the common saying: "This may be true in theory, but it does not apply in practice"', in H. Reiss (ed.), *Kant: Political Writings*. Cambridge University Press, pp. 61–92.

Kazemi, F. 2002. 'Perspectives on Islam and civil society', in Hashmi (ed.), pp. 38–55.

Keane, J. 2000. 'Secularism', *The Political Quarterly* 71: 5–19.

Kelsay, J. 2002. 'Civil society and government in Islam', in Hashmi (ed.), pp. 3–37.

Kepel, G. 1994. *The Revenge of God: The Resurgence of Islam, Christianity, and Judaism in the Modern World*. University Park: Pennsylvania State University Press.

Kessler, C. S. 2006. 'Cartoons and caricatures: dignity and respect, sanctity and humour; or, Is there "something rotten in the state of Denmark"?' Unpublished paper.

Khan, M. 2003. 'Constructing the American Muslim community', in Y. Hadad, J. I. Smith and J. L. Esposito (eds.), *Religion and Immigration: Christian, Jewish, and Muslim Experiences in the United States*. Walnut Creek: AltaMira, pp. 175–98.

King, D. S. 2000. *Making Americans: Immigration, Race, and the Origins of the Diverse Democracy*. Cambridge: Harvard University Press.

King, R. 1999. *Orientalism and Religion: Post Colonial Theory, India and the Mystic East*. London and New York: Routledge.

Klausen, J. 2005. *The Islamic Challenge: Politics and Religion in Western Europe*. Oxford and New York: Oxford University Press.

2006a. Contribution to an email exchange on the 'Danish cartoon controversy' among some members of the Ethnicity and Democratic Governance Project (an international Canadian-based five-year major collaborative research project detailed at www.edg-gde.ca), 13 July.

2006b. 'A Danish drama', *Prospect* (March).

2006c. 'Rotten judgment in the state of Denmark', *Spiegel Online*, 8 February.

Klug, B. 2003. 'The collective Jew: Israel and the new antisemitism', *Patterns of Prejudice* 37: 1–19.

2004a. 'Anti-Semitism – new or old? Klug replies', *The Nation*, 12 April.

2004b. 'The myth of the new anti-Semitism', *The Nation*, 2 February.

2004. Öffentliche Konflikte um die Inkorporation muslimscher Minderheiten in Westeuropa', *Journal für Konflikt- und Gewaltforschung* 6: 85–100.

Kolanad, G. 2001. *Culture Shock: India*, rev. edn. Portland, OR: Graphic Arts Center Publishing Company.

Kukathas, C. 2003. *The Liberal Archipelago: A Theory of Diversity and Freedom*. Oxford: Clarendon Press.

Kurien, P. A. 2005. 'Being young, brown, and Hindu: the identity struggles of second generation Indian Americans', *Journal of Contemporary Ethnography* 34: 434–69.

Kurzman, C. 1998. *Liberal Islam: A Source Book*. New York: Oxford University Press.

Kymlicka, W. 1989. 'Liberal individualism and liberal neutrality', *Ethics* 99: 883–905.

2002. *Contemporary Political Philosophy: An Introduction*, 2nd edn. Oxford University Press.

2005. *Multicultural Citizenship: A Liberal Theory of Minority Rights*. Oxford University Press.

L'Hospital, M. de. 2001. *Discours politiques, 1560–1568*. Clermont-Ferrand: Editions Paléo.

Lalouette, J. 2005. *La séparation des églises et de l'Etat*. Paris: Seuil.

Landman, L. 1968. *Jewish Law in the Diaspora: Confrontation and Accommodation*. Philadelphia: Dropsie College for Hebrew and Cognate Learning.

Lapidus, I. M. 1975. 'The separation of state and religion in the development of early Islamic society', *International Journal of Middle East Studies* 6: 363–85.

Laqueur, T. W. 1976. *Religion and Respectability: Sunday Schools and Working-Class Culture, 1780–1850*. New Haven: Yale University Press.

Larmore, C. 1987. *Patterns of Moral Complexity*. New York: Cambridge University Press.

1996. *The Morals of Modernity*. Cambridge University Press.

Laursen, J. C. and C. J. Nederman (eds.). 1998. *Beyond the Persecuting Society*. Philadelphia: University of Pennsylvania Press.

Law Commission. 1985. *Criminal Law: Offences against Religion and Public Worship*. London: Her Majesty's Stationery Office.

Law Reform Commission of New South Wales. 1992. *Blasphemy*, Discussion Paper 24 (1992), www.lawlink.nsw.gov.au/lrc.nsf/pages/DP24CHP3.

Lawrence, B. B. 2002. *New Faiths, Old Fears: Muslims and Other Asian Immigrants in American Religious Life*. New York: Columbia University Press.

Le Tourneau, D. 1997. 'La laïcité à l'épreuve de l'Islam: le cas du port du "foulard islamique" dans l'école publique en France', *Revue générale de droit* 28: 275–306.

Lefort, C. 1986. *The Political Forms of Modern Society: Bureaucracy, Democracy, Totalitarianism*, ed. and trans. J. B. Thompson. Cambridge: Polity Press.

1999. *Fortdauer des theologisch-politischen?* Vienna: Passagen Verlag.

Lemann, N. 1996. *The Promised Land: The Great Black Migration and How It Changed America*. New York: Vintage.

Leonard, K. I. 2003. *Muslims in the United States: The State of Research*. New York: Russell Sage Foundation.

Levey, G. B. 1997. 'Equality, autonomy and cultural rights', *Political Theory* 25: 215–48.

2006a. 'Identity and rational revisability', in I. Primoratz and A. Pavkovic (eds.), *Identity, Self-Determination and Secession*. Aldershot: Ashgate, pp. 43–58.

2006b. 'Judaism and the obligation to die for the state', in M. Walzer (ed.), *Law, Politics, and Morality in Judaism*. Princeton University Press, pp. 182–208.

2006c. 'Symbolic recognition, multicultural citizens, and acknowledgement: negotiating the Christmas wars', *Australian Journal of Political Science* 40: 355–70.

2008a. 'Multicultural political thought in Australian perspective', in G. B. Levey (ed.), *Political Theory and Australian Multiculturalism*. New York and Oxford: Berghahn Books.

2008b. 'Multiculturalism and Australian national identity', in G. B. Levey (ed.), *Political Theory and Australian Multiculturalism*. New York and Oxford: Berghahn Books.

Forthcoming. 'What is living and what is dead in multiculturalism', *Ethnicities* 9.

Levey, G. B. and A. D. Moses. Forthcoming. 'The Muslims are our misfortune!', in G. Noble (ed.), *Lines in the Sand: The Cronulla Riots and the Limits of Australian Multiculturalism*. Sydney: Institute of Criminology.

Levy, L. W. 1994. *The Establishment Clause: Religion and the First Amendment*. Chapel Hill: University of North Carolina Press.

Lincoln, E. C. 1984. *Race, Religion, and the Continuing American Dilemma*. New York: Hill & Wang.

Locke, J. 1963. *A Letter concerning Toleration*, ed. Mario Montuori. The Hague: Nijhoff.

Loobuyck, P. 2006. 'De plaats van levensbeschouwelijk geïnspireerde standpunten en argumentaties op het publieke forum Bijdragen', *International Journal in Philosophy and Theology* 67: 3–22.

Macedo, S. 1990. *Liberal Virtues: Citizenship, Virtue and Community in Liberal Constitutionalism*. Oxford: Clarendon Press.

1997. 'Transformative constitutionalism and the case of religion', *Political Theory*, 26: 56–80.

MacIntyre, A. 1988. *Whose Justice? Which Rationality?* Notre Dame, IN: University of Notre Dame Press.

Madan, T. N. 1998. 'Secularism in its place', in Bhargava (ed.), pp. 297–320.

Madeley, J. and Z. Enyedi (eds.). 2003. *Church and State in Contemporary Europe*. London: Cass.

Mahajan, G. 1998. *Identities and Rights: Aspects of Liberal Democracy in India*. New Delhi: Oxford University Press.

Malik, I. H. 2002. *Religious Minorities in Pakistan*. London: Minority Rights Group International.

Mandair, A. 2006. '(Im)possible intersections: religion, (post-)colonial subjectivity and the ideology of multiculturalism', in N. Ali, V. Kalra and S. Sayyid (eds.), *A Postcolonial People: South Asians in Britain*. London: Hurst, pp. 93–107.

Maréchal, B., S. Allievi, F. Dassetto and J. Nielsen (eds.). 2003. *Muslims in the Enlarged Europe*. Leiden: Brill.

Marshall, W. 1993. 'The other side of religion', *Hastings Law Journal* 44: 843–63.

Martin, D. 1978. *A General Theory of Secularization*. New York: Harper & Row.

2003. 'Religion, secularity, secularism and European integration', self-published web-based 'think-piece'. Available at http://ec.europa.eu/research/social-sciences/pdf/michalski_210503_contribution02_en.pdf.

McCloud, A. B. 2003. 'Islam in America: the mosaic', in Y. Hadad, J. I. Smith and J. L. Esposito (eds.), *Religion and Immigration: Christian, Jewish, and Muslim Experiences in the United States*. Walnut Creek: AltaMira, pp. 159–74.

McConnell, M. W. 1992. 'Religious participation in public programs', in G. R. Stone, R. A. Epstein and C. R. Sunstein (eds.), *The Bill of Rights in the Modern State*. Chicago and London: University of Chicago Press, pp. 115–94.

Mead, S. E. 1976. *The Lively Experiment: The Shaping of Christianity in America*. New York: Harper & Row.

Mellinkoff, R. 1970. *The Horned Moses in Medieval Art and Thought*. Berkeley and London: University of California Press.

Melton, J. V. H. 1988. *Absolutism and the Eighteenth-Century Origins of Compulsory Schooling in Prussia and Austria*. Cambridge University Press.

Mendelssohn, M. 1986. *Jerusalem; or, On Religious Power and Judaism*, trans. A. Arkush. Hanover, NH: University Press of New England.

Meyer, M. A. 1967. *The Origins of the Modern Jew: Jewish Identity and European Culture in Germany, 1749–1824*. Detroit: Wayne State University Press.

Michaelis, J. D. 1995. 'Arguments against Dohm (1782)', in P. R. Mendes-Flohr and J. Reinharz (eds.), *The Jew in the Modern World: A Documentary History*, 2nd edn. New York: Oxford University Press, pp. 42–44.

Mignolo, W. 2005. *The Idea of Latin America*. Oxford: Blackwell Publishers.

Mittleman, A., R. Licht and J. D. Sarna (eds.). 2002. *Jews and the American Public Square: Debating Religion and Republic*. Lanham, MD: Rowman & Littlefield.

Moch, L. P. 2003. *Moving Europeans: Migration in Western Europe Since 1650*, 2nd edn. Bloomington: Indiana University Press.

Modood, T. 1992. *Not Easy Being British: Colour, Culture and Citizenship*. London: Runnymede Trust/Trentham Books.

  1994. 'Establishment, multiculturalism and British citizenship', *Political Quarterly* 65: 53–73.

  (ed.). 1997a. *Church, State and Religious Minorities*. London: Policy Studies Institute.

  1997b. 'Difference, cultural racism and anti-racism', in P. Werbner and T. Modood (eds.), *Debating Cultural Identity*. London: Zed Books, pp. 154–72.

  2003a. 'Muslims and the politics of difference', in S. Spencer (ed.), *The Politics of Migration*. Oxford: Blackwell, pp. 100–15.

  2003b. 'Muslims and the politics of difference', *Political Quarterly* 74: 100–15.

  2005. *Multicultural Politics: Racism, Ethnicity and Muslims in Britain*. Minneapolis and Edinburgh: University of Minnesota Press and University of Edinburgh Press.

  2006a. 'The liberal dilemma: integration or vilification?', in Modood *et al.*, pp. 4–7.

  2006b. 'Obstacles to multicultural integration', in Modood *et al.*, pp. 51–62.

  2007. *Multiculturalism: A Civic Idea*. Cambridge: Polity.

Modood, T., R. Berthoud, J. Lakey, J. Nazroo, P. Smith, S. Virdee and S. Beishon 1997. *Ethnic Minorities in Britain: Diversity and Disadvantage*. London: Policy Studies Institute.

Modood, T, R. Hansen, E. Bleich, B. O'Leary and J. Carens. 2006. 'The Danish cartoon affair: free speech, racism, Islamism, and integration', *International Migration* 44: 3–57.

Modood, T. and R. Kastoryano. 2006. 'Secularism and the accommodation of Muslims in Europe', in T. Modood, A. Triandafyllidou and

R. Zapata-Barrero (eds.), *Multiculturalism, Muslims and Citizenship: A European Approach*. London: Routledge, pp. 162–78.

Mohsin, A. 1999. 'National security and the minorities: the Bangladesh case', in D. L. Sheth and G. Mahajan (eds.), *Minority Identities and the Nation-State*. New Delhi: Oxford University Press, pp. 312–33.

Moore, L. R. 1986. *Religious Outsiders and the Making of Americans*. New York: Oxford University Press.

Müller, A. 2005. 'Ist der freiheitliche Staat auf vorpolitische Ressourcen des Religiösen angewiesen und welcher Platz soll den Religionsgemeinschaften im öffentlichen Raum zukommen?', in R. Mortanges and E. Tanner (eds.), *Kooperation zwischen Staat und Religionsgemeinschaften nach schweizerischem Recht*. Zürich: Schulthess, pp. 35–90.

Murphy, A. 2001. *Conscience and Community*. University Park: Pennsylvania State University Press.

Nagel, T. 1987. 'Moral conflict and political legitimacy', *Philosophy & Public Affairs* 16: 215–40.

1991. *Equality and Partiality*. New York: Oxford University Press.

Nandy, A. 1998. 'The politics of secularism and the recovery of religious toleration', in Bhargava (ed.), pp. 321–44.

2002. *Time Warps: Silent and Evasive Pasts in Indian Politics and Religion*. New Brunswick, NJ: Rutgers University Press.

Neal, P. 1997. *Liberalism and its Discontents*. Basingstoke: Macmillan.

Nederman, C. J. and J. C. Laursen (eds.). 1996. *Difference and Dissent: Theories of Toleration in Medieval and Early Modern Europe*. Lanham, MD: Rowman & Littlefield.

New Immigrant Survey (NIS). http://nis.princeton.edu.

Niebuhr, H. R. 1929. *The Social Sources of Denominationalism*. New York: Henry Holt & Co.

Nigam, A. 2006. *The Crisis of Secular-Nationalism in India*. New Delhi: Oxford University Press.

Novotny, H., P. Scott and M. Gibbons. 2001. *Rethinking Science: Knowledge and the Public in an Age of Uncertainty*. Cambridge: Polity.

O'Leary, B. 2006. 'Liberalism, multiculturalism, Danish cartoons, Islamist fraud and the rights of the ungodly', in Modood *et al.*, pp. 22–33.

Parekh, B. 2000. *Rethinking Multiculturalism: Cultural Diversity and Political Theory*. Basingstoke: Macmillan.

2006. 'Europe, liberalism and the "Muslim question"', in T. Modood, A. Triandafyllidou and R. Zapata-Barrero (eds.), *Multiculturalism, Muslims and Citizenship: A European Approach*. London: Routledge, pp. 179–203.

Perry, M. J. 1991. *Love and Power: The Role of Religion and Morality in American Politics*. New York: Oxford University Press.

1993. 'Religious morality and political choice: further thoughts – and second thoughts – on love and power', *San Diego Law Review* 30: 703–27.

1997. *Religion in Politics*. Oxford University Press.

2003. *Under God?* Cambridge University Press.

Pfeffer, L. 1967. *Church, State, and Freedom*, rev. edn. Boston: Beacon Press.

Pluralism Project CD-ROM. 1997. *On Common Ground: World Religions in America*. New York: Columbia University Press.

Portes, A. and R. G. Rumbaut. 1996. *Immigrant America: A Portrait*, 2nd edn. Berkeley: University of California Press.

Poulter, S. M. 1986. *English Law and Ethnic Minority Customs*. London: Butterworths.

Protero, S. (ed.). 2005. *A Nation of Religions: The Politics of Pluralism in Multireligious America*. Chapel Hill: University of North Carolina Press.

Pufendorf, S. 1934. *The Law of Nature and of Nations in Eight Books*, trans. C. H. Oldfather and W. A. Oldfather. Oxford: Clarendon Press.

2002. *Of the Nature and Qualification of Religion in Reference to Civil Society*, ed. S. Zurbuchen. Indianapolis: Liberty Fund.

2003. *The Whole Duty of Man According to the Law of Nature*, ed. I. Hunter and D. Saunders. Indianapolis: Liberty Fund.

Quinn, P. 1997. 'Political liberalisms and their exclusions of the religious', in Weithman (ed.), pp. 138–61.

Ramadan, T. 1999. *To be a European Muslim*. Leicester: Islamic Foundation.

Rawls, J. 1971. *A Theory of Justice*. Cambridge, MA: Belknap Press.

1985. 'Justice as fairness: political not metaphysical', *Philosophy & Public Affairs* 14: 223–51.

1993. *Political Liberalism*. New York: Columbia University Press.

1999. *The Law of Peoples*. Cambridge, MA: Harvard University Press.

Raz, J. 1990. 'Facing diversity: the case of epistemic abstinence', *Philosophy & Public Affairs* 19: 3–46.

Reames, K. 1998. 'Metaphysics, history, and moral philosophy: the centrality of the 1990 Aquinas Lecture to MacIntyre's argument for Thomism', *The Thomist* 62: 419–43.

Rickard, J. 1996. *Australia: A Cultural History*. London: Longman.

Roelker, N. L. 1996. *One King, One Faith: The Parlement of Paris and the Religious Reformation of the Sixteenth Century*. Berkeley: University of California Press.

Rorty, R. 1989. *Contingency, Irony and Solidarity*. Cambridge University Press.

1994. 'Religion as a conversation-stopper', *Common Knowledge* 3: 1–6.

Rose, F. 2005. 'The face of Muhammad', *Jyllands-Posten*, 30 September.

2006. 'Why I published those cartoons', *Washington Post*, 19 February.

Rosenblum, N. 2003. 'Religious parties, religious political identity, and the cold shoulder of liberal democratic thought', *Ethical Theory and Moral Practice* 6: 23–53.

Rosenthal, J. 2006. 'Do the *Jyllands-Posten* cartoons resemble "Nazi cartoons"? Judge for yourself', *Transatlantic Intelligencer*, 13 February, www.trans-int.com/news/archives/141-Do-the-Jyllands-Posten-Cartoons-resemble.html.

Roy, O. 1994. *The Failure of Political Islam*. London: I. B. Tauris.

2004. *Globalised Islam: The Search for a New Ummah*. London: Hurst.

Runnymede Trust. 1997. *Islamophobia: A Challenge for Us All*. London: Runnymede Trust.

Ruthven, M. 2002. *A Fury for God: The Islamist Attack on America*. London: Granta Books.

Saeed, A. 2006. *Interpreting the Qur'an: Towards a Contemporary Approach*. London: Routledge.

Salmon, J. M. H. 1975. *Society in Crisis: France in the Sixteenth Century*. London: Methuen.

Sandel, M. J. 1993. 'Freedom of conscience or freedom of choice', in T. Eastland (ed.), *Religious Liberty in the Supreme Court: The Cases that Define the Debate over Church and State*. Lanham, MD: National Book Network, pp. 483–96.

1994. 'Review of Rawls' *Political Liberalism*', *Harvard Law Review* 107: 1765–94.

1998. *Liberalism and the Limits of Justice*, 2nd edn. Cambridge University Press.

Savage, T. M. 2004. 'Europe and Islam: crescent waxing, cultures clashing'. *Washington Quarterly* 27 (summer): 25–50.

Sayyid, S. 2000. 'Beyond Westphalia: nations and diasporas – the case of the Muslim Umma', in B. Hesse (ed.), *Un/settled Multiculturalisms: Diasporas, Entanglements, Transruptions*. London: Zed Books, pp. 33–50.

2003 [1997]. *A Fundamental Fear: Eurocentrism and the Emergence of Islamism*, 2nd edn. London: Zed Books.

2004. 'Slippery people: the immigrant imaginary and the grammar of colour', in I. Law, D. Phillips and L. Turney (eds.), *Institutional Racism in Higher Education*. London: Trentham Books, pp. 149–59.

2006. 'Introduction: BrAsians: postcolonial people, ironic citizens', in N. Ali, V. Kalra and S. Sayyid (eds.), *A Postcolonial People: South Asians in Britain*. London: Hurst, pp. 1–10.

Schilling, H. 1988. 'Die Konfessionalisierung im Reich: religiöser und gesellschaftlicher Wandel in Deutschland zwischen 1555 und 1620', *Historische Zeitschrift* 246: 1–45.

1995. 'Confessional Europe', in T. A. J. Brady, H. A. Oberman and
   J. D. Tracy (eds.), *Visions, Programs and Outcomes*, Vol. 2 of *Hand-
   book of European History 1400–1600: Latin Middle Ages, Renais-
   sance and Reformation*, 2 vols. Leiden: E. J. Brill, pp. 641–82.
Schlaich, K. 1997. 'Kirchenrecht und Vernunftrecht: Kirche und Staat in der
   Sicht der Kollegialtheorie', in M. Heckel and W. Heun (eds.), *Klaus
   Schlaich, Gesammelte Aufsätze: Kirche und Staat von der Reformation
   biz zum Grundgesetz*. Tübingen: J. C. B. Mohr, pp. 179–203.
Schmitt, C. 1996. *The Concept of the Political*, trans. G. Schwab. University
   of Chicago Press.
Schneewind, J. B. 1987. 'Pufendorf's place in the history of ethics', *Synthese*
   72: 123–55.
   1996. 'Barbeyrac and Leibniz on Pufendorf', in F. Palladini and
   G. Hartung (eds.), *Samuel Pufendorf und die europäische Frühaufklärung:
   Werk und Einfluß eines deutschen Bürgers der Gelehrtenrepublik nach
   300 Jahren (1694–1994)*. Berlin: Akademie Verlag, pp. 181–9.
Schneider, H.-P. 2001. 'Christliches Naturrecht', in H. Holzhey and
   W. Schmidt-Biggemann (eds.), *Die Philosophie des 17. Jahrhunderts,
   Band 4: Das heilige Römische Reich deutscher Nation, Nord- und
   Ostmitteleuropa*. Basel: Schwabe, pp. 813–35.
Sciolino, E. 2004. 'Debate begins in France on religion in the schools'. *New
   York Times*, 4 February.
Scot, J.-P. 2005. '*L'Etat chez lui, l'Eglise chez elle*': comprendre la loi de
   1905. Paris: Seuil.
Seidler, M. J. 1996. '"Turkish judgment" and the English Revolution:
   Pufendorf on the right of resistance', in F. Palladini and G. Hartung
   (eds.), *Samuel Pufendorf und die europäische Frühaufklärung: Werk
   und Einfluß eines deutschen Bürgers der Gelehrtenrepublik nach 300
   Jahren (1694–1994)*. Berlin: Akademie Verlag, pp. 83–104.
   2002. 'Pufendorf and the politics of recognition', in I. Hunter and
   D. Saunders (eds.), *Natural Law and Civil Sovereignty: Moral Right and
   State Authority in Early Modern Political Thought*. Basingstoke: Palgrave,
   pp. 235–51.
   2003. 'The politics of self-preservation: toleration and identity in
   Pufendorf and Locke', in T. J. Hochstrasser and P. Schröder (eds.),
   *Early Modern Natural Law Theories: Contexts and Strategies in the
   Early Enlightenment*. Dordrecht: Kluwer, pp. 227–55.
Sen, A. 2005. *The Argumentative Indian: Writings on Indian History,
   Culture and Identity*. London and New York: Allen Lane.
Shah, T. S. 2000. 'Making the Christian world safe for liberalism: from
   Grotius to Rawls', in D. Marquand and R. L. Nettler (eds.), *Religion
   and Democracy*. Oxford: Blackwell, pp. 121–39.

Shah, T. and M. D. Toft, 2006. 'Why God is winning', *Foreign Policy* (July/ August): 38–43.

Shaw, B. 1999. 'Habermas and religious inclusion', *Political Theory* 27: 634–66.

Shue, H. 1995. 'Thickening convergence: human rights and cultural diversity', Amnesty Lectures, Oxford, 6 November.

Smith, J. 1999. *Islam in America*. New York: Columbia University Press.

Smith, T. L. 1978. 'Religion and ethnicity in America', *American Historical Review* 83: 1155–85.

Smith, T. W. 2001. *Estimating the Muslim Population in the United States*. New York: American Jewish Committee.

Smith, W. C. 1991. *The Meaning and End of Religion*. Minneapolis: First Fortress Press.

Solum, L. 1990. 'Faith and justice', *DePaul Law Review* 39: 1083–106.

Spiegel Online. 2006. '*Jyllands-Posten* rejected Jesus satire', 8 February, www.spiegel.de/international/0,1518,399840,00.html.

Spinner-Halev, J. 2000. *Surviving Diversity: Religion and Democratic Citizenship*. Baltimore: Johns Hopkins University Press.

Stark, R. and R. Finke. 2000. *Acts of Faith: Explaining the Human Side of Religion*, Berkeley: University of California Press.

Stolleis, M. 1995. 'Jus publicum und Aufklärung', in N. Hammerstein (ed.), *Universitäten und Aufklärung*. Göttingen: Wallstein Verlag, pp. 181–90.

Sunier, T. and Luijeren, M. von. 2002. 'Islam in the Netherlands', in Haddad (ed.), pp. 144–58.

Sydney Morning Herald. 2005. 'Madonna sacrilege row', 10 October.

2007. '"Burkini" comes to Aussie beaches', 16 January.

Tambiah, S. J. 1998. 'Crisis of secularism in India', in Bhargava (ed.), pp. 418–53.

Taylor, C. 1992. 'The politics of recognition', in A. Gutmann (ed.), *Multiculturalism and 'The Politics of Recognition'*. Princeton University Press, pp. 25–74.

1994. 'Justice after virtue', in J. Horton and S. Mendus (eds.), *After MacIntyre*. Cambridge: Polity Press, pp. 16–43.

1997. 'Nationalism and modernity', in R. McKim and J. McMahan (eds.), *The Morality of Nationalism*. Oxford University Press, pp. 31–55.

1999. 'Democratic exclusion (and its remedies?)', in R. Bhargava (ed.), *Multiculturalism, Liberalism and Democracy*. New Delhi: Oxford University Press, pp. 138–63.

The Age. 2006. 'Publish and be damned: the fight for freedom of expression', 7 February.

The Australian. 2004. 'New recruit's headpiece sets her apart', 27 November.

The Sunday Times. 2004. 'Blackadder fights comedians', 5 December.

Thiemann, R. 1996. *Religion in Public Life*. Washington, DC: Georgetown University Press.

Thomasius, C. 1950. 'Von der Historie des Rechts der Natur bis auf Grotium. (Foreword to the first German edition of Grotius' *Law of War and Peace*)', in W. Schätzel (ed.), *De jure belli ac pacis (Drei Bücher vom Recht des Krieges und des Friedens)*. Tübingen: J. C. B. Mohr, pp. 1–28.

1994. 'Vom Recht evangelischer Fürsten in Mitteldingen oder Kirchenzeremonien', in W. Schneiders (ed.), *Auserlesen deutsche Schriften, Erster Teil*. Hildesheim: Georg Olms, pp. 76–209.

Thomasius, C. and E. R. Brenneisen. 1696. *Das Recht evangelischer Fürsten in theologischen Streitigkeiten*. Halle: Salfeld.

Thompson, M. P. 1986. 'The history of fundamental law in political thought from the French Wars of Religion to the American Revolution', *American Historical Review* 91: 1103–28.

Tibi, B. 2002. 'Muslim migrants in Europe: between Euro-Islam and ghettoization', in AlSayyad and Castells (eds.), *Muslim Europe or Euro-Islam: Politics, Culture, and Citizenship in the Age of Globalization*. Lanham, MD: Lexington Books, pp. 31–52.

Tocqueville, A. 1945. *Democracy in America*. New York: Knopf.

Tully, J. 1999. 'The agonic freedom of citizens', *Economy and Society* 28: 161–82

Turner, B. S. 2001. 'Cosmopolitan virtue: on religion in a global age', *European Journal of Social Theory* 4: 131–52.

Unger, R. M. (1983). *Critical Legal Studies Movement*. Cambridge, MA: Harvard University Press.

US Commission on Civil Rights. 1983. *Religion in the Constitution: A Delicate Balance*. Clearinghouse Publication 80. Washington, DC: US Commission on Civil Rights.

Valadez, J. 2001. *Deliberative Democracy, Political Legitimacy, and Self-Determination in Multicultural Societies*. Boulder, CO: Westview.

Vanaik, A. 1997. *Communalism Contested: Religion, Modernity and Secularisation*. New Delhi: Vistaar Publications.

Veer, P. v. d. 2001. *Imperial Encounters: Religion and Modernity in India and Britain*. Delhi and Princeton, NJ: Permanent Black and Princeton University Press.

Vertovec, S. and C. Peach (eds.). 1997. *Islam in Europe: The Politics of Religion and Community*. Basingstoke: Macmillan.

Waldron, J. 1993. 'Religious contributions in public deliberation', *San Diego Law Review* 30: 817–48.

2000. 'Cultural identity and civic responsibility', in W. Kymlicka and W. Norman (eds.), *Citizenship in Diverse Societies*. Oxford University Press, pp. 155–74.

Walzer, M. 1992. 'Comment', in A. Gutmann (ed.), *Multiculturalism and 'The Politics of Recognition'*. Princeton University Press, pp. 99–103.

1995 [1980]. 'Pluralism: a political perspective', in W. Kymlicka (ed.), *The Rights of Minority Cultures*. Oxford University Press, pp. 139–54.

1997. *On Toleration*. New Haven and London: Yale University Press.

2001. 'Nation-states and immigrant societies', in W. Kymlicka and M. Opalski (eds.), *Can Liberal Pluralism be Exported?* Oxford: Oxford University Press, pp. 150–3.

2005. *Politics and Passion*. New Haven: Yale University Press.

Warner, R. S. 2005. *A Church of Our Own: Disestablishment and Diversity in American Religion*. New Brunswick: Rutgers University Press.

Warner, R. S. and J. G. Wittner (eds.). 1998. *Gatherings in Diaspora: Religious Communities and the New Immigration*. Philadelphia: Temple University Press.

Weisbrod, C. 1989. 'Comment on Curry and Firmage articles', *Journal of Law and Religion* 7: 315–21.

Weithman, P. J. 1991. 'The separation of church and state: some questions for Professor Audi', *Philosophy & Public Affairs* 20: 52–65.

(ed.) 1997a. *Religion and Contemporary Liberalism*. Notre Dame, IN: University of Notre Dame Press.

1997b. 'Religion and the liberalism of reasoned respect', in Weithman (ed.), pp. 1–38.

Westerlund, D. 1996. *Questioning the Secular State*. London: Hurst & Company.

Williams, B. 2005. *In the Beginning Was the Deed: Realism and Moralism in Political Argument*, ed. G. Hawthorn. Princeton University Press.

Williams, M. 1998. *Voice, Trust, and Memory*. New Haven: Yale University Press.

2000. 'The uneasy alliance of group representation and deliberative democracy', in W. Kymlicka and W. Norman (eds.), *Citizenship in Diverse Societies*. Oxford University Press, pp. 124–53.

Williams, R. B. 1988. *Religion of Immigrants from India and Pakistan: New Threads in the American Tapestry*. New York: Cambridge University Press.

Wood, F. G. 1990. *The Arrogance of Faith: Christianity and Race in America from the Colonial Era to the Twentieth Century*. New York: Knopf.

Wood, J. E., Jr. (ed.). 1985. *Religion and the State: Essays in Honor of Leo Pfeffer*. Waco, TX: Baylor University Press.

Wyduckel, D. 1996. 'Die Vertragslehre Pufendorfs und ihre rechts- und staatstheoretischen Grundlagen', in F. Palladini and G. Hartung (eds.), *Samuel Pufendorf und die europäische Frühaufklärung. Werk und Einfluß eines deutschen Bürgers der Gelehrtenrepublik nach 300 Jahren (1694–1994).* Berlin: Akademie Verlag, pp. 147–65.

Young, I. M. 1992. *Justice and the Politics of Difference.* Princeton, NJ: Princeton University Press.

Zagorin, P. 2003. *How the Idea of Religious Toleration Came to the West.* Princeton University Press.

Zarka, Y.-C. (ed.). 2005. *Faut-il reviser la loi de 1905? La séparation entre religions et l'Etat en question.* Paris: Presses Universitaires de France.